SEA-STEADING

SEA-STEADING

✦

A LIFE OF HOPE AND FREEDOM ON THE LAST VIABLE FRONTIER

Jerome FitzGerald

iUniverse, Inc.
New York Lincoln Shanghai

SEA-STEADING
A LIFE OF HOPE AND FREEDOM ON THE LAST VIABLE FRONTIER

iUniverse books may be ordered through booksellers or by contacting:

iUniverse
2021 Pine Lake Road, Suite 100
Lincoln, NE 68512
www.iuniverse.com
1-800-Authors (1-800-288-4677)

ISBN-13: 978-0-595-38758-8 (pbk)
ISBN-13: 978-0-595-83141-8 (ebk)
ISBN-10: 0-595-38758-6 (pbk)
ISBN-10: 0-595-83141-9 (ebk)

Printed in the United States of America

This book is dedicated to my Mom and Dad.

and

The Bellingham Oar Club Gang

To Perry, who really does give a shit,
To Mike Baker, who somehow makes nice seem bad-ass,
To Tom, who eventually might get around to it,
To Mike Rostron, who proves up-tight can be cool,
To Robert, who will be one hell of a mentor some day soon.

Contents

This is an Oar Club Book

This book is dedicated to those who sail and appreciate the beauty inherent in sailing. This book is dedicated as well to promoting the skill, character, and seamanship displayed by those who sail in its traditional fashion—without the aid of engines. This book affirms the rigors of true sailing—the attentiveness they demand and the strength they contest—as rewards: This is what makes the experience meaningful. We cannot imagine demeaning our experience by making it trivial or common. That does not mean that we demand that we cross oceans (though some do) or rashly brave storms (though some have) but rather that we do what we do, in a manner real and meaningful, and eschew that which is not. Perhaps fifty percent of seamanship occurs within fifty feet of a dock…

Notes on the Text

I'd like to explain a little bit about this book. This book is rough, cheaply printed, and poorly edited, just like the rest of my books. I've got no apology for that. Here's why. A book like this is bound to sell to a very limited market, from my personal experience perhaps two dozen copies a month world wide. Thus, in terms of royalties I'll get perhaps 10 percent of the wholesale cost of this book. Fifty bucks a month, then, if I'm lucky. I've got perhaps 400 hours of work involved in this text—if I were working at minimum wage flipping burgers I'd make at least 2000 dollars in this period of time. It will take me 5 or six years to even break even with the time involved—so I'd be an ass to spend any more time on polish than is absolutely necessary. Besides, I hate writing. I'd rather flip burgers, actually.

This book is also self-published. The same reasons apply. If I self-publish my royalties are nearly twice what anyone else will offer me. Of course I've got no editor. That much will become clear. That being said—I've got no editor—which means I can say whatever I damn well want without worrying what the editor thinks about the market appeal of this "product."

Lastly, in my heart of hearts, I actually think typographical errors are great. At least they force the people who plagiarize my stuff to take the effort of cleaning up the text a bit before they publish it elsewhere.

So there you go. If this bugs you—to hell with you. I'm writing this book out of a sense of ethical obligation more than anything. Certainly not cash, certainly not fame. I'm writing this book because I think the information within it is critically important to a certain sort of person in this day and age—I think this lifestyle I advocate is one of the last options for liberty left in this world...

Time's a wasting...

Preface

Yeah, yeah, yeah, it's another one of my crazy books. You who have read the others will find there's a good bit of the same crap in this one that was also in the other ones. That's just the way my brain works, I'm afraid, and I've got to admit to it. Besides, I really think there is good reason for it. What evolves from watching these books arise is a glimpse not only into the ideas in the books, but also how these ideas mature and change, and become more accurate and valid. Perhaps more than what *is in these books again—perhaps more interesting is what is not...*

There is, however, a great deal of material in this book that some might feel unrelated to the topic at hand. I disagree. Many, many people catch the dream of the freedom of the sea. Not a few make some effort to make this dream a reality. Most, by far most, fail at this task. I have lived for the last five years at one of the largest marinas of the United States, the fourth largest on the West Coast. I have been very involved and aware of the sailing population and the plans of those to "sail away." Of the 3000 boats and hundreds of cruising boats, I only know of one couple—*ONE!—who has been able to achieve the means to cut the strings permanently and sail away!* Why? Many reasons. The main reason, however, is that people tend to be large on passion and short on follow-through. If one only dreams of and desires the freedom of the seas, dreams are all one will ever have. One must finally lay hand and make the deed happen. Sailing away is harder than you think. It's harder yet to do it and enjoy yourself. This takes more than passion—it takes a measured, thoughtful conviction that provokes and guides action. Hence the heavy dose of not only how, but *why as well.*

Hence, the purpose of this book is not to convince anybody to build or rebuild an engineless sailboat and to take up the lifestyle of the cruising sailor in its idealized form, although that is exactly what this book is about. Rather, *realistically,* the purpose of this book is to aid those who already recognize why it is that they should do exactly that, who desire to do exactly that, and are likely to do exactly that anyway. The goal is to aid, and to provide a like mind and a friendly voice of candor—so perhaps on those dark nights after a tough passage when one faces exhaustion and a crowded anchorage full of howling generators and buzzing inflatables one can feel, at last, that the effort involved in that passage was worthwhile, even though obviously no one else felt so, and that one isn't *entirely nuts...*

What is a Sea-Stead?

A Sea-Stead is a homestead at sea. It is an attempt for an individual, a couple, or a family to attempt to create for themselves a better life. Perhaps this means more financial independency. Perhaps this means more emotional independency. Perhaps this means seeking a more real and viscerally rewarding lifestyle: a frontier existence. Certainly it contains elements of all of these. Whatever notions the term "homestead" brings to mind, I embrace: the only difference being that this new frontier is the oceans of the world. The urgency apparent in the realization that the oceans are the last viable option for a frontier lifestyle is part of our discussion as well.

This book was written with the purpose of creating a network of competent, like-minded people interested in investigating the progressive vision of a frontier lifestyle at sea. The frontier life beckons to all that seek freedom, independence, the rewards of self-reliance—the oceans of the planet are quickly becoming the last remaining area of the planet where such a lifestyle is both viable and practical. *It is my personal goal to create the meeting place for those who seek to develop the skills necessary to live within this environment.*

While some eight billion persons compete for the resources of one quarter of the Earth's surface area—and perhaps only half of *this* is *desirable* for human habitation—three-quarters of the planet remain empty for a few thousands who have the skill and means to live upon it. The oceans are truly vast. Hundreds of thousands of miles of coastline remain uninhabited because the skills have not been acquired to live within this sometimes harsh environment. Thousands of islands as well remain empty due to lack of infrastructure and modern conveniences. These areas are rich indeed, teeming with food and resources for those with the skills to gather them—who will settle these last frontiers?

Properly and thoughtfully equipped, a modest sailboat can be a very nearly self-sufficient entity suitable as a life support platform for exploring these areas. Skillfully handled and relying on a minimum of fuels and supplies, such a sailboat can be the successful means to independent survival. My intent is to provide the elementary skills required to get one started.

Different than the sailing cruiser, the needs of the Sea-Steader are unique and progressive. It is the also the goal of this book to define and attempt to discover the most effective way of meeting these goals.

Several key aspects of self-sufficiency at sea at once stand forth for consideration:

1. **Financial Viability:** No one has ever gone to the frontier because they were already well-to-do—rather they went there as a means to discover some sort of better life for themselves. The same is true of the Sea-Steader—if the initial cost of the Sea-Stead is too high, it becomes unviable. Thus, an effective Sea-Stead must demand as little financial support as possible while creating the means for independent income.

2. **Quality of Life:** It is pointless for us to seek this lifestyle if the quality of life that we receive for our efforts is not at least as rewarding as a conventional life on land. Life can be drudgery anywhere—the sea is no exception. It must be important for us to recognize from the beginning that alienation, loneliness, and boredom have always been as great a hazard to the homestead lifestyle as crop failure and violence. We must be aware of this risk and look for ways to minimize it.

3. **Mobility:** In no other subsistence lifestyle is man capable of being so effectively mobile—it is possible for *this* homestead to perpetually live within the ideal seasons—to always live at harvest. Mobility made possible by the modern sailboat—likely constructed from modern materials and requiring a minimum of expense and care for up-keep.

4. **Skill:** The self-sufficient life, of course, relies on few others for support. This demands a great deal of skill, both in particular and in scope—one must be capable of a great many things.

The model of Sea-Stead I suggest is based upon a sailboat that has been built or modified to provide an individual or family a home on the sea. More than a cruising sailboat or a recreational vehicle, this vessel is designed and equipped to provide for both shelter and livelihood, allowing its residents to live perpetually, albeit semi nomadically, where fortune and safety might lead them. This is a very special kind of vessel and a new one—although many traditional lessons learned through vessels of other types might well be of use.

There has been, in the last ten years, a sort of movement within the idea of Sea-Steading that has attempted several different forms. Several sorts of modified oil-rig platforms and other very complicated structures have been posed. Without exception they have been expensive and ungainly. What has mystified me is why the obvious solution—the sailboat—hasn't been much considered, although perfectly functional and non-experimental examples exist.

However, while successful case examples exist, let us clearly consider one point before we begin. Pursuing the "Sea-Stead" is a new and relatively uncommon phenomenon. Not to say that people haven't been actively cruising for a hundred years. Nor to say that people have not made sailboats their permanent home. What is *very* uncommon to find is people that do both. If one carefully examines the issue, one will find many that have boats that have traveled widely—but the vast majority of these people maintain a land based home base. The boat is not a "homestead", it is a vacation home. Likewise, one can find those who make a sailboat a home—but for them even day sailing is a real rarity. Of the long time liveaboards in my harbor that I know of—and I know most—in the last 5 years I'm the only one who has done any extended cruising (meaning more than a month)—and not a few have *never* left their slip! There is simply very little information to draw upon as to what it takes to create a successful Sea-Stead, so we will start from scratch in our analysis. The choice to build a "Sea-Stead" is a deadly serious game—much like generations before encountered in the homesteads of the unspoiled West. Again, let us not forget, *most failed.* Let us then, before we take off towards the horizon put some very careful thought into our project. The reasons for failure were many—practical, material, environmental, and psychological.

What sort of vessel is the ideal Sea-Stead? My current boat project was created to find out.

This question is far more complicated than one might initially think. The needs of the Sea-Steader are different than those of the yachtsman, or even the conventional world cruiser. Economy and rugged durability are perhaps the most primary concerns. So is seaworthiness. Capacity to carry stores, cargo, tools and gear are issues to consider as well. Certainly some types of sailboats are definitely not appropriate for this task. We will discuss this in detail.

Economy—meaning purchase cost and cost of maintenance—is affected primarily by the size of the boat and the complexity of its systems. Economy can also be affected by the potential of some boats to earn an income—thus perhaps offsetting to some degree the costs inherent in their size and complexity. I will discuss two basic types of Sea-Stead. The first, which I'll call a Phase One Sea-Stead, is appropriate for a beginner. A Phase One Sea-Stead provides home and shelter but perhaps not income. It is important to be efficient and cost effective. I'll suggest the Phase One Sea-Stead be a boat of under 32 feet and under 10,000 pounds is a reasonable place to start. Properly equipped, well handled, such a boat can easily take a couple anywhere in the world for very modest costs. Typically, our Phase One boats have been 28-30 feet in length, sloop rigged, and without auxiliary engines to save cost and to vastly increase storage capacity. The "lack" of auxiliary engines has *proven* to not be an inconvenience in boats of this size, and encourages the development of the skills of seamanship that Sea-Steading demands. Such a vessel can often be purchased and refit for under $20,000—and is an excellent and prudent place to start for an individual or couple of ordinary means. My "RENEGADE" followed this model, and I cruised and lived aboard more or less independently for eight years.

"MACHA", my new boat is a Phase Two Sea-Stead. A much larger and capable vessel—MACHA is based on a traditional Colin Archer hull. Ballasted to 32,000 pounds displacement, carrying the large traditional gaff-cutter rig with working lowers of 1350 square feet, MACHA is 38 feet on deck, 11 feet 8 inches abeam, and 50 feet overall. Designed to be a workhorse—MACHA is fitted with the simplest and most practical gear possible of adequately performing the task, with an eye always cast to economy and self-sufficiency. "MACHA" is a much more capable vessel, and its greater abilities provide some income able to offset its greater costs of ownership.

What we are trying to organize at the moment is the Phase Three Sea-Stead. Can a vessel such as MACHA be used to provide support for a fleet of smaller Phase One Sea-Steads? Can a community of frontiersmen be created on the oceans, reaping the benefits of shared infrastructure and resources? In essence, can there be created a floating frontier town? Can such a community be created that could have its own self-sufficiency and income generating potential? *I think so*, and I believe the potential to be great. It is impractical, for example, for a fleet of six small boats to carry individual water-makers, especially when smaller water-makers are less rugged and reliable, when one larger vessel could carry one large unit and thus be the well-maintained "well" for the group. It is impractical also for each boat to carry dive tanks and gear, when one boat could carry a few tanks and perhaps a compressor. The potential is great, and the possibilities for increases in safety, independence, and quality of life are such that this potentiality must be investigated. We are not at this point convinced that larger boats are more effective Sea-Steads. It is possible that a larger boat's capacity to carry gear—especially income generating tools and stores—may make a larger boat in some ways more viable. But the costs of a larger boat are larger, and incomes must be larger to support them. This may be an unnecessary encumbrance, and the expected gain in quality of life assumed by many may not be justifiable. We expect to resolve an ideal size through this project. Further investigation is required at this point.

Figure 1: Big and Little Sisters—AVALON careens against MACHA to effect rig repairs after a difficult passage.

Consider this very carefully:

Is it reasonable to expect petroleum dependent machinery to remain a viable tool for the Sea-Stead in the long term? Are diesel engines for propulsion reasonable aids or encumbering luxuries? Certainly, talented crews on engineless sailing vessels have proven again and again that engines are *not* necessary to effective boat handling. We much consider very carefully in this turbulent age with uncertain supplies and rising costs whether we want to put this potentially very unreliable and expensive machine at the heart of our project. Many successful Sea-Steads have no propulsion power other than sails, and my current vessel is no exception.

A large portion of this book is about the act of sailing. There are a lot of books on the shelves that have something to do with sailing—but the "sailing" I'm going to be talking about in this book seems to have become a lost art. Again, when I speak of sailing, I mean just that—sailboats, not motor boats. This distinction is important to the concept of the Sea-Stead, for reasons both financial and psychological. This discussion will be surprising to some, and some will take issue with the points that follow. I have no apology for this. I'm not certain how many more centuries of successful voyaging must still take place wholly under sail to prove to the doubters that it is possible and viable. Still, even the unconvinced may well find useful information here.

The "sailing" world has been well marketed and merchandised—boats are bought off the line just like the new model of cars—boats are designed to be as accessible and turn-key as possible. Sailing has become more accessibly casual. Yacht design is far more influenced by interior accommodations and ease of docking under power than seaworthiness or anything else. This has created a new kind of yachtsman—one who has by and large forgotten many of the skills and lessons that a yachtsman of fifty years ago might have had. Fifty years ago it took more ability and commitment to sail than it does today. The yachtsman of fifty years ago learned from this commitment—whether he wanted to or not. Today this is no longer the case. The yachtsman of today has not felt the need to learn the skills of the past—*he simply hasn't had the need*. The influence of the "work boat" world of sailing—that might have served as an example to the yachtsman of years past—with all its practicality, functionality, and knowledge has all but disappeared. It is of inestimable value to gain a instinctive, visceral understanding of what might not be ideal, *but what works*. We have lost this with the lost of our working sailboats. We have those, in places, which try to keep these nautical arts alive in one forum or another—but more often than not the efforts take the form of exhibition rather than demonstrations of viability.

<u>*This*</u> is not to be a book of academic interest. This is to be a very practical text with the intent of introducing the reader to the practical skills of handling a sailboat. A sailboat, as defined in this text, is a boat powered by sail. It is not a powerboat. It is not a power-assisted sail craft. It is powered by sail, and controlled by the human beings that ride upon it—not synthetic electromechanical crew. Some would say that this "sailing purism" is at best an esoteric exercise—exhibition again—but we say it is not. There are <u>*very practical reasons*</u> why one might—upon

choosing a sailboat with which to see the far places of the world—decide to choose a pure sailing craft. There might be more reason for it all the time…

This book is written for one who has learned some about sailing, has done some sailing, and is perhaps considering taking up cruising or perhaps purchasing a boat. It is not a primer—it assumes the reader has some knowledge of the basics of sail. This book will likely be of great use to this individual. This book is also written from the perspective of the coastal or inland sailor—as it presents the most complicated tactical problems that a sailor faces—and teaches the most pertinent points. Sea-Steading, as I currently envision it, will most often take place near land, for this is where the food, supplies, and camaraderie is to be found—not in the deep ocean. One must be able to sail the hard waters, amidst the fickle winds and relentless currents—at least some part of the time. The vessel must be capable of this as well. This skill is often overlooked and even discounted in today's yachting print. My observations consistently show me that in technical inland waters less that 5 percent of the sailboats sail in any other than ideal conditions—probably not more than 20 percent in ideal conditions. In the last two years, I haven't seen a single sailboat anchor under sail. I've seen 3 sail off of moorings. Yes, I am keeping track because it is truly shocking. Sailing is simply something that very few people do.

So while not a "primer"—for many this book *will* be an introduction. It is an introduction to sailing in its true form, and the attitude sailing requires. It is an introduction to the attitude that motors aren't even a consideration. Sailing is not learned by power-assisted voyaging, nor is it learned by maneuvering around a few yellow buoys in a bay. These teach something, of course, but what these activities teach are certainly not a complete representation of the activity we call "sailing." This book has no pretense to be complete either. Not intended to be comprehensive, it is intended to be facilitating. If we raise issues that are often ignored—and to point the way to discovering the solutions to these issues, by oneself and one's experience—one may, through time, be on one's way to learn what sailing is all about. That is the goal of this book. There is no way to learn to sail, or any skill for that matter, but by doing it…

The Choice to Exist is Inherently Irrational...

Introduction

February, 2004.

So here I am, underway aboard my tight little sailing sloop *"RENEGADE."* Above me my six year old standing rig still holds a sparkle in the bright February sun. A cold, heavy, frontal wind fills the sails; cold water boils on the starboard side, roiling away to looward. Bronze, steel, leather—The craft in the splices and the meticulously measured stitches in the latigo have served me well thus far—these archetypally appropriate materials for both the aesthetic as well as the structural. This rig—and the sails that hang upon it—my web for catching the zephyrs—still appears as I feel a rig should; it is beautiful, and it is my still my best bid against the uncertainties of the sea. Perhaps more so, if we imagine steel might be fortified by carbon, chromium, *and good memories as well...*

Much has occurred in the last few years. The world is a harder and meaner place than it was when I last wrote; I feel the wear this has had upon me—of course we spoke of the inevitability of this trend toward conflict, so for those of us who keep an eye on the horizon we are perhaps not too surprised. Much change is afoot—I really do believe that we may have passed a very critical point in human existence. Change in my life as well—little *"RENEGADE"* is sold and this is likely my last sail aboard her. She, thankfully, goes to a good capable friend, but I am melancholy just as well. I have purchased as of last December a abandoned hull project for very little money and I am setting forth on a new task. This new task reflects a new understanding of the world and our place in history, and in my life, and I am moving forward.

I now believe we have seen the beginning of the end of the oil age already—and with it we have seen the beginning of the end of the greatest period of wealth that the world has ever seen—and indeed *may ever see again.* Civilizations have always been built and empire created upon the ready access of resources—free from the earth for the taking, and these resources—all of them—are rapidly being used up. We as a culture refuse to learn anything at all from our mistakes and our atrocities, we deliberately ignore the fact that the world is a zero sum game with only a finite amount of resources—that at some point that ultimate barrier to expansion must be reached. We are indeed now approaching this barrier. Since the majority of our culture is afflicted with an

1

obsessive compulsive disorder that demands and drives the acquisition of property and wealth to the exclusion of all else, at some point *it is a necessity* that as goods become rarified the only means left to acquire yet more from one's self is to steal from others...

And the affluent are stunned by the hatred the poor feel towards them? That the West and the American people in particular are stunned that much of the world bears so much resentment towards them? Why? It is indeed a religious (un) holy war on all sides—of fundamentalist capitalist consumerism against all other fundamentalist religions. There is no surprise in this conflict—materialism against "otherworldlisms"—they are certainly mortal rivals, aggressive and mutually exclusive. This I fear to be the precursor of the final global conflict. I say final because in *this* conflict will be consumed the wealth and resources necessary to fight a second global conflict—as well as the necessary wealth and resources to recover from this conflict. I do not see an apocalyptic cataclysm—although this remains a possibility—but rather a day is reached in which there no longer exists the fuel to fly the bombers, the battle tanks rust where they ran dry—and except for the petty and vicious small scale warfare that likely will trend on into perpetuity—little of scale will ever rumble again.

> *This is the way the world ends*
> *This is the way the world ends*
> *This is the way the world ends*
> > *Not with a bang, but with a whimper...*

I do not wish to participate in this conflict. I do not, however, believe it is possible to prevent it. The conflict, in fact is *necessary* as we finally writhe free from the fantastic religious values that entrap us. God no longer speaks to us—we are abandoned as orphans to ourselves as we tumble through the cosmos—that realization shakes the heart of most all who live today. The fight is not so much for this or that but rather for meaning itself—for affirmation of existence. There is none. There is nothing. *This must be realized.*

The time has arrived for we courageous among men to squarely face the fact that we lack any "metaphysical" basis for our actions, we must also abandon our preference for the "otherworldly" and finally get beyond primitive concepts of "good and evil" once and for all. Again, this *must* occur, for we know this reality—and the denial of this reality makes many of us ill. The desperate grasping towards the divine affirmation that will never come is bent into desperate grasping in many forms. Some shuffle for miles in the hot sun to a shine in bare feet in grasping for affirmation. Some beat their bodies and cut themselves and wail in the dark in this grasping for affirmation. In our culture, we work long hours at the detriment at our health and our relationships—we attempt to build grand temples and homes in this grasping for affirmation. This is hollow and empty, for certain, and bears the marks of madness.

None-the-less, the fact that we lack any "otherworldliness;" that if any god or other or spiritual realm exists it remains inaccessible to and unfathomable to us—and as such, *does not exist by definition*—this reality does not preclude the necessity that we must still lift ourselves by our own bootstraps and find reason and criteria for our actions lest we lose volition altogether. We have not the luxury of doing else wise. Fortunately, while this is a difficulty, I believe it need not be an impossibility. Without reliance on any "spiritual" assumption, one can still form a reasonable ethic—indeed the *only* reasonable ethic, although this ethic may fundamentally *not be rational*. Yet is there a vestige of rationality in the recognition that we do not have the luxury of *not* projecting some value, even though the value we project may ultimately be nothing more than a preference? I hope so, for there is nothing else.

There can hardly be a debate that even in a world without meaning or god that some actions are, at least on a personal level, more constructive for me than others. As well, that some actions can seem as helping the continuance of my existence more than others and some actions that, again, at least from *my personal perspective*, do the same for "others"—and *this* may be interesting because these actions may also be beneficial to me. Indeed, the entire natural world exists on such an ethic and carries along marvelously without a single conscious thought. We should examine and affirm this same principle—the principle of the successful—which is what I will call within the context of consciousness, to affirm life.

When I say "affirm life" I certainly do not mean to suggest any leap back into the otherworldly. I do not suggest that life has any inherent value except for those involved in it—and then irrationally—every thing that lives has an interest in its own existence or it wouldn't live. When I say "affirm life" I simply mean this—to pursue, in our case consciously and deliberately, what all other living things do: to grow, to create, to become ever stronger and more expansive. To do so as well in a manner that trends towards my personal evolution: to my every increasing personal complexity and diversity: of course in doing so I create an environment around me of complexity and diversity for my own benefit as I reach ever higher…We can, with very little discomfort, live within the same ethic as does a tree—the tree, to survive, must reach ever higher towards the sun, with ever stronger branches, and with ever greener foliage; we must drop our fruits about us for both ourselves and the small creatures lest we *both* perish; we must grow high and broad until we seem to support the stars and the heavens themselves...I hardly speak in metaphor...

More practical—you cry! Rightly so! I agree. Certainly; practicality. This is to be a supremely practical book and is meant to be applied: What is thought without applications? I'll answer that—we call it "pretentiousness."

We must as more or less conscious human beings grow to survive. I will not claim to be a higher or even more complex creature than the tree—but I will claim to be different. While using the same ethic, still the tree requires stimulus from the sun and nourishment from the soil—I require stimulus in different ways. In fact, in essentially three ways.

1. The physical

2. The intellectual

3. The social

The physical: We are physical beings. Since we must abandon the indefensible concept of a mind body duality with all other otherworldly concepts, we must assert this truth—we are our bodies. If one can even speak of mind without being inconsistent, we must certainly realize that a mind existing as part of an unhealthy body will not remain healthy for long. We require good food, clean air, good exercise and freedom from stressors and pathogens in order to reach our fullest potential. Our physical health, or the degree of it, limits our ultimate holistic health.

The intellectual: We require intellectual stimulation and exercise as well. Our neurons die and pathways fade daily if not used. Thus our health suffers. We must seek for the highest order of clarity, expansiveness, and accuracy—correspondence with actuality—in our mental constructs. We must strive for acuity and mental prowess—these are only to be realized in a fertile environment relatively free of drudgery and where learning is meaningful, applicable, and as such rewarding.

The social: We are social beings. We require each other for both mutual affirmation and comfort—we will not progress far in our academic pursuits without the challenge of peers—we will not build much of note without the hands of others to help with the heavy loads. It is healthy and productive for us to care and be cared for in the largest sphere of meaningful relationships we can maintain.

Of course these three areas are so intertwined as to be functionally insepara-ble—the relative health of each area affects and limits the health of the other and practically should be viewed as a composite—still it is reasonably useful to dissect as to define.

Now then, to say to "affirm life" again—to maximize my growth and health as defined in these three ways. I consider an action, predict its effect upon my gen-eral health—if the actions seems beneficial—I go ahead and act. While the pre-dictions of the results of my actions can be complicated and difficult, most often it is not. For example, I might ask whether or not I should own a car. From a context of what a car does to my health—assuming I would walk or bike other-wise—assuming it is going to cost me an appreciable amount of money that I cannot then use more constructively ort at least will require me an extra amount of hours in a stupefying job environment—this is time lost to spend with my loved ones—assuming I've got to breathe the exhaust—it becomes clear pretty quickly that unless I can come up with a major positive the car is a fast track to becoming fat, stupid, poor, generally unhealthy, and likely alienated as well. On the other hand, does it make sense for me to make an agenda out of this—and say deliberately never learn how to drive a car or refuse to have a driver's license to make some sort of social point? No, of course not. Merely having a driver's license has no effect on my health at all. Not knowing how to drive at all or being unwilling to for some ill-defined ethical reason may well be rude and inconve-niencing to others, for at some point driving a sick friend to the hospital might be the best thing to do. *There is no point to be made after one abandons the other-worldly and primitive concepts of righteousness.* One does what is best because it is best—and this, ultimately, is an entirely practical issue.

While, again, not all ethical considerations are this clear—it is definitely against my best interest to own a car but an indulgence in arrogant luxury to not know how to use one—I think that we will find that MOST of them are. I expect, however, that initially many of us may not appreciate the answers we find. Still, the fact that occasionally one bumps into a close call doesn't mean that we should abandon our considerations: it means rather we should consider all the more carefully...

Now it is very apparent that within our culture we've been sold a pile of shit on what's important—and as a result we're pretty unhealthy. No surprise, when the only aspect of our life that is given a significant shake is the attempt to amass a big pile of cash—we've been told that financial success is the means to physical, intellectual, and social health. I'm going to state that living a life striving for financial gain is a far greater hindrance to health than poverty might be. This assumes even that one strives and is relatively successful in money—the reality is more depressing: upwards of three quarters of the people in this obscenely wealthy country in the most wealthy of ages die completely broke…even here! Even now! These are the odds—would you take these on the risk of losing one's life and having nothing to show for it?

Now I would never suggest that one should not earn his or her daily bread, or that one need not work in some fashion to do so. All living things must do so, why should man be exempt? Rather, I am calling for a great deal of moderation; I am stating that it is foolhardy and grotesque to spend one's "life working oneself sick laying up goods against a sick day." To value a feeble and insipid existence where one is never too hot or too cold, where one never need exert oneself, where one lives without either risk or challenge; is this not quite close to the ideal of what we call success? And so we live in a culture where we are lonely and unhealthy, and wheeze when we walk, and even our exotic, expensive, over bred pets die of obesity…I cannot confront this with any feeling other than nausea. What is obscenity or perversity other than the elevation of the ill at the expense of the healthy?

It is good for me to be wet and cold on occasion. It is good to walk uncomfortable distances. It is good for me to work and to suffer a bit at times. As a sailor, it is good for me to make mistakes on reading the weather and to end getting a little punishment for my lack of attention. All this makes me stronger—I should embrace it as a means to becoming the best I can. Even among the feeble of the world I feel I can boast even by their values—to stand among the best of the bean counters and business men, whom I will point out to that I can keep my home in good repair and my welfare intact on nickels and dimes while they in their lack of skill require millions to do the same…

I don't see an honorary MBA coming any time soon.

Now, the crux. There is a great danger in what I advocate here, and I wish to introduce this danger immediately. While I am convinced that what I advocate is the best and even a necessary course of action, it may at long last be of no use at all. If the ethic here has no use, I see very grim prospects for the future of mankind. I do not believe we can take this issue too seriously, and I ask that this issue is kept present as we work through this discovery.

Some of you who have walked with me thus far will have sensed where we are headed. Here lies the monster that destroys most that come this way. Here is its riddle:

Does one live a life of honesty, integrity, and strive for personal growth—knowing full well the rest of mankind does not and will not—and knowing that this choice will make one a lonely hermit and an outcast?

OR

Does one realize that one hasn't the strength to carry on alone—and thus choose to remain ill in company rather than to carry on alone?

The higher one elevates oneself—the more alienated one becomes. We have been told that as one grows one becomes more self-fulfilled—I would say not—but one DOES become more full. This means the yearning to give and share ones wealth with others becomes ever stronger. One desires to share the wonders one has seen; but one's eyes see further than others: they cannot hear what you hear—you long to take others to the heights you have ascended to but the air is to cold and rare for them. Too often your offer of gifts are taken as taunts and threats even—and one learns to be silent. Or as one who speaks to children too much. As one grows, those that one can hold communion with grow fewer and fewer—or perhaps disappear. Then what? What now? Eventually the alienation one feels eats away like a poison and one's health suffers for it—eventually one reaches as far as one can. The beauty of the forests become wilderness with no one to share it with—and one proceeds along one's path no further. Do we know this person? Is this not true? Careful, as we hunt for objections—careful let us not mistake the eternal cheeriness buoyed by strength of the hardened traveler for the joy of the traveler who has found his home…that smile may be a virtue, but not represent fulfillment.

After a good deal of very cautious and despairingly rigorous thought, I have decided that the idea of "self-affirmation" is a philosopher's phantasm. I do not believe we can feel affirmed alone. I believe this is due to how we are wired in terms of our social needs, and that we only feel affirmed within a society when we perceive our self to be a genuinely valuable member of a group involved in a genuinely valuable pursuit. We mask this reality, because most of us are not genuinely valuable nor are our pursuits—and we attempt to make them appear more so by giving ourselves grand titles and projecting ill-fitting and grandiose imagery upon our endeavors. Again, as we will examine, there is no inherently valuable experience outside of subjective experience, which ultimate is an irrational preference, but again necessity insists…The use of the motif of sailing as a vehicle for this discussion will make this apparent, as the motif is so concise and simple—but for a beginning, let us say that a "good" man has no value on a sailboat at all, but a "skillful helmsman" certainly does. Can we hear this distinction?

A potential for despair, yes, *but imagine the coldness of a world where no one needed or desired the affirmation of anyone else…*

All voyages of discovery require traveling companions. All ships require crew to stay their course. And again, after all this ramble, back to sailing: Few activities in this world symbolize the life of mankind as a sailing ship on its way to uncharted regions. Few groups of people relate together as effectively of a crew pursuing a meaningful end. This is why I started this forum—this is its purpose. The way is, or should be, hazardous: we must expect and will see casualties. I'm sure we all have, friends, at this point—I'm sure we all have. And the world wonders why sailors are prone to cursing: what other response is reasonable in the face of diabolical injustice other than to spit?

Hopelessness? Nearly. Of course—but hopelessness is why people have always put to sea. It is a calculated risk, we choose hopelessness nearly over hopelessness certain and damn the alienation in hope of that oh so fine hope…We cannot abide the rabble ashore for long. We tread among them with caution when we must…the disparity of man is astounding—imagine that as we navigate by the stars and even now by the stars we have built with our own hands that there are still men who might well argue that peanuts have souls—and as such wouldn't be chased away as the village idiot but rather receive a seat on the supreme court…realizing that the masses of mankind have such a vested interest in myth and fraud, in so much blue smoke and bullshit that anyone who sees more clearly is hardly likely to be admired—remembering this; stand tall but tread with caution!

So this is why I live like I do. I live on my little boats not for any particular love of the sea but rather that it is the healthiest environment that I have found for myself. I live what is basically a minimalist, ecologically friendly lifestyle not in any attempt to save the world, but rather in an attempt to save myself. This is also why I preach like I tend to do—the task we have at hand at this point in our development—this awe inspiring difficult task—the task of creating meaning for ourselves now that we've discovered ourselves to be orphans in this enormous universe: to pause, to say—yes indeed, orphans. Most have believed that they were heirs. Orphans. Orphans need a different set of skills than an heir might, I think. Those skills lend themselves well upon the sea...Orphans are more likely to look for a traveling companion than an heir might as well...

Orphans as well are those likely sorts that would seek the frontier. Can we sense the urgency of this endeavor?

Remember as we voyage together that the sea is only the first step...

1

THE TASK

One meets a lot of people traveling. One meets people in a manner different than one does if one is a local resident. There is a certain amount of confidence and trust that is automatically granted the archetypal wanderer—the image is full of the concept of a sage in disguise—and the fact that one is unlikely to see this wanderer again makes them an ideal recipient of a confession. It seems to me that most people today have a confession that they are simply bursting with. This is not a confession that they can share with their friends—as the confession would destroy the friendship. This is not a confession that they can share with their spouse, as it would destroy the relationship. This is certainly not a confession that they can share with a priest or a councilor, because the confession itself is very near a challenge—an attack even, an admission of the falsehood of the great lies that we live under…

This confession? *That I feel so hollow…so empty…so lonely…*

And expecting an answer perhaps, my response of "of course you do!" is perhaps not too comforting—but it is fair and accurate.

We only have meaning in our lives insofar as we create meaning. Meaning is nothing more than what can be termed "emotive import", or a fancy way of saying the "event at hand makes me feel." It doesn't really matter *what* a particular event makes one feel, only that it does. We only notice, are conscious of, the emotion of the moment.

Let us be frank. Much of the time in our interaction with the world the emotion we experience is not positive. If we were to carry a pair of stopwatches with us, and during the day keep track of each moment we were experiencing a negative emotion and each moment we are experiencing a positive emotion—I think that many of us much of the time would come up pretty heavily on the negative side. At least I think this is a fair bet for most people in most conventional lifestyles. This problem has been a problem for mankind forever, of course, and the religions of the world have tried to confuse the basic issue of the fact that for most people, most of the time, life stinks. There are all sorts of mental tricks that are taught to blunt the edge of reality, to numb the mind with ideas of acceptance and detachment—or otherworldly justice that at some fictitious point in the future makes all the pain one experiences in the now justifiable—of course these are the worst, the most evil of lies. To ignore—which in essence what religion teaches to do—towards what religion calls "evil" is unimaginable to me; to perform task and ritual that over a lifetime piths the emotions to achieve a quiet, even, and wholly useless personal glow is grotesque in the extreme. Imagine that if mankind had faced squarely the issues of the difficulty of life for ten centuries rather than trying to evade them, where we might be today? Rather they teach being bad cooks we cut out our tongues…We will evade no longer—or at least I will not. This book is an attempt to move down this new path.

I have always had this bias in my life—dissatisfaction and a striving towards a better way. George Bernard Shaw made the quip "The reasonable man conforms his ideas to fit the world, the unreasonable man expects the world to conform to his ideas: Thus, all progress is affected by the unreasonable man." I think this sums up my temperament pretty effectively.

And it may not be all that unreasonable after all. I was raised in a fairly religious environment, matured out of that non-sense to humanitarian atheism—mostly matured out of that non-sense: in many ways I feel that I've walked a good deal of the spectrum and seen and studied a lot of creeds. I must admit, as I think most anyone will do, that most of the lot are pretty ineffectual. Of course, one finds particular cases in all belief systems where things more or less seem to work, but still huge numbers of people often flounder around the edges. I've come to the point that *since* I've found that most people in any given system of thought neither understand nor believe what they say they do that in a lot of ways—excepting cases where the belief system is aggressive and combative—*that it really doesn't matter much what one believes*, because again, almost no one does. At least to say that almost no one believes anything of any sort in such a manner of confidence to effect how they live their lives. Of course there are certainly crazy fundamentalists—yes, you get these whenever a belief system is threatened and no longer makes sense—hence, today—but among people in reasonable circumstances and in reasonable comfort most are pretty apathetic.

I have come to the conclusion that more than what one believes or the ethical system one holds, the *environment one lives in* has more of a bearing on how one views the world—I think the meaning one feels in one's existence is much more carried in where and how one exists than what one thinks about it. Thinking about it makes for very little. In a good environment, where one lives well, the occasion to think about ethics seldom arises. A bad environment, and desperation in general, make one tend to grasp at any hope, and one is likely to find god. If hard pressed enough, one's mind will reach towards any salvation. They say there are no atheists in foxholes, and to some degree I admit as an atheist this is true—religion of course recognizes this and seems to figure a good solid shelling is better means of proselytizing than a sermon ever was. Certainly better than a bowl of rice. Religion requires desperation for its existence—what is the offer of a redeemer to one who feels no need of redemption?

Therefore, I would suggest that if one finds that one is thinking about ethics much, it means that one's environment isn't too good, and the ethic that is developed should be one that instructs one to move towards a good environment, or, back to Shaw, to make one's world conform to one's idea of what would be good.

And what would be a "good environment?" One where we felt that our lives had meaning in a positive way: that we were healthy and the environment encouraged our health; that we were skilled and learned and the environment encouraged this growth; that we had role and purpose within a group of respectable peers—seeking a meaningful end: if we live in such a place, what need have we of any sort of creed? Again, religion and its kin only make sense among the ill and the desperate...

I will suggest that health, intellectual skill, and social role are relatively simple and quantifiable concepts. As such, the rational work of forming the ethic is relatively simple as well now that we have driven off the smoke. Health means that I am as strong, viable and free of disease as possible for as long as possible. Intellectual skill means the collection of things I know how to do and how well I learn to do new things—as opposed to effete academia, which is something else entirely. A social role means just that—I have a position in a group that is granted to me because I am valuable within that group—probably directly relative to how healthy and skilled I am—and *my existence is affirmed in this.* There is no pretense in this anywhere—these values could very nearly be enumerated on a balance sheet.

The environment of the Sea-Steading lifestyle is very much like this ideal, and I found it has been very effective in achieving all these ends, and more so all the time. This much would seem obvious, but there are very serious traps. The most serious trap is this: the pursuit of health and skill often involve a good deal of very hard work. Very many people do not like hard work—in the conventional world it is possible to achieve at least the appearance of skill and health and worth without much substance to it at all. An illusion, for certain, but many people—their sensibility likely clouded by erroneous world views as we have said—are simply unwilling to lay their hand to the task of right living. Also, again, the image competes with the reality. This as well is certainly the case in the image of sailing itself.

What is sailing?

Commonly, I suppose, "sailing" means traveling in a boat under sail. When one asks a man on the street what sailing is, this is what he will say. This means using wind as propulsion, weather and tide as the variables that determines the route and the tactics—it implies an intimate knowledge and involvement with the natural world. As such it is certainly a much different activity than simply "boating." The symbolism and the level of involvement is the key. Perhaps one could suggest that sailing necessitates a higher level of participation with one's environment than many other forms of travel might—like riding in an airplane or on a bus, or careening down the freeway in a motor home. There is an implicit value in this; to say that while one *could* go to island X, for example, by taking a flight, the "sailor" who travels by means of sail wants to go there in a matter that *teaches, tests, and proves something.* This also suggests that that if one really wants to experience something, then one must have a bit of an investment in it. One might even go so far to say that the quality of the experience is relative and *dependant* on the amount of effort involved as well as the amount of skill exercised. An experience may be had in a manner so much more meaningful than another—that it might casually resemble—that it may *no longer even be the same type of experience.* If one walks over a mountain rather than drives around it, one sees indeed a <u>*different*</u> mountain. Most of us would suggest a greater mountain at that.

We can reasonably suggest that "sailing" is, in many ways, and perhaps even fundamentally, an "aesthetic" activity at its core. For "cruising under sail" to be meaningful—more than a mere lark or some lackadaisical diversion for unimaginative folks with too much time and money on their hands—it must fit within a certain symbolic framework. One is drawn to the activity because one finds it appealing—this suggests a lack somewhere that wants to be filled. If one ignores this symbolic framework—if one ignores the stimulus that gave rise to the effort—the resultant experience will certainly be less that satisfying.

Figure : "Pristine" harbor, and a no-wake zone. Can you believe they get away with this? A boat like this is dumping perhaps 2 gallons an hour of unburned fuel in the water as it runs, burning another 14 gallons to blow into the air. It leaves a slick behind it as it runs—but the "zero discharge" people can't see any of this, apparently.

I do not think that anyone with sense can say that there is much aesthetically pleasing or symbolically constructive about the sort of people that blast around in huge motor yachts. While this activity obviously appeals to a certain tasteless segment of the population—its popularity is no testament to the quality of the experience. Experience requires sensitivity: Power-boating demands one shut one's senses off. It is <u>necessary</u> within the experience to ignore the noise, the vibration, the ride of the boat. It is necessary too to ignore the smoke, the oil slick, and the beach erosion that one's passage causes. It is necessary too to ignore the statement of such a passage makes: belittlement of the local peoples homes and environment as secondary to one's own jollies, and to frankly discard any care about courtesy or meaningful interaction with other people. Power-boating demands, then, that one be a sort of person with poor awareness. It demands of its adherents little, except that they be some sort of semi-functional deaf-mute idiot...a demand met and all too often evinced by their level of boat-handling skill and shore side behavior.

Some people with more taste claim to still cruise what passes for "sailboats," although this number is dwindling in comparison to their noisy bastard cousins. "Sailing," I will insist, however, has become an activity seldom practiced. Many "cruisers" who claim to "sail" today gloat with pride if their passages make the fifty percent mark in terms of their ratio of sail miles covered to power. This ratio of fifty percent has become reasonable to many. Not only this, it has also become reasonable to *expect* to only sail when it is *convenient,* and the wind and weather are within a very narrow range of conditions. When seamanship is called for, or when speed drops below an arbitrary number—indeed when most perform the very act of setting sail—the engine comes on. These boats are designed, crewed and "cruised" in a manner that makes "sailing" impossible, thus they demand auxiliary power. People say it is only reasonable to have an engine on board a "sailboat." Reasonable? Since the engine removes the greater need for seamanship, for knowledge, even for *personal investment,* thus the resultant experience is fundamentally changed. Is it reasonable to ignore the fundamental reason why one might want to sail at all?

Most people one meets are avid "motor-sailors." Most people have "motor-sailor" craft where the auxiliary engine is *critical* to the function of the vessel. It is necessary for propulsion, as well as for the power to drive convenience systems. It is the artificial crew that allows sail changes to be made. It is the hands that set and haul the anchor. It is the eyes that keep watch. This is obviously the case. This is indeed typical and expected.

Yet if you were to call one of these "sailors" a "motor-sailor" or refer to the boat as a "motor-sailer," as it *obviously is*—by every potential definition—most of these "motor-sailors" would bristle. They would take this as an insult.

Why should this be troublesome? Either one "sails" a "sailboat" or one does not. This is a pretty simple concept. If one "cruises" under sail—then one is a cruising "sailor." Again, not a difficult concept. Why then do not most people freely admit they are "motorsailors" and not "sailors?" Why do people get hot under the collar when called a "motor sailor?" Why should this be construed as an insult? *Because we all recognize that it takes more skill and ability to handle a sailboat under sail than it does to handle a motor sailor, and we respect that.* We recognize that it takes more investment to make passages under sail than it does under power-assisted sail. We recognize that a person who has the will, ability, skill, and stamina to do so has more will, ability, skill, and stamina than one that does not. We understand that a "sailor" is in many ways a more skilled human being than is a "motor sailor." Understanding this, many people *do desire* to be sailors and to sail. Unfortunately, however, many of these same people do not care to make the investment necessary, nor they do not have an interest in the amount of sweat and effort involved. Still, they desire the status of skill and so have learned to merely _presume_ to be "sailors." They pretend. Thus the insult of inherent in the term "motor sailor." It calls a spade a spade.

This is fraud. We all know this. We, once again, are drawn to this activity for a reason: a lack. If we do not fulfill this lack—our activity is a failure. Among those that fail—it is common to preach the method of failure for it masks one's own. To preach failure is dangerous. Yet this is what drives the boating world…We know all too often the silliness of our activity—hence the vast array of "boat things" that we purchase and bolt to our boats in an endeavor to make them appear more "serious" or more "seaworthy"—as if a "motor-sailer" needed more gear to become more a "sailboat."

"Cruising under sail" is an aesthetic activity which ends can only be met by aesthetic means. Sailboats—straight sailers now—are aesthetic to their essence. They are motive shapes—a complex collection of curves that creates motion out of force by sheer being—it is difficult indeed to find a creation of the hand of man that is as exquisite an example of form following function following the forces of nature that equals the sailboat. We sense this—it is an appropriate vehicle for an aesthetic task. Our senses need not rebel at its proximity. It is an appropriate ally in our endeavor.

It would be difficult to argue that activities that challenge our skills and encourage development of strength and character are *not* good for us. In "cruising" again, we agree it is fair to say that the "challenge" of the activity is an inherent part of the quality of the experience. I must point out, however, "challenge" is a relative concept, and what might be routine for one might be high adventure for others. We see that in the adventures many have simply getting on and off the dock. Yet there is no inherent virtue in incompetence—even though I admit incompetence might often make things more exciting. Neither is there inherent virtue in not evincing any progression in one's abilities—for one who has spent a few years on the water, passage-making in a powered craft must be nothing if not simply boring and unrewarding. We do not feel a sense of pride (I hope) in successfully driving our cars fifty miles without mishap—although once in our lives, years ago, driving was high adventure.

Sailing is not like that at all. Each passage is a new experience. The number of variables one must take into consideration in making a successful passage under sail—variables the presence of the engine makes insignificant—makes every passage a challenge. While after time an acquisition of local knowledge may diminish the level of adventure in one's native grounds—there is always the next fifty miles of water to explore and its particular characteristics. It is simply much more difficult to make good passages under sail. It is mentally tougher and physically tougher. Those who eschew the engine certainly will become mentally stronger and physically tougher as a result.

The purest and most rewarding form of travel must be walking. This is difficult to do on the water. For those of us drawn to sea, sailing is the next purest thing. Some of us need desperately to escape the triviality of daily life. Engines make trivial.

The degree to which engines make power-assisted sailing trivial is disguised. Sailing, in good conditions, takes nearly no ability at all. One can log off a thousand miles under the keel with hardly touching a sheet. One could be asleep, or dead even, and the boat would have continued along its way. While this sort of sailing is pleasant, it is certainly not challenging, nor does it teach or demand much of the sailor aboard. No, sailing, and "seamanship" does not so much involve the thousand mile passage in ideal conditions, although it is involved in producing it—"seamanship" involves much more that hundred feet of contrary current off the point that one cannot make way against. It involves getting under sail in good manner and entering a harbor with proficiency after a passage. People like to think of themselves as a 80% sailor, and a 20% motor-sailor—although such a ratio is dangerously close to a "yachtsman's gale." They like to think in terms of hours underway, or miles underway, for this ratio. This disguises or belittles the fact—that without the engine, had they encountered that hundred feet of the contrary current and not been able to deal with it—even after a thousand miles, they still would have *failed* to make port. Properly, then, their ratio should be expressed as 100% power-assisted sail, as they would have been helpless without the engine. It is important to note that in any activity that is judged by its completion, a 1% failure means a 100% failure...Let us make being 100% sailors our goal...

Sailing requires of and rewards those who reach towards health and skill—the environment demands it. Among those that are sailors, and there are still a few of those, the skill and strength useful on one ship is useful on the next—the knowledge one sailor has is certainly useful to another. This usefulness is meaningful—those that *are useful have a role that is undeniable within this group, the affirmation that comes from this usefulness is undeniable as well.* In sailing, and within the group of people that do it, there is meaning written symbolically into the task itself. What does sailing mean as a symbol other than to head away towards hope and promise? Is it not a symbol of expansion and growth at its core? Does it not carry the meaning implicit in it that we that do so are underway towards better and greater things? This is certainly significant, for if this analysis is correct, we are describing a lifestyle in which health and strength are necessary, learning is required, tested and rewarded, where group and role still means something, and the entire activity as a whole at its very core is an expression of the ideal of life…how many other activities of life come this close to the ideal? I can not think of another that even approaches this. Certainly, there is discomfort a plenty to be had, certainly there is a good deal of sweat involved, certainly there is fear and anxiety—certainly there will be those that fail. This is to be expected—we are speaking of life after all. Nonetheless, that which is good for us is inherent in the environment, as sailors we grow whether we like it or not, and we are all the better for it.

Figure 3: If accessories make a boat seaworthy, then this is the most seaworthy boat I've ever seen. See what we've come to?

2

A SAILBOAT

A sailboat is a craft powered by wind. Its efficiency is dependent on how effectively it harnesses the power of the wind. The voyages it makes, the far ports it visits—are dependent largely on how well it harnesses the power of the wind. A "good" sailboat is one that effectively fulfills its purpose.

We have an ethic then, contained in the sailboat. A sailboat is designed to go places under sail. To do so, it must manifest certain "virtues"—it must be fast, efficient, weatherly, safe, reasonably comfortable, durable, and cost-effective. If it lacks in any of these "virtues" the sailboat is less "good" and its efficiency suffers. With the suffering of efficiency, the purpose that the sailboat was designed for is unlikely to be met.

Virtue? Of course from our atheistic perspective the ideas of "good" and "virtue" seem a little queer. There is a purpose to the use of these terms. To claim that "goodness" is dependant on the effectual fulfillment of a purpose is not a new idea, but it is in many ways a forgotten idea—at least to many of us. In many "primitive" cultures and primitive religions human "goodness" has exactly that same form as does our analysis of the sailboat. A "good" man might be one who is an effective hunter, or a warrior. Effectuality in these environments is easily quantifiable—a man who is a good shot with a bow exists under the same ethic as the sailboat that sails well to weather. As society and religion evolves, the idea of goodness becomes much more complicated—or we might say easier to evade—and "goodness" becomes more of a nebulous concept. Purpose changes as well, from a man who daily must gather food for his family—again, easily understandable—to a man who "fulfills the unfathomable purpose of God", which might as well mean anything, or perhaps nothing at all. Complication of an idea does not always mean a more evolved presentation of an idea. In this case, especially, since most of us fall short of the idea of being good in the world of the hunter/gatherer/warrior society, there is a distinct incentive to create some worldview where we are "granted goodness by grace." Is this good for us? Hardly. Does it encourage us to be effectual human beings? Hardly.

But more on this later—back to sailboats. Let us discuss our idea of designing a "virtuous" sailboat. Since the Sea-Stead is the topic at hand (remember?), let us say our design parameters are to design a sailboat that carries a couple around the world in the most "effectual" way possible. Let us design a fast, efficient, weatherly, safe, comfortable, and cost-effective boat for this purpose.

Now where are we to begin? This is not a trivial task...

It is curious to note that if we had asked to design a boat for a very limited environment, not a global one, this would have been a much easier task. Let us say we want to design a boat that is fast around the buoys in 10 knots of air on flat water, and we want it to sell. This is easy. An easily driven hull with a minimum of wetted surface area, a high aspect keel to make it stiff and weatherly—the extra ballast can be made up for by crew—and a tall rig to cheat the summertime inversions. It has to look a certain way above the waterline—it must look flashy and somehow radical but still conform to the current idea of what is "speedy." It needs to be as light as possible to keep the sail sizes down so the rig loads aren't heavy enough to strain the backs of the bankers that will own them. Light, as well, means expensive, as exotic materials are called for. This adds to the idea of being conventionally "speedy" but helps keep the exclusive nature of sailing that so many people want to preserve. This boat has no need of being comfortable, as no one makes it their home, it need not be durable, as it is only used for a couple of hours a week. It need not be safe, ultimately, as it never faces difficult conditions. It need not be cost-effective as it is a simple toy for rich boys. Yet for peculiar reason these types of boats abound and are revered—there is a curious cultural value here...

This value not only exists in sailboats. Let us look to biology as an example. We for some reason are drawn to admire those evolved organisms that inhabit very narrow ecological zones—finding the course of evolution amazing that created them. Perhaps the course is not so amazing after all. Perhaps there is a parallel here. Obviously, evolution finds it relatively easy to create an organism that lives in a "special purpose" environment. This may suggest, curiously, that the species of exotic orchid that only lives on one sort of tree in one certain area and blooms only once a decade under exacting conditions may well not be a very remarkable or highly evolved creature at all. At least when compared to something like a seagull, which seems to be able to flourish anywhere and on anything. We seem to carry this same preference for the specialized to our society as well, preferring a person who is wholly ineffectual except for one peculiar ability—in fact we encourage this sort of development. Why is this the case? Upon examination, it makes very little sense. Is this again a preference born of evasion—and attempt to escape an ethic that would demand we "tell the truth and shoot well with arrows?"

But again back to sailboats—designing our world cruiser. Obviously we must take a much more careful analysis than to simply suggest something like "moderate displacement, an easily driven hull, a generous rig, etc." We must be much more deliberate than this. We are pursuing an ideal—and this ideal will certainly be not a particular but a composite...

Then again—let us start by looking a couple of boats.

Casually, the first task of the boat is to float—so we need hull with a good deal of buoyancy. Secondly, it needs to carry some sail area, so it needs to have reasonable beam and depth to support a generous rig...this all to the good as the boat we're designing is going to have tremendous volume inside for comfortable living and plenty of stores and gear. In fact, we may as well make it a double ender for traditions sake—it seems like we've designed something that looks like a Westsail 32. A wonderful boat...that is, until the couple on board attempts to sail anywhere, and the huge rig (that proves too small) exhausts them in short order—they end up motoring a lot instead of sailing—the fuel costs eat their meager cruising budget and when the engine wears out prematurely the cost of the repair equals a full year of cruising and that's the end of it for them...not that it's a real loss at this point—as they gave up the idea of sailing on the first trip to the islands...2 knots as a VMG to weather can get disheartening indeed.

Perhaps this design is not the way to go. Let's face facts about heavy displacement—heavy displacement means heavy everything—including labor. It also means heavy wear and tear, which then invariably means heavy costs.

Let's not make this mistake again. Let's go for lightweight, a minimum of wetted surface area—a broad beam, a high freeboard for reserve buoyancy—a high-aspect keel and rig—it seems like we've designed something that looks a lot like a J-30. Our new couple gives this boat a try. They leave the harbor in the early morning breeze and are off like a gunshot. This is better, as our other couple wouldn't have even got out of the slip.

They make a good first passage to the islands and feel pretty good about themselves. On the way back, though, things blow up a bit—and they reef down, feeling more manageable. But the boat is very lively indeed, and the bouncy ride begins to take its toll. They spend a couple of days weather-bound in a poor anchorage and the constant veering and rolling become exhausting. No one sleeps, he's even a little sea-sick. They tough it out for a couple of days, but they're becoming really tired. Below things are crazy—they can't really cook well—no body really feels like eating. They leave and exhaustion comes home when they make a navigational error, and the long keel taps a rock that the West-sail would have sailed clear over (and likely not even had felt if it hit it)—but on this boat it feels like a car wreck and the keel bolts are making water. Once back home, and in the yard, the repair bill comes to a year's worth of cruising, and that's the end of it. It's just as well, for the survey finds that the bulkheads are working out, the mast step is distorted, and things are simply coming undone...

Now, to be fair—I sail an engineless heavy displacement double-ender and have successfully gone many places in it. I do, however, admit, that it can be a awful lot of hard work in some conditions. I am willing to take on that hard work, I am willing to take on that hard work as I'm reasonably athletic and still reasonably young. As I teach sailing in this boat, it has room for stores and nice berths for crew. It is a compromise. I also know a guy who sails an engineless J-30. He is, however, a fanatic, and keeps the boat in racing trim everywhere he goes—he lives aboard but one would never know it as it is so spartan inside. He also admits that it is expensive, but he can afford it and it is the sort of boat he likes to sail.

The point of this ramble is perhaps this—there is not a right kind of boat, nor a right way to sail, as long as what and how one sails is wholly consistent and coherent with their task. To talk about the boat in absence of the context of the crew on board makes little sense—as their preference in the inevitable compro-mise that must be made by the limiting environment is key. So again, let back away once more and simply talk of particulars, and what they mean, and make our choices from that. The confusion we have with the concepts of "good" and "effectual" and even "virtue" seem to come whenever we move away from the particular. Let us the stay with the particular.

Figure 4: MACHA as we bought her, complete with pilot house, rotten decks, and bat colony.

The Hull:

There not as many hull forms as one might think when one begins to look. This is reasonable as well when one begins to realize that there are not many environments that a boat inhabits—and thus must conform to. Traditionally, there was little in the way of sail but fishing vessels, freight hauling boats, and warships. Fishing vessels needed to carry a good deal of weight, but they were most often day sailing or at least near shore most of the time—as such they required the ability to be handy and relatively weatherly even centuries ago. Speed meant money to the fisherman, and fast meant stiff and well canvassed. This was not a problem necessarily as the boats were generally strongly crewed. Safety wasn't much of a concern as people were cheap. Remember that to take a "fisherman's reef" originally meant to carry away a spar...

A freight hauling square-rigger had different requirements—it needed to be less weatherly but more powerful to carry the tremendous weight of cargo under sail. The hulls were simple and optimized for volume above all else. Again, safety and comfort were secondary concerns. Warships were different yet, could carry even more canvass as they *very* heavily crewed—modifications in rig were possible that simply could not be handled on a merchantman.

When it comes to *yachts*, however, there is *much less* of a tradition. The idea of people going to sea in small boats for pleasure or a lifestyle is scarcely a hundred years old, the idea of "cruising" under sail becoming popular enough to be more than a rare stunt is hardly more than fifty years old. Most of the early cruising sailboats were fishing boats or modeled after fishing boats—even today many masquerade in that trim. But this is likely an inappropriate design for "cruising." A cruising boat is unlikely to carry a highly powerful crew—so large rigs are probably not manageable. If a large rig is not manageable, then heavy displacement is probably not feasible. If heavy displacement is not feasible, full, deep keels are likely not going to be part of the design. This is just as well, as we are not designing a boat to haul cod but people, and perhaps we should start at the bottom up and talk about the environment that a cruising boat inhabits and what attributes are likely most effectual in it.

Let's talk about the keel, as this is the backbone of the boat and is in some ways the foundation...

The purpose of the keel is twofold; to provide lift and resistance to lateral motion—leeway—as well to provide stability. Most any keel does both of these jobs to some degree but how they do so varies widely. One speaks of depth, aspect ratios, keel length, etc, but it is useful to think in concise statements as to the role the keel plays and what it does—which is to say, it is a lever and a wing.

Wings vary from each other in shape, the most meaningful variance in shape being called it's "aspect ratio." Although the technical definition of the aspect ratio is slightly more complex, for our purposes it is useful to describe the aspect ratio of a wing being its ratio of width to its length. It is obvious important to a sailboat to be able to sail to weather, this requires lift generated by the keel. But what kind of wing shape—or airfoil—generates the most lift, or is the most effectual form? This now becomes complicated...

People often refer to high aspect airfoils and keels—like one might see on a buoy racer—by claiming they generate more lift than low aspect keels. This is not necessarily true. High aspect airfoils do not generate more lift—they generate more lift for a given amount of surface area—which is to say they generate proportionally more lift. High aspect airfoils are also often capable of higher speed potential than low aspect airfoils—why that is we'll address in a moment—in fact they are generally dependant on speed to generate useful lift. High aspect keels allow greater speed because they present less drag, and less wetted surface area, which is all to the good…at least on paper, or in a special niche environment.

If we look at airplane wings this becomes obvious, as the wing shape follows the function of the airplane. Taking the U2 spy plane as an example, we have very high aspect wings. The U2 flies very high, very fast, and is quite efficient. If we look at a crop dusting biplane, however, we see much slower, much less efficient airfoils. Is one better than the other? Now the question emerges.

It all depends, again, on what one plans to do with the airplane. For spying, the U2 makes much more sense, for crop dusting the bi-plane (imagine flying thirty feet off the ground and dodging powerlines at mach 2). If you tried to fly the U2 at low speeds, it would fall like a brick and if you tried to take the bi-plane to speed you'd blow the wings off. But what if we wanted a plane that was to be used for traveling the world, and to be functional in the widest variety of conditions possible? This would mean it would need to be able to take off on marginally smooth and clean runways at times—often short ones. Often it would need to burn less than perfect fuel and might need to not burn as much of it as one would like. It would also need to be serviceable by reasonable means…so while our "hypothetical" plane might not look like either the bi-plane or the U2—it will probably look *more* like the bi-plane than the U2. In fact, I'd guess it would look a hell of a lot like a DC-3—the airplane that has probably hauled more gear to more places for more years than any other, and as I understand is the only airplane to have ever documented a successful landing with one wing missing…imagine that!

Back to discussing boats again—a sailboat does more than just sail to weather. If so, it would be easy to design that keel. High aspect—as much as is functional, and we're done. But if we need a boat that can sail to weather, but also sail slowly through a anchorage or feel out a reef—lower aspect keels can earn their keep. A lower aspect keel, just like the wing of a bi-plane, retains lift at lower speeds and thus control. Low speed control in the real world is often important, so we might want to make a bit of a compromise. If our anchorage is shoal, having a shorter keel might be worthwhile for that reason as well, as there are certainly more places one can go in the world with a short keel than a deep one.

So a compromise begins to form, again, away from the technical ideal towards the functional ideal. Obviously, again, weather performance is critical. Moving away from a high aspect keel towards lower aspect we do loose some weather performance. But we also gain critical functionality without which we might not be able to sail at all.

A few more compromises that work into the design:

A high aspect keel generates proportional more lift for wetted surface area, but generates less yaw resistance—or resistance to changing course—so then the high aspect keel demands a much larger control volume of the rudder to maintain course—increasing wetted surface area to some degree.

A high aspect keel will generate lift at high angles of attack but will much more readily with large changes in the angle of incidence of the flow. So then while the keel points higher, only if it can be kept steadily on course, again, with a good deal of work and a large control surface. It is questionable, then, in circumstances with very turbulent water and low boat speeds how much lift such a keel is capable of making.

A high aspect keel generates more lift at speed but much less at low speeds. Thus a boat with a high aspect keel will be difficult to control at low speeds. At zero forward motion it provides no lift at all, it's resistance to lateral motion is solely dependent on its area. So then, if you don't want to go sideways when you're not going forward—or are for some reason not able to carry sail, a high aspect fin keel is of little use.

Think on this for a bit, and how it matters to the cruising environment—let's talk about the function of the keel as a lever.

The keel as a lever is the pendulum that keeps the boat upright. Keels again, can be shallow or deep. Deep keels obviously have a longer lever arm so they provide more stability—more righting moment—than short keels. Stability is all to the good, at least on paper…

But in the real world, that long lever arm has to be fastened to something, which anymore is most often fiberglass, which is a rather floppy material. The problem of mounting thousands of pounds of weight on a narrow face that gets lifted and bounced is far from solved, as a quick walk through any boat yard will testify to. That long lever arm becomes less of an asset as well if one might happen to hit bottom at speed—the lever arm serves its function there nicely in the role of creating damage.

Displacement:

Relative displacement is a very important issue for us to consider. Here again one hears great oversimplifications about one thing being good and another being bad. Mostly what people hear is that heavy boats are comfortable and slow and light boats are bouncy but fast. A ridiculous oversimplification, this, and we need to consider it.

Without worrying about hull to displacement ratios and that sort of stuff, we can first make the observation, fairly, that larger hulls have more volume than smaller hulls. Of course. But since a boat must sail, its shape to a great degree is confined by the needs of reality, and it matters a great deal where that volume lies. Volume is a good thing for certain. It provides living space and room for stores. But if it is up too high it provides a great deal of performance destroying windage. Volume up high, as well, created storage areas and living space that, when filled, diminish stability and sail carrying ability. This, of course, is a bad thing. In order to get the volume lower, this will require a shape conducive to being partly submerged and ballast with which to get it there. This, means, in turn, what we call a heavy displacement hull form.

True, heavier boats, in moderate conditions will ride less roughly than lighter ones, but I personally feel that this difference is overstated—I feel that in rough conditions most everything rides rough. More importantly, heavier boats—with the appropriate hull form, can carry necessary gear without unduly effecting sail performance. For a study of appropriate hull forms one might take a look at two vessels of same displacement—perhaps my Atkins Ingrid and a Coronodo 41. Is there any question about what boat will carry gear more effectively without harming hull performance? There simply isn't any stowage area on the Ingrid at all that is above the water line! All cargo is effectively ballast on hulls of this type. Because of this, the more heavily loaded MACHA is, the more sail carrying ability she has—and *very* minimally more wetted surface, a ton of cargo adds less than one square foot!—you can hardly tell anything has changed.

So then, in terms of performance under sail and the charge of being slow—heavy boats *are* slow if the weight they carry is placed so that it doesn't provide sail carrying stability. There are slow as well if they do not carry adequate sail area in the rig itself. Both of these traits can easily be compensated for by proper designing.

The point of all this—if we want to evolve the keel for a cruising boat—we can see that if our keel is too long, we'll fail and stay home, and if our keel is too short, we'll fail and stay home. Some where in there is an keel—an underbody that is just right—not too long and complicated, not too short and primitive—but as the *world* is still primitive—is still made of rocks, waves, and wind, our ideal keel, our most effectual keel will likely be nearer the primitive than the refined…

Having considered a keel, let us talk about the other wing of our fantastic bird that glides on the interface of two fluid mediums…

Sailing, kernalized, is simple. It is simply motion—hopefully forward—generated by the forces of wind. Controlled sailing is the act of balancing all the forces acting upon a boat—not just wind but the forces that come from the boat itself moving through the water—both simple hydrodynamic lift as well as wave action. All forces acting upon the boat in total contribute to the boat's course and speed.

The most difficult and interesting case to explain—as well the most important—is the case of a boat sailing to weather. This is the case where wind blows across sails rather than to into them, where lift is generated rather than drive, and where the balance of all forces acting upon a boat become most critical and important. This is where we begin our conversation.

Basically, of course, when a wind stream encounters an object, it separates and flows around it, re-connecting with itself on the downwind side at some distances and after generating a good deal of turbulence. If the shape happens to be an airfoil, basically meaning any asymmetrical shape where the flow on one side of the object must travel a greater distance than the airflow on the other side—lift is generated. This lift is simply a conservation of energy issue—Bernoulli's principle of high speed creating low pressure, low speed creating high pressure—thus the greater distance side requires a higher speed of the airflow, thus lower pressure, thus "suction," thus lift in that direction.

A relatively simple concept. The difficulty is that the amount of lift generated has a direct impact on the speed of the boat, and of course, due to the nature of "apparent wind," the speed of the boat has a direct impact on the amount of lift generated. The velocity made good to weather is the quantity we seek, and this is dependent on a great number of variables.

Thus sailing, again, simple in theory, difficult in practice. Many problems arise in application that detract from the efficiency of this windward lift. First off, the sail is not a rigid object, and the shape of it itself is determined by a certain angle of attack to the airflow—likely less than ideal—which is required to keep the sail set. The sail has irregularities to it, and a surface that has some amount of friction to it, which causes turbulence and interrupted airflow, again destroying lift. The speed and density of the air itself is hardly constant, nor is it often a true laminar airflow—thus turbulence is introduced even before wind meets sail. The angle of attack of the sail to the wind, at least in any sort of seaway, is not constant either, and thus the sail must be oriented for "optimum" drive, not "ideal" efficiency. Thus a good deal of guesswork is involved—theory can be a effective guess, but it is still a guess, and the main trick to sailing any boat well, is to learn the boat and find what peculiar combination of sail and orientation is best.

Still there are certainly issues which are relatively constant. Sailing closer to the wind gets us up wind quicker than sailing further off the wind. Sailing on the wind, the sails are trimmed, more or less, as inboard as possible without inducing stall. Stall? Stall occurs when the angle of attack to the airflow is too great, and the air stream on the high-speed side is in essence flung off the sail due to sheer inertia—resulting in turbulence and loss of drive. This occurs near the section of the sail with maximum camber, as one might expect, as here the centripetal acceleration is the greatest. Stall occurs quite often in sails, but its effect is often invisible and only shows up as reduced speed. Yet much can be learned by studying stall. Though not we're not going into this in great detail, we will address the issue. A sailor in a pure sailing craft has a need for speed—he is always in a race against the elements—he races both with and against the tide, the wind, with storms and calms. There are good reference texts on this material if further study is desired. Rather than reading, however, I will always recommend sailing…

Since we've already determined that while the high aspect keel is the most efficient, it is not the most effectual. We will sacrifice a bit in weather performance—little, actually—to gain a great deal in practicality and versatility. We need a rig that matches, there is no since in placing a over designed sail plan on a boat that cannot stand up to it, no matter how impressive it might look in the slip. While the multiple spreader tall rig of the racer is questionable, so then is the very low aspect primitive rig of the lugger. But again, like the keel, the rig must live in a world of wind and wave and the lee shore—all primitive concerns, so it is likely that in this physical world of reality that our rig we choose will again resemble the primitive perhaps more than the hypothetical ideal—choosing again effectuality over efficiency.

How big should this boat be? This question is important our discussion of keels and sails. My answer is *not very*. I know this is going to be unpopular, but contrary to what the yacht press wants you to believe, now stating flatly that one cannot cruise in anything of less than 38 feet in length—small boats are by far the most effective cruisers. By leaps and bounds far. Most of the argument for the big boat masquerades under the guise of seaworthiness, but this seaworthy case is absolute nonsense. I really do not believe that MACHA is any safer, ultimately, than RENEGADE. The main reason that the minimum length of a cruiser has gotten so huge is that the people on them cannot exist without gobs of crazy mechanical systems—thus one needs a huge boat to house the icemaker. People have come to expect the ability to take a land based lifestyle to sea with them—this is impossible without making grave compromises to the safety, quality, and performance of the craft.

Diatribe:

Setting the pretense inherent in the yacht world aside for a moment, and again addressing the issue of seaworthiness: small boats can be very seaworthy, in fact more so than large boats in many circumstances. The size of a boat is a factor in its ultimate seaworthiness, but only one factor, and not one of the more important factors—not nearly so important as, for example, quality of construction. Seaworthiness itself, as I see it, is a factor of safety and not the other way around, but again perhaps not the most important factor here either. One will, or should, face few storms. The storms that one will face likely will not be of a catastrophic magnitude. One could engineer an unsinkable boat—a ballasted steel sphere would be a good start, it would handle the worst storms and stay afloat. But it wouldn't sail worth a damn, and on a lee shore would be a terribly unsafe boat. Safety, that attribute of being not likely to hurt you in any way, you then see, is a factor in the effectiveness of one's choice of a boat. Obviously, if one's boat sinks—it's a failure—and not an effectual design. *So to is it a failure if it breaks, injures you, and ends your sailing days. So is it a failure if it is too large to comfortably handle. So too is it a failure if it is too heavy to make passages under sail. So too is it a failure if it is too complex and expensive to maintain that you never go anywhere with it.* Big boats, regardless of what anyone says, are much less safe than small ones, even IF we admit that they may be less likely to sink in a very few rare circumstances.

Continuing with that thought, as I work into a bit of a rave, let me point out that very few boats sink in *any* size, and most people who die in boating do so by falling overboard drunk, accidents, and gear failure, and in that order. The drunken thing seems to be an unavoidable part of the boat lifestyle but it can be moderated a bit with some maturity and prudence. Accidents, like the poor bastard I just read about, circumnavigator, great sailor, careful prudent seaman, gets run over by a powerboat while snorkeling—these are often unavoidable as well, assuming one lives one's life and doesn't just hide in a padded cell. Gear failure, such that everything was right and something just broke—this may well be ultimately unavoidable also: no matter how careful one is eventually something is going to break up. On a small boat, however, loads are small and Norwegian Steam goes a long way towards making them right. On a bigger boat, however, when things break they'll just rip your arm off.

Not a problem, you think? Ah, voice of a novice! Many people think this, and they learn their lesson just like everyone else. People buy the big boat, they quickly discover that they won't be able to handle it—the day job they've got to have to pay for it will keeps them soft and incompetent as well. It will wear them out to take the boat out for a casual a day sail—and so, do what the petty yachtsmen do, on one's allotted yearly weekend they motor someplace, find there's no berthage for the big boat, and motor back. Next year, they'll just stay home. By the fourth year the boat is for sale.

Here's the big obvious bugaboo: ground tackle. As with many things in this world, it is so with good anchors—there ain't no substitute for displacement (this statement makes a excellent mantra, by the way). Among anchors, the primary virtue, their effectuality, so to speak, is their weight, pure and simple. Sure, types and styles have pluses and minuses, and yachtsmen like to gas about them, but heavy is good and don't let anyone tell you otherwise. Two things cause an anchor to fail. The first is that it drags, meaning that it never got properly set. A heavy anchor sets easier because it simply bites through the grass and crud easier. Secondly, assuming the anchors are set properly, they break. Strong is good, and strong means heavy—pure cross sectional dimensions. Think on this.

On my RENEGADE, I had a 20 lb. Bruce with 30 feet of 5/16 BBB chain and 300' of 5/8 nylon for my primary hook and a 33 lb. Bruce with another 250 feet of ¼ HITI chain and 250 of ½" nylon for my hurricane hook. This is certainly not overkill, most cruisers with experience would say I'm on the light side—for my area, however, it is adequate and practical. Yet the yacht literature will rate this setup as adequate for as much as a 36' 30000 lb. boat! That's 4 times her displacement…I'll tell you why they say that too, because my little anchor set up is about the top limit of what a normal guy can drag off the bottom without screwing his back up. This probably 60 to 80 pounds worth full of mud. The big Bruce is tougher yet. MACHA carries a three 44 pound Bruce anchors, a 55 pound fisherman, and 400' or 5/16 high test chain. I have hauled this anchor from sixty feet once hand over hand but this was an absolute killer and only reasonable in extreme circumstances.

Windlass? A necessity on MACHA. Of course the mechanical advantage comes from being slow, and sometimes a guy has a need to deal with the hook with alacrity. It takes at least 5 minutes to haul the hook in 50 feet of depth. An anchor is a piece of safety gear, by the way, and all that might stand between safety and grief: no power, no wind, no oars, a reef, and a 4 knot current. If you can't deal with it in a rush it is of no use. You may as well leave it at home. While I can't haul the hook quickly, I can drop it in a gunshot but stand clear of the chain. RENEGADE, of course, had none of these problems. The answer for the large boat is two ready drop bow anchors. It is unlikely to foul both, and truthfully, two large fouled hooks are likely to hold me anyhow.

Power windlass? Obviously not an option for non-auxiliary sailboats, but it's the thing that allows a lot of people on the water. It's expensive. Can you afford a tow if it buggers up? Can you afford a new boat? I saw a new powerboat go on the rocks just last weekend because of this. Think about it. To rely on a power windlass isn't prudent, but neither is it prudent to be on the water uninformed, in denial, and with one's head shoved up one's ass.

Diatribe II:

Sinking again. Everyone is really scared about sinking. This is reasonable, but the response to it is not. Sure, the thought of getting the hell beat out of you in a small boat in storm conditions is highly unpleasant. Yes, one can imagine the huge wave coming, here comes the One Wave, and that's it. But the truth is most people, in most boats, survive this event relatively unscathed—assuming that the boat is strong enough to bear the shear impact of the waves. People use this excuse to buy big boats—ignoring the consequences and the reality.

But here's the reality. Most sinking is not caused by the One Wave. It is caused by the collision with some floating object, such as with the One Freight Container. The collision with the freight container is caused by not posting a watch AT ALL TIMES. Not posting a watch at all times is caused by a cruising couple on an all too big boat—loaded with gear and running on autopilot—not possessed with enough stamina to maintain the required four hour on and four hour off sailing routine—let alone handle sail proficiently alone most of the time. Coming away from a collision with a hole is caused by having a boat that goes too fast with too thin of a hull. Do you really want a large, light displacement cruiser? As I read the argument; big boats cause accidents—and thus—less safe.

One other dose of reality. One of the best arguments for big boats is the greater potential speed under sail. Of course they are; this is purely a function of waterline length. This is a legitimate observation, and it is indeed an argument worth thinking through. Within safe parameters—this a big question in itself—a faster boat is indeed safer than a slow one for no reason other than it is less likely to be exposed to hazardous conditions—it spends less time passage making. Contrary currents are also less likely to cause hazards even if one has, by error, found oneself in these conditions.

All of this is true. A large vessel, driven well, with an able crew, will make better, faster passages than a smaller one in ideal circumstances. However, if there is no crew, or the crew is not able to drive the large vessel at the same level of proficiency as the smaller one—this is not the case. If due to crew strength, the large vessel is most often under shortened sail, or is simply not as handy in stays, it will—in practicality—*not* be faster, and its potential gains in safety will not be realized. Practically speaking, on a short day passage of 50 or so miles, the time it takes to set sail on the bigger boat eats all of the speed potential that it has over the smaller boat. Comparing MACHA with my old 28-foot boat—in good conditions to weather I might average 5 knots, the large boat 7 knots—though in truth these are both optimistic figures. That makes my passage a 10-hour passage, and the larger boat makes a 7.5 hour passage. The larger boat, however, will take longer to get underway—by perhaps 15 or 20 minutes on either end—making an 8-hour passage. In reality, the wind will shift and change—all of these adjustments destroy the lead of the larger boat. With a short crew, if the large boat is Bermudan rigged and requires headsail changes—switching from a genoa to a smaller jib and back a time or two will make the overall time considerably slower. In light air, definitely so. Downwind, in less than 10 knots of air, which is more common than people think, most all boats are just about the same speed. In reality, large boats are not too often much faster.

If it is too much boat to tack smartly, it is frankly foolhardy to assume one has the capacity to beat off a lee shore. Not seaworthy, nor safe.

Marketing—have you been suckered, you free-thinker you? Everybody is uptight about gales and hurricanes and such. Talking about storms sells more gear and books than anything else. Yes, for sure, the storm is a legitimate concern. Let me state for the record, however, that somewhere between about 35 and 40 knots lies the point at which most boats, power, sail, traditional or otherwise, won't make way to weather anymore. A lot of them won't make any long before that. Truthfully as well, a true 40-knot blow is uncommon save in squalls and can be avoided as long as one sails the proper seasons. One may and expect to see solid 30's the year around, but 40 knots is a lot of wind and can most always be avoided in coastal sailing if one pays attention. The real truth is that most sailing is done at the other end of the scale, in the 0 to 10 knots category. A small smart sloop is always faster than a bigger one in these conditions and far more handy. Surprisingly, all of the boats I've personally seen go on the rocks did so in less than 15 knots of air…

So what sort of boat are we evolving? Many people when they think of pure sailing craft think of purists aboard gaff-rigged pilot cutters, Ingrids like mine, and the like. Heavy cruisers are indeed popular as motorsailors but uncommon among sailors. Why? Most of these vessels were designed as working craft and with the intent of carrying great amounts of stuff—also popular among the motorized cruising set—and their rigs and sail plans reflected that in their day. The working canvas of a true pilot cutter would likely be double what passes as a pilot cutter today—sailing them was difficult, strenuous, and tiring work. They were certainly not designed as pleasure craft. The best of them, rigged properly, made remarkable way to weather, but like MACHA, it was a wet and rugged ride. MACHA will make eight and a quarter to weather in good conditions while taking through 90 degrees, which is performance on a par with any heavy displacement hull I know of. Many, however, don't do that well. Contrary to the popular myth, most pound hard on the wind, ride rough in a seaway, roll ponderously, and are fearsomely hard on their own gear. If wooden and yachty, they are also mightily expensive to keep up. As a working boat, with hired crew, none of this is objectionable. Personally, since I'm a bit nuts, I love it. For the average small crew of retirees interested in a pleasant time, however, it is a bit much. Those who sell the modern versions of the boats know this and again keep the sail plans very modest—too much so to really expect to make way in most conditions—so the work of sailing these things is manageable. Properly canvassed, heavy displacement engineless boats—with a strong crew—can weather gales comfortably, many of them will keep themselves off a lee shore in more extreme conditions than perhaps any other type of vessel—but again, driving them hard in inland waters can exhaust a weak crew in short order. For most applications, then, I still say they are unacceptable craft. They are definitely, wholly unacceptable for those new to sailing. They are big and powerful and unforgiving. MACHA, for a novice, would simply be a good place to get killed.

Figure 5: MACHA one year later.

Now as I say, I currently own such a vessel. I sold my small "*RENEGADE*" for such a project. "*MACHA*", my new boat, is precisely the kind of boat I'm telling you not to acquire. *MACHA* is 38 feet on deck, 52 feet overall, displacing 15 tons unloaded. Why do I own such a boat? I wanted a larger boat for my partner and I, and this project was available very inexpensively. I finished it, rigged it, built all the sails and the end result came in at my benchmark of under a dollar a pound—labor of course not included. This is a big, heavy, monster boat with a high performance gaff pilot cutter rig. We set nearly 2000 square feet of down-wind canvas. Again, this boat with a 22 foot boom and flying topsails is absolutely unsuitable as a first boat for anyone. It is raw and robust—a sailor's dream machine but lethal and unforgiving in handling. I feel it is acceptable for me for two reasons. First, I am no longer a novice sailor and have years of non-motor assisted cruising under my belt. Second, I have my Sea-Steading lifestyle developed and I know that this lifestyle is a reality—not a distant dream. I am living it today. Because of this, I have a very clear vision of what I can, have, and will do with this boat, and what it needs to be capable of. If you lie in the same situation, a deep sea dreadnaught like this might be viable. Still I think this is a very wrong boat for most people. More on all this later.

A very common misconception—used as an argument for large heavy craft—is involved the effect of displacement on sea kindliness. There is a relationship, but not what is typically stated. In a true sea, where ride matters, any boat much under two hundred tons is tossed pretty badly. Comparing 28 foot light displacement boats to 50 foot heavy displacement boats is not as significant as many would think. The absolutely worst riding boat I've ever been on weighed in at 230,000 pounds! In comparably mild conditions, however, the ride for the small boat gets busy quicker, this is certain. It is also buttoned down and ready for a blow in next to no time, while the larger boat is an exercise. It is doubly difficult on a rolling deck. I personally feel that the ride of a moderate displacement small boat to be far more comfortable that of the heavier vessel—the motion may be quicker at times, but less "powerfully ponderous." This has to be felt to be described; my point is to insert a word of caution.

A light boat is far, far, less likely to drag its hook in a blow than a heavy boat, by the way. A lighter boat simply surges less powerfully. The hook that a light boat drags is also much easier to deal with in an emergency.

On to the other end of the spectrum: racing boats. One might think that in light of the previous argument, there is something to be said for a race boat as a cruiser. Indeed there is—especially an engineless boat—as long as the hull form is not radical enough to produce handling idiosyncrasies. This eliminates many of the most modern racers from consideration—most are simply too squirrelly to handle short-handed. Unfortunately most of them are also built too light to handle the wear and tear a true sailboat suffers. Still, I have met sailors cruising on fairly radical race boats, single-handed and engineless—something I can't say for the heavy boats. Again, the fellow with the J-30 in particular stands out—an excellent sailor—and was willing to live with the very rigid demands of keeping his boat light and sailing it in race trim everywhere he went. Most sailors are not so disciplined nor as vigorous a sailor; I am personally willing to sacrifice a degree of pointing for the ability to carry an extra case of beer. I am not willing to sacrifice 3 degrees—but 1 degree I will: This is really all one gains by going with a radical boat as opposed to one that is simply well proportioned and sailed well. This is the case even with multihulls, which, I must admit, in some ways appeal to me greatly. Still, I find really them really impractical. Regardless of the hype, in the majority of conditions, any multihull with a sincere capacity to cruise isn't really any faster than a good monohull, and its living spaces and load carrying capacity are minimal compared to a monohull even of like displacement. But note I'm saying that I think they're impractical, not that I don't like them. At this point, I simply don't know of any case examples of success—and for myself I don't feel the need to re-invent the wheel when good alternatives exist. While performance is critical, speed costs money: how fast do you want to go? In the sailing world, very, very small increases in boat performance cost large amounts of money. Most of the time, these modifications make little sense.

In the mid 1960's and early 1970's a type of boat was developed called the cruiser/racer. There were a number of boats designed and manufactured that are of this type. Carl Alberg, William Shaw, a great deal that came out of the influence of Olin Stephens; these are representative designers of this type of boat. Each had particular signature styles but one thing in common: balance. The hulls were balanced, the interiors modest, the ballast ratios excellent, the rigs moderate in aspect. Many of these boats are extremely handy and fast sailors—in my mind representing close to an ideal—the most boat one can get without sacrificing any one characteristic. Many of these boats reflect an era in which the engine truly WAS an auxiliary, and ARE capable of functioning in absence of it—seldom seen today. Few boats of this type are manufactured today—I would advise buying an original—start with the Pearson Triton as a paradigm and develop one's preference from there. As I said, I cut my teeth sailing a Pearson "RENEGADE," if you care about my preference.

Shall I finally describe my ideal boat for the new singlehander with big dreams? In my mind, for a single handing sailor an ideal boat would be 28 feet overall, 8 ½ feet abeam with a symmetrical waterline that ends up being about 22 feet on the water in cruising trim. I'd expect the boat to weigh about 6800 lbs. light. Any more boat than this and any single handed sailor who is *actually sailing* is going to have a tough go of it until he or she becomes really skilled, and the pure intimidation of the larger boat will make this skill harder to come by. This may depend a bit on where one sails, but for inshore work, tacking up passages, handling in close quarters—in short all those places where a sailor is most likely to wreck a boat—a bigger boat will be much more difficult to manage, less handy, and thus slower. Again we're designing an effectual boat for the real world—so we must keep it small.

I'd expect this boat to draw about 4 feet. At least 2300 lbs. of that should be lead in an encapsulated keel. There are an awful lot of places in the world where the water is thin, there are an awful lot of uncharted rocks. A shallower keel is less likely to hit bottom than a deeper one, for obvious reasons. Not too shallow, however, as we need to go to weather well, so we will need a relatively large keel with a good airfoil shape to carry powerful lift. The Cal 40 keel might be a good example—strong, and is certainly no slouch. The encapsulated keel makes a lot of sense too, as it is part of the boat rather than just bolted on—even a moderate encounter with a submerged rock is not too likely to do much more than remove a little gelcoat.

To continue with weather performance, we'll want a well sprung and low sheerline—as we too often forget that the hull is sail area too, but sail area that doesn't help going to weather—so let's keep a low profile. To keep reasonable volume in this low slung boat, I'd like to see a fairly good sized under-body—again with a modified full keel with a cut away forefoot. I'll probably opt for a balanced spade rudder in a boat of this size, as this is certainly the most weatherly configuration—and build it strong enough not to worry about it. Of course our displacement is now heavy enough that solid scantlings are not a problem. From a fish-eye's view things would appear not quite wineglass but close, with a nearly flat run at the boat's optimum angle of heel.

The rig will be balanced to this hull, with nearly half-beam spreaders and about a height of 32 feet off the total deadrise. Relatively large main—capable of sailing under a reefed main alone or trysail in heavy air…

Am I not describing a beautiful boat? This sounds like an absolutely classic yacht. We know the best examples of this style—the finest examples seem almost natural, organic, and alive. We feel almost a sense of presence and life within them—and why should we not? The fact is, that if a sailboat, or any machine for that matter, is engineered in such a manner as to appropriately fit within its environment of function to the highest degree of effectuality possible—it has in essence evolved in the same manner as *a living being, and we should expect it to carry that same sort of natural grace.*

Figure 6: RENEGADE at rest.

In fact, I do no think we will find it too much of a stretch to say that in many ways—the most beautiful sailboats are the *best* sailboats—not just aesthetically so, but *functionally* so as well. Most of the time, a boat that looks like a good performer indeed is. The same may be said for our other example, airplanes—it might be difficult to find more aesthetically beautiful representations of piston driven power than the great radial engined warbirds of late World War II. Are there many machines more graceful than the Corsair? And not only graceful, but powerful, and *lethal*. Indeed, again, the Corsair was simply one of, if not the best fighter plane of its era. It reflected functionality within its environment perfectly…

Do we have an innate perception towards the ideally functional? Perhaps. It certainly seems we have an innate *preference* towards the ideally functional. In fact, I would suggest that in most cases, that which we call beauty has function and effectuality at its core. Let us examine this for a moment.

I believe the emotion or the sensation of beauty is tied directly to survival. How? I'll demonstrate:

Rose
Mountain
Sailboat

Each of these terms invoke a mental image, do they not? I will not suggest that your mental image corresponds to mine—this does not matter; all this path does is lead us into a labyrinth of metaphysical fallacies—nor will I suggest that one mental image is in anyway better or worse that another. Your concept "rose" is your concept "rose"; mine is mine, all that matters is that indeed we have one, whatever it is.

Rose. You can see it in your mind's eye. Now suppose you are walking through a garden, and you see a rose that in many ways resembles your conceptual rose. The objective approximates the conceptual. You are reinforced in your worldview. You feel the rose is beautiful, the "is" of it resembles the "should be." This reinforcement is important because it proves you are not off in crazy land and are dealing effectively with the universe you live in. Also, while color might vary, and while style might vary, I think it is reasonable bet the rose is a picture of health, a bright solid bloom; I'll bet there is no wilt to it and no aphids either. Of course, that idealized rose is doing exactly what it is supposed to—attract attention for pollination. It obviously works.

How about mountain? This is a visceral one for me, as I'm a child of the mountains. I can certainly see in my mind's eye this mountain, as it stands in its remote and savage grandeur. But what happens to the mountain when you put a ski lift on it? How about a parking lot near the summit with a whole host of bourgeois assholes parading around in brightly colored Lycra outfits? How about a clear cut or two, or a lot of them all around the base? How about an exclusive gated community on what was once public land? Is the mountain beautiful any-more? Not for me—any more than any other rape victim.

Try sailboat. We all can easily see that one, as we've been talking about that for a while. Here are the questions about it, however: is your idealized sailboat under sail or at the dock? Mine is definitely underway, as I suspect yours will be, or at least somewhere having just arrived there. Is it under power or under sail? This much is obvious. Still, we see we must be careful here—sometimes images are composites and they contain values, which is fine, as long as we understand that they often do. In this case, the "should be" of "sailboat" does not include sit-ting at the dock, neglected. Nor does it include motor sailing. In fact, we would say that even a very fine sailboat, obviously never put to use as such, is quite a sad sight. There is function often in beauty, and we must be careful to look for it.

Of course, one of the critical points that follow is that we also have an image of self. We incessantly check and double-check our actual self against our ideal-ized self. A good deal of our quality of life comes from the results of this compar-ison. We often hide from the results of this comparison—the whole of our society hides from the results of this comparison—and interesting dynamics arise as the result.

Even within our perversely materialistic culture I would be hard pressed to accept that anyone is so stupid as to believe that one's possessions make them more of a person: To believe that between two identical men the one with the new pick-up truck is more of a man than the man with the old pick-up truck. That the man with a big house is more of a man than he with a small house. That the rich man is necessarily a better man that the poor man, etc. Yet most all of us play this game to some degree or another. Why? Because each of us, individually, fools excepted, recognize how depraved we are in reality, and how little we can actually claim as our own. Yet we have such a huge vested interest in this game. We must play the game—the materialism that we see is a compensation for this terrible lack—with it we can buy for a while a little bit of praise from others. How weakly satisfying and only for the shortest while. Yet we keep at it. We have no self—so we buy one or another expensive masks to substitute for character. We wear one or the other costume; try on this or that persona. This book is likely an exercise in such vanity as well—I admit I am in the same boat.

This is an insidious lie. It is insidious because it is so difficult to escape from and requires the most immense personal strength. Suppose one calls bullshit on the fancy new house or the big-name career and attempts to face life personally, honestly, and with integrity. Suppose one want to be oneself first, and the expec-tations of others second. Do you expect that this man will be admired by his peers? Hell, no! His peers understand completely what he is doing—they understand in some small part of their mind that they should do the same—yet they haven't the strength and they greatly resent his will to do what they cannot. They see the assault that he has made upon the walls of his prison—they feel the force of his hammer blows and it rattles their cells as well—and they fear and hate him. They have been so long inside their dungeon that they cannot survive outside. The sun is too bright. Never mind our hero's pain—the jump from alienation in the dark to alienation at dawn is of dubious value—yet this is necessary for any sort of hope, however distant. Still, among those that hold a collective lie he that admits that the lie is a lie is the greatest of blasphemers—this is the only unforgivable sin.

It is far more difficult for a man to be himself than to do anything else. Hence the masks.

Some of us know our worth in spite of them.

I desire greatly to be a beautiful human being. I desire to be beautiful in the same manner as is the sailboat, the Corsair, the bright red rose—in the same manner than any object is beautiful when it effectually functions within its environment. I have an image of what I should be if I were my ideal self, I have a sense of what I should be capable of in that state—yet I find myself far away and struggling. I think most people feel that way, *and the rest probably should*. It has been difficult for me to reach for health in the past, as it seems to be for many. Why should it be so difficult to become what we have the ability to be?

An answer; perhaps what we have is the situation of that beautiful sailboat which we have described lying on its side in the middle of a Kansas wheat field. Is the sailboat still beautiful there? It seems curious to even ask that. It seems almost absurd. The sailboat that a moment ago was beautiful floating in a protected bay now seems more a tragic creation than anything. *No attributes of the sailboat have changed, what has changed is the environment.* Obviously a sailboat has no business in the middle of a Kansas wheat field, all the virtues it has in terms of keel shape and helm balance are of no consequence. Certainly, one may come and observe the sailboat—lying on its side in the field—and may admire it even in some hypothetical sense, but still, outside of the context of function, the virtues of design and effectuality are pointless.

I think this is exactly the case for most of us. I believe the environment that most of us live within does not at all support at all the idealized aspects of humanity. We admire strength, of course, but few of us have any real need for strength in our lives—perhaps we play at sport but it is still play. We admire intelligence, of course, but most of us have seldom a reason to think seriously about anything and we soon lose the ability. We admire a sensitive and intuitive mind, but a sensitive mind is positively a handicap in modern life—the roar and buzz and confusion and pain of the mob requires us to keep our senses shut off to cope—we soon lose the ability to turn them back on, or become afraid to try. We admire integrity and honesty, or at least say we do, but the reality is that integrity and honesty is certain a faster track to alienation and poverty in the modern world than even the "vice" of sloth. The environment we live in not only doesn't require our idealized selves; it is positively hostile to health.

Those of us who care fight and fight to win against this hostility. We recognize that we should be a certain way and strive to be so with all our might in spite of adversity. Is this sane? We've asked this question already...

I am going to suggest at this point that there is very little sense in becoming the human analog of the landlocked sailboat. I will say as well that the virtue as a mere accessory is more fopism than health. It seems to me, at this point, that if we accept the idea that environment plays a key role in describing that which fits and functions within it, perhaps we should take a good look at a couple of other environments than the one we currently live in. Perhaps rather than to use our energy to strive against adversity, we should seek to find environments that support our health. I think it makes far more sense to seek that environment that makes us strong, healthy and wise than to try to be strong, healthy, and wise in a lifestyle that does not.

Run while you still can...

Figure 7: We don't even remember what we've lost. You'll think we still have forests until you see a snag like this one, a dead, haunting reminder of once was. Most of these reminders, even are gone.

3

CONSIDERING THE SELF

So a couple of years ago I was out cruising. I had been out a little over a week, sneaking through the islands—not working too hard, not going too far. The weather was nice, for certain, but lousy sailing as the wind was awful light. I had done a fair bit of rowing, but I had expected that, and it wasn't a big deal. At this time of year rowing typically means a laid-back sweep of a couple hundred yards from one place where the wind blows, barely, across an area where it doesn't at all, to an area where it barely blows again. I had chosen a time for the cruise when the tides were relatively small—meaning less than five feet, and one didn't encounter currents of much more than a knot and a half. A knot and a half of current can be plenty if the wind isn't blowing, of course, but if one plans accordingly, actually quite fine passages can be made if one plans to sail riding the tide sailing to weather—and a solid speed of advance can be realized. This I'd been doing, and I'd knocked off quite a few miles.

I've got a sailing buddy up here that's some sort of peculiar Buddhist—which is amazing—and not amazing that he's a Buddhist but rather than I can tolerate a Buddhist as a friend. I'm highly anti-religious, if I haven't effectively communicated that yet (snort)—and it doesn't take a lot of otherworldly nonsense spicing the conversation to really make my skin start to crawl. Religion is a lie, an understandable lie for certain, but a lie nonetheless. It's tough to make friends of liars—but it's easier to make friends of the slightly insane—and here's where I in an attempt to maintain a friendly manner categorize these sorts of people, at least for a while. But with either liars or those people that are nuts—of course at some point the resulting confusion is bound to compromise the relationship. For this reason alone religion should be condemned—if one wants to build the central tenets of one's life around personal confusion and project that as truth—in absence of discourse or any attempt at agreement with the rest of mankind—it seems to me that finally religion is nothing more than a deliberate choice to tell the rest of the world to go to hell. Masquerading behind humility is only appalling arrogance. Can we ignore the really aggressive religions or those that refuse to eat other people's food, as it is beneath or *unworthy* of them? This isn't very friendly, for certain—and religious people only get along in this world because nobody really takes them seriously. This of course includes *other* religious people, who assume that people that don't participate in *their* religion are either liars, or are simply nuts just like I do...

But at times, I've got to admit, that those escapist "acceptance and detachment" creeds, like Buddhism, have the temptation to make sense. Sailing in the summer in the Puget Sound stinks, and there is indeed nothing you can do about it. You'll get nailed by a huge powerboat wake the second you get up to speed, there is nothing you can do about it. Becalmed, adrift, you'll be plagued by black flies, which I could easily believe are the reincarnated souls of these powerboaters—as they only venture forth with the sailing is terrible and the water flat...they seem attracted to shiny shit—and there is a hell of a lot of them...seriously, there are things that happen that one does have precious little control of.

But seldom is this the case. There is no good in saying that I cannot control the winds and the tides and to rest back in "enlightened resignation" when it was I that decided to go sailing in the first place. Certainly, life is battered at the whim of fate—absolutely—the discussion of free will and determinism, of freedom and responsibility is nearly as old as critical thought. Some people believe these issues have not been resolved. This is an error—this issues have indeed been solved—the results of the solution have not been accepted, however, and so the debate continues. For those of us who reach towards integrity, however, the question of life and of the level of involvement I have in my fate is relatively simple. The answers can be resolved simply as well by a simple method of residues. One may well argue that my life is wholly determined, one may well argue for acceptance and detachment, one may well argue (weakly) for a galactic teleological fate. One may even convince someone here and there. The point, however, that I would like to make, is of all the philosophical positions that exist, and among all the grand arguments, there are precious few of them that are both *valid and meaningful.* Which means to say that to believe and espouse the given position is *both* rational *and* makes some sort of difference. Which is to say, again, that the position is *effectual.* To be effectual means that to hold the given position must then effect change in behavior.

Of course we are free. Man is indeed condemned to be free. Of course we are responsible for our actions—who else would be? It would be useless to deny the propositions—for the denial would be ineffectual—the law of excluded middle prohibits any other explanation. Would we live differently, would we act differently? We cannot live any differently. Can we pretend for a moment that we are not responsible for our actions, and that some grand puppeteer is pulling the strings? Of course not. And it makes no difference whether we call that grand puppeteer god, or fate, or genetics, or what have you.

The absurdity, of course, is exactly this (as I continue to rip off Sartre)—we are free and self-motivated in a world with no point at all. None what so ever. Dostoyevsky protested "without god, anything would be permissible." This is of course true. Of course there is no god. This much is obvious. Many of us live in denial of this reality because we are so afraid of the *very meaningful rational result of this reality*. And we are afraid of this for good reason—the fear is enough to drive men insane. What form should life take in response to being free, responsible, not morally culpable as morals cannot exist—in a vacuum of meaningless temporal existence? This is not a rhetorical question—I ask this pointedly and personally—what should I do today in light of this reality?

As I continue to press to the point—there are really only two rational responses to this reality. The first is suicide. Why, indeed, not elect suicide? I cannot answer that. There is *no* answer to this question. This question becomes increasingly difficult when one moves away from my personal candy-assed existence to the manner how I observe *most* people live. The squalor and pain of the vast bulk of human existence can be seen as nothing other than awe-inspiring. What indeed is the *reason* to carry forward in an existence of pain towards an inevitable death anyway when there is no point to do so? What is the reason?

The *only* response to the question of suicide, and it isn't a strong one, and it isn't a lasting one, is this—I simply don't want to kill my self. It is a *preference* at this point in my life, and largely due to the fact that I am having a pretty good time of it. Again, exercising my freedom to choose against my non-existence, now I must embrace my responsibility to live—as again we encounter that law of excluded middle—either I am going to live my life or not; either I am going to attempt to be the captain of my fate or not. It makes no difference in objective reality whether *I am really free to choose this or not, or whether I have any real control of my fate or no*. I must live as if I do. To do otherwise is denial, inconsistent, and lacking in integrity.

Effectuality again. This reality does make a functional difference—at this point our *relationship* towards our universe is firmly established—we stand before ourselves as our own future. We must embrace this wholly, fundamentally, and in its stark reality. We must embrace the reality of the environment that we must be effectual within. Elsewise, what is the context for our effectuality?

And so I left Port Townsend on the early morning ebb out through Admiralty Inlet to make my way back up north. I hadn't been to Port Townsend in several years, and it was a surprise. For those of you who don't know the area, Port Townsend is the center of the Pacific Northwest's wooden boat scene, and it is as peculiar a place as any. I spent a couple of days anchored on the waterfront, watching the world go by, and would observe the craziness. Through the binoculars I would see a "classic" yacht approach the waterfront. Under power of course, sail covers on. At a discrete distance, the sail-covers could come off, and a gratuitous sail would be made along the waterfront, close in, with obvious intent of showing off the boat. The boat would then sail up to the marina, sail would be struck—*but not furled*—to present the complete image of a sailboat which had just complete a passage. The only sight more laughable than this were the gaff rigged boats—out for a day sail—which would motor up the harbor a good distance away from the waterfront, to weather only to then set sail out of sight and to come back again, under sail, down wind—until they were more or less out of sight again. Sail would be struck, they would motor to weather again—sail back through…astounding. I can call it nothing else. I had sat through hours of this until the bars opened—I was a bit dismayed to discover than the only real bar left in town had sold and was now replaced by yet another "brew pub" selling muddy ales for far too much money—I wandered a bit to find the cheapest place and took a stool. I had a good rousing drunken discussion with an old fellow who was as disgusted as the pretentious scene as I, who ended up selling me a very nice Plath sextant for very little money—as, he said, I'd actually appreciate it—I almost fell in the water on the way back to the boat that night but the only casualty was a nice pair of Ray-Ban's—ah well, an occupational hazard.

But leaving that morning, with bright skies, with a good forecast that made sense—I did not know I was in for a bit of an adventure. I rolled out the inlet past Point Wilson into one of the thickest fog banks I had ever encountered, on a stronger than predicted tide, and of course the wind completely died, although strong westerlies were predicted. I spent two hours in a kelp patch with a couple of knots of current rolling through it, until the wind filled in enough to barely make way, sneaking along the beach just outside of the invisible breakers, following the bottom contours and the sound of the surf—all the while listening to the horns and sounds of the propellers of passing ships. I became very fatigued of this by late afternoon, as the fog still hadn't lifted by six o' clock and I hadn't more than perhaps 5 knots of wind since I had left in the morning, although a heavy roll was coming in from the Straits where obviously it was blowing as predicted—I had noticed on the charts a small shallow bay that I could at least pretend was an anchorage—I'd have to leave if any wind filled in at all but that seemed unlikely. As it happened, the fog broke and the wind filled in just as I reached my "anchorage;" I took advantage of the situation and the slick underbody of an engineless boat and sailed hell-bent for Squim Bay, which I made just at dark—drifted in the narrow entrance on the late flood, dropped hook and crashed for the night.

The question here: in what way was I responsible for my fate within the context of this passage? Precious little—except that I was there, and my carrying on had brought me there. Within the context of adventure itself, there were only two rational courses of action, carry on and try like hell to not get run over by a freighter or go on the rocks—or to give up. This is my point, and my illustration. This day was, by far and away, the most challenging passage I had ever made. Doesn't sound like much on paper, but sea stories never do justice to the reality of the moment. I have been through the same passage of water dozens of times and these times were not challenging. This day, however, was different: this day was challenging and was made challenging purely by a confluence of events. Without trying very hard, I would have wrecked my boat that day, very likely—and that is the only time in thousands of miles of sailing that I have ever felt that to be the case. Acceptance and detachment would have gotten me nowhere—the attitude given me by this denial may just have been what it would have taken to lure me into waiting another thirty seconds before I broke out the sweeps and humped in an ape-shit serious manner for the kelp—what then? Was this passage any more complicated than any other? Perhaps not, except to say that it was transparent in its hazards. The hazards that were there, and are always there, made their presence known, and in unison, in a manner that seldom occurs.

Try, try hard, or *give up then*—the motto we must embrace. When we embrace our task, our role, our responsibility, we must embrace the *means* to that end as well. "Acceptance and detachment" in most every form is simply an attempt to dodge the personal responsibility, to say at some point that things don't matter. Granted, they don't. But within the context of carrying forth *in spite of that—we must try our utmost in the most effectual manner possible, or it doesn't make sense to try at all.*

◆   ◆   ◆

We often consider that we at every moment are intimately conscious of what we call self. We assume we are aware of the existence of the self and we feel its existence within time is continuous. We have spent most of our lives feeling rather content at our understanding of this identity, even though consciousness itself is a phenomena which as yet is well outside the various methods of test or demonstration. The reality, I may suggest, is much different. We have very little understanding of what self is, or how it exists, or even more than a very vague means of explaining what we might mean by the very word.

Is the self an emotive sensation? We may consider that this is a possibility, as it has been suggested as such by many philosophers. But sensations are not constant and immutable. We sense love and hate, sense pain and pleasure, we sense all sorts of passions and sensations—although not all at the same given moment. We must also recognize at this point the polar quality of these sensations—hate and love are in many ways the same emotion—but the terms hate and love may as well be different colors upon the same spectrum. Pain and pleasure very much the same as well. Indeed, we can see that our emotive sensations—our pure passions—occurs as spectrums. Not so with the concept of self—we do not have a corresponding sensation of "not-self" or "negated-self"—thus the existence of the self concept must be very different than pure emotive sensation.

But clearly, self and self symbol and consciousness itself is highly attached to emotive import. If we consider our self in our mind's eye, we must recognize immediately that we never catch ourselves as existing in absence of emotional response. We may find ourselves feeling heat or cold, pain or pleasure, love or hate—but never do we see ourselves existing in a truly neutral state in absence of what we assume to be external stimuli. If we remove ourselves from the presence of stimuli, we may very well assume to no longer exist.

We may do very well to suggest at this point we exist as a composite structure—that our consciousness is more or less an amalgam of a particular, individual set of perceptions. As our perceptions are changing rapidly and from moment to moment, so to are we. We cannot take a single breath without changing our universe. The nature of the universe as we experience it is much as a peculiar television show, where perceptions sequentially make appearances—where they pass, re-pass, move away and return to associate in a manner that we more or less force coherence into. There may be no inherent consistency to any of existence at all except that which we insist upon. There may well be no plot to this program, there may be no script to follow—yet we look for it, and in our looking create meaning where it did not exist, and create ourselves then in response to this self-created meaning…

We do carry consistency and coherence forward temporally through the concept of object—we ascribe form, identity, and symbol to consistency and sameness. We have an idea, indeed, of objects other than ourselves, and objects relating one to another. Yet we must understand the utterly fluid nature of existence. As each idea comes to exist, it does so from the context of only our own personal existence—which must by necessity change from moment to moment. One never observes the same object twice—object A can only be defined by placing it within a temporal context. Hence, object A must be defined as "object A at time X"—*of course to do so denies the basic nature of objective reality.* Yet we irrationally insist that we do so, we insist on the persistence of object. Why? Preference engendering denial. *Because to accept the reality of the temporal, non-persistence of reality is to accept the non-persistence of self.*

One of the most difficult to understand aspects of existence and consciousness is this: the unidirectional, solipsistic nature of the universe. For any given consciousness, it alone is the only subjective entity within its universe. All other "entities" are objects, subject to interpretation by the perceiving eye of the consciousness in question. To be exact, there is only one conscious being within the universe—and that is you. The universe, as defined, is only the universe you observe. You have no access to any other perspective to speak of "other" consciousness. You have never had an experience of "other" consciousness, you have only had experience of "other" through what was assumed to be the manifestation of consciousness—actions that you assume do not come from the self. It must be admitted that there is no basis for this assumption. There is no rational reason to assume the existence of other minds at all—to do so is merely preference. Rather than to make assumptions of whether in "my personal universe" there do indeed exist other minds, it is far more important to realize that the existence of other minds is a null set equation—it does not matter at all whether there are other consciousness or not. The phenomenology of my observed existence will remain the same in either state—and herein lies the answer: again it does not matter at all.

Still, it is fundamentally critical to realize that there is not, nor can there be, any sort of intersubjective agreement, as again, within every given universe, which must be personal, there is only one conscious subject. Existence proper within any given universe is wholly dependent upon perception—to be is indeed to be perceived. The nature and state of one's universe is dependent on the perceptions as well—one's preferences shape the reality of one's universe as much as the effect of any given hypothetical object.

A case example to illustrate—perhaps an early human decides to try his hand at fishing. He leaves in the morning with a spear and heads to a local pond where he has seen large fish before—imagine even that he has never eaten fish or fished but it seems like a reasonable idea considering how hungry he currently is. He understands very little about the world—for him the world is a blurry, blooming confusion of ghosts and demons—some may have basis, some may be imagined—for him all at this point real. He doesn't think about this much, or anything much, on his way to the pond—and in an hour or two he arrives and begins to walk the perimeter to look for fish.

Stepping up on a rock, he looks down into the placid water of the early morning, and to his shock, he sees another hairy warrior staring out of the water at him, and brandishing a spear as well! He raises his spear in warning, the other warrior does as well—obviously nothing left to do but throw—he does—at the same moment as the watery warrior launches his weapon as well. He jumps back to avoid the missile, but sees the tip of his spear hit the water and the other warrior shatters into a million pieces and odd jumbles of light. Kicked *his* ass, he thinks, smugly.

The question may be, however, how this event will be interpreted, and how it will then be incorporated into the primitive man's universe. Will the universe become one in which gods rule the ponds and one must beware—only to be able to approach on windy days, overcast days when the gods are not present? Will there be rumors of a strange tribe that lives under the pond, who can be chased away with a spear throw? Will the pond be considered haunted and fishing never be attempted again? Will there arise a concept of optics and reflection, a movement to a more complicated and predictable understanding of the observed universe? Hard to say, and in many ways the answer is dependent on the personal preference of the warrior—but this preference will create the universe that he indeed lives in. Is there any effectual difference in these interpretations? Hard to say. Is one more valid than another? Certainly to us, but within the personal universe of our primitive, all are equally valid in a very important sense. Perhaps the only real critique that can be applied to all explanations is once again the critique of effectuality. Either an explanation works, is functional and has predictive ability or no, or perhaps less so than another hypothesis. I once considered writing a sailing book under this sort of idea—that explained sailing as a magical ritual that compelled aquatic demons swimming under the boat to push on the keel, which then propelled the boat. The demons liked certain shapes better than others, they liked certain symmetries better than others—and producing these symmetries got the demons all excited and they pushed all the harder. The curious point being that perhaps this book, although to my mind wholly invalid because my world embraces explanations of fluid dynamics much easier than the presence of demons—could be completely effective in teaching people how to sail. For many people, Bernoulli and Abraxas have a good deal in common, and likely understand neither. Preference again...

It soon becomes obvious why our preference in explaining the nature of the universe tends toward polarity and dualism—it is perhaps the influence of consciousness itself. If one makes choices towards health and life—health and life become an integral part of one's personal universe. It is from then a fundamentally more healthy universe that on views all else—and the choices indeed created the meaning that the universe will have. Conversely, this is true as well—choices against life and Effectuality as well reinforce themselves—and the further down the path of darkness one goes the darker the universe does indeed become. These effects are ultimately real, these are not states of mind—except to say that states of mind must be seen as just as real as any other hypothetical form of reality. Indeed, states of mind, or precisely, the state of one's own mind, is the only reality that we can insist upon with rational integrity. Descartes' assertion, "I think, therefore, I am" is perhaps the first and only rational epistemological conjecture. Beyond this point may lie only idle speculation.

What then might be left—why is it that some of us might prefer to embrace life and others choose to embrace annihilation? Both positions must be equally valid, as we now understand. Certainly, we also see that when many react toward the world with hatred, in large degree these reactions are understandable and justified. Of course as well, a mind that chooses nothing lives within a universe that means nothing and will tend towards nothingness. Still, it must be realized that a choice towards life is self-affirming, and a choice towards death is self-disaffirming. If the universe chooses to mean life—it will continue. If the choice is to mean death, it will end. Is there an inherent value in this, is a choice that self affirms greater than one does not? Perhaps...if nothing else a self-disaffirming choice does not make a very strong case for itself. Suicide is not effectual, and makes no case for itself. The only case left is that of life...and once that case is made, there is only one rational conclusion to that argument.

So what is the point? Exactly that—to give life a point. *This is the implicit purpose of human life; to create meaning. A beautiful human being is one who, having arbitrarily chosen to exist, projects meaning into existence in the most effectual way possible.*

4

EFFECTUAL LIVING

Much has been said about effectual living in recent years—the majority of which is flaming bullshit. The failure of most treatises on effectual living is due to a number of errors. The first error, a grand and pervasive one, is to attempt to convince through the idea of some higher principle, or in the name of causes or under the some idea of the beauty of mankind. It is suggested that we are beautiful beings and we must—because of an inherent ethical imperative—fulfill our glorious nature. Nothing could be further from the truth. Mankind is hardly glorious. The bulk of mankind is foolish, mean-spirited, unexceptional in talent, and repulsive. To revel in the glory of mankind because some very few human beings have indeed performed deeds that were remarkable—to then project that glory to ourselves—is simple self-indulgence.

We inherit no value through simple existence: the origin of beauty must be entirely personal. It is no good to suggest that we have the meant to be fast runners simply because we were born with feet, and that some very few people with feet as well have been able to run sub-four minute miles. Or, more to the point, to suggest that the mere fact of owning a sailboat makes one a sailor. We can see why, however, we may prefer to do so. Denial once again. We want to believe that we can create value for ourselves—we want the immediate gratification of creating meaning for ourselves—we want the creation of value and meaning to be accessible. But the creation of a meaningful existence is supremely difficult. It is difficult enough that one may run a fair opportunity of trying for a lifetime and failing after all. This is the risk we take when we decide to live, and decide to create ourselves.

The second error that is commonly made, which is engendered by the first error, is this: an erroneous understanding of the nature of the world we live in. Too commonly those who seek the effectual, enlightened life trend towards a rather heady, psuedo-trancendental sort of existence. But we have discussed sailboats—we may already see this error. We, if we decide to live within this world, as a beautiful organism, must do so effectually in the same manner as the ideal sailboat. We must not make the mistake that one might when designing a boat or an airplane—we must not either attempt to become the radical race boat nor the U2 spy plane. Neither is effectual, except in the most limited environment where it undeniably excels. Yet we do not live that special environment, nor should we seek to do so. As such, to suggest that enlightenment comes from the lifestyle of the priesthood—whether as an actual priest in a monastery or a scientist working for a foundation, or perhaps a university professor in the humanities—is to make the same error as suggesting that an Ultimate 30 might be the best sailboat to make a circumnavigation in. We should hardly laugh at this suggestion—designers of sailboats are coming dangerously close to this assertion already.

Again, we do not live in a monastery and should not seek to do so. Our desire to do so most likely stems from lack and denial. I have certainly asked this question before: does one become a scientist because one loves the sciences or because one is socially inept? This is not a rhetorical question at all—and I believe in most cases the answer is the latter. We attempt to escape from what we are not talented at to areas where we have ability; we attempt to hide from our weakness. What is a monastery, ultimately, but an infirmary? And of course, remember, I use the term monastery in its widest sense.

Our good friend Henry David went to the woods on Walden pond, as he said, to live deliberately. As such, we should pity him and his need to do so—but we should also *understand* his *need* to do so. Yet we must admit, as we attempt to build this lofty structure of personal meaning, the height of any construction is ultimately limited by the breadth of its foundation. Our first choice when living responsibly for ourselves should not be to draw away from the world as some hermit—but to embrace the reality of the world and our existence.

Some might suggest that living on a small sailboat and traveling the world might be considered a withdrawing from reality—the point might rightly be asked—what is reality? I certainly feel we must believe that reality fundamentally is as much wind and wave, rock and surf, of sails and lines, of sweat and fear as anything. It is also of moments of discomfort, and moments of bliss. It is of fingers bruised by hard labor, it is walking in the cold rain. It is sometimes of pain and empty stomachs. It is sometimes of forlorn loneliness and sometimes of drunken camaraderie. I have had people inform me with a straight face that my living on a small sailboat in the manner I do is simply my manner of hiding from reality—while a desk job in suburban white middle class America is not…Passion is meaning—passion is emotive import. I advocate sailing simply for this reason—I know of know other activity where the aspects of life are so immediate—where my involvement with my world is so necessary and intimate. As such, I must admit, that sometimes, even a lot of the time, the sailing life is a bit much. One does not always get to pick and choose when one partakes. I am not certain that I particularly enjoy it, ultimately, but this is hardly the point. We are discussing meaningfulness, not pleasure. I have made the irrational but conscious and deliberate point of living; it would be of no use at this point to hide from life.

Clearly, the choice of a pure sailing craft as one's home carries one towards this end a good ways, and within that motif an ethic does begin to emerge. A case example: I had a small woodstove on my boat that I had used for cooking and heat for years. I had installed a set of propane burners inside of it so the stove would effectively use propane or solid fuel, and was very convenient. For coastal rambling, however, it was simply too difficult to keep a pot on top of, and I wasn't particularly excited about the possibility of a lurch and embers flying out of the stove or other objects flying on top of it. This never happened, but a full pot of hot chocolate did indeed come adrift in the middle of a hard beat and the hours of cleanup gave me a good deal of time to thing about how I was going to remedy the solution. I purchased an ancient Optimus Sea-swing that has given me reliable service in this aspect ever since—I still kept the woodstove because I do sail year-round as well as live aboard and the woodstove in a snowy anchorage burning driftwood is as symbolic of comfort as anything I know. The question that arose, however, was this—keep the propane? Being the minimalist I inherently am, and knowing I didn't want the weight aboard, I removed the propane system. What I immediately discovered, however, was I was extraordinarily poor at building fires in the context of a woodstove that needed to produce heat throughout the night. The propane, before, had always kept the stove lit and going regardless of fuel. I had been around woodstoves in cabins and such before, of course, but these were invariably large and had better flues and draw than the small boat stove. There was no use in pretending I could place a huge hardwood log in the stove and clamp the damper down—the stove is no larger than a small mailbox. Once the stove began to cool, it got cold, and ceased to draw, which filled the boat with smoke and was extremely annoying. But after several weeks of cussing I learned to build a proper fire, with carefully chosen and tended materials—I learned to wake for moments in the night and refresh the fire—and to immediately be asleep again upon returning to bed—this ritual became no inconvenience what-so-ever. The result was that I learned a *skill*, I learned much about fire. I learned much that almost no one in the developed world knows any more. I saw many beautiful moonlit mid-nights that I otherwise would have slept through and have missed—as a result my life was greatly enhanced. Now, the use of the stove seems trivial, but the choice of removing the propane was right and effectual. My life has more meaning for it.

The same is true, once again, for the sailboat. Having taught sailing on pure sailing craft for a few years now I see much the same evolution in perspective in handling the boat. When one first learns to sail—the handling of the boat is a great adventure. It certainly was for me as well—especially those difficult times of entering and leaving the harbor. I rowed way, way, way too damn much. But the adventure has its roots in the fact of lack of skill—this quickly becomes mundane and a trivial effort. Once boat handling becomes routine, one begins to head further and further afield—the job of learning to read weather becomes the next challenge. This can be difficult for certain—but once again, after a season or two of extended time on the weather—the reality is that a good sailor can usefully predict wind and conditions within 5 knots of air and within a half an hour of resolution perhaps 95 percent of the time. This makes passagemaking, in good non-engine assisted vessels, more or less mundane and trivial as well. Once one learns this—one begins to feel confident take chances in a whole host of conditions—after all, what can really happen? At this point, I am certain and confidant that my passages in my sailboat under sail could easily be *less* effort than they would be with an engine on board. They only are not, sometimes, because I have chosen to push the envelope in the conditions and play a bit of a hot dog. Should I then install an engine on board to make my boat sail poorly and so I would have an expensive device to require maintenance and to worry about? Hardly—I've done plenty of mechanical work in my life and I'm done with that. Perhaps I might work one some else's boat for fee and challenge if I feel the need. More likely, however, having recognized the scourge of the internal combustion engine—not that it is inherently evil, it is not, it is a highly useful tool—but rather that it provides an easy means for many people to escape the immediacy and importance of the experience of non assisted travel. If we all walked in the rain on a regular basis the world would be much better for it.

Diatribe:

Not many things make me cringe as much as seeing a "think green" sticker on the back of a car. It would be funny as a joke—appalling in reality. I cannot understand the mentality of those who would deliberately seek out pristine places in the quest of good experience and defile these places with their presence. Make no mistake about it—diesel engines are terrible polluters. Many people don't care. My only assumption about this is that those that don't suffer from the damage that they cause must be significantly insensitive—I'm not sure what these insensitive people are accomplishing on the water other than damage. If one is insensitive to the damage, they must also be insensitive to the experience. Are they having a good time? In a trivial way?

As I see it, and as I think reasonable, thinking people do—ecological and environmental issues are secondary issues rather than primary ones. This is to say that we see an ecologically beneficial lifestyle as a fundamental aspect of "right living." For any healthy human being, "Right Living" is the first task—environmentalism follows. We might even feel this is seldom the case in what we see; seldom the case in the shill cries we hear for "save the 'X'". As the careful and reasoned mind sees it—our ecological responsibility is not nearly as simple as many would have us believe. The claim that we often hear—that the "environment" is being "destroyed"—this is an intellectually indefensible claim. It is a spiritual/religious claim that begs a lot of questions—and like all spiritual/religious claims—its presumptuous presuppositions breed much contention. The environment is indeed not being destroyed, but it is unquestionably being *altered*, and altered in a manner that is quite likely to be damaging to many species—including humans. From a holistic sense, however, for life itself—most of which is comprised in the form of some worm or bug—very little of note is likely to occur.

But for myself, since I don't flourish under high levels of ultra-violet radiation, nor does my system effectively metabolize PCB's—I think I am in for a world of hurt. I am indeed disturbed by the environmental trends I see. So then, disaffirming the spiritual/religious arguments towards conservation, I will affirm some highly personal and selfish ones. Every organism that lives has an understandable desire not to see its home, habit, health or life destroyed, no matter whether it is cognitive of the fact or not. Also, no matter whether cognitive of the fact or not, every species clambers after the propagation, survival, and elevation of itself. This is inherent in life, and necessary to its existence. To say that life seeks itself is a tautology: would life possibly seek death?

Everything that lives, as well, creates a bit of corruption and stink around it as it moves through life. This is another inescapable fact of existence. Nothing runs at 100% efficiency. Entropy is a fundamental reality of the universe. The issue is not IF we corrupt our home but whether we do so in such a way that corrupts us with it as well. There is a danger to that end contained in life. Large numbers of species—yeast, carp, and humans all come to mind—show a tendency to run unrestrained, to eat themselves to death and die in their own excrement. I'd like to think that humans are more farsighted than yeast. Time will tell.

Stating that scale of consumption is the key issue—everything that lives is entitled to a little bit—we have an enormous problem on our hands. This problem is that the world is a zero sum game. With a finite amount of space and resources—as population increases, all get poorer. This is inescapable. When one member of the species gathers a disproportionate amount of wealth and resources, the others suffer for it. This too is inescapable. Although the richness and abundance of the past obscured and took the edge off of this reality—richness and abundance is no longer the case. It is time to admit that the acquisition of disproportionate wealth is **violence**, indistinguishable from any other sort of violence in the harm it causes. Indeed we judge violence <u>by</u> the amount of harm it causes. It would be difficult to find a greater source of woe than that caused by our rampant materialism…Wealth is indeed the greatest single cause of poverty.

We have a very entrenched, erroneous, and self-indulgent view towards wealth in our culture. We'd like to believe that the acquisition of wealth is somehow related to natural selection—that the financially successful are entitled by nature to consume—that somehow a "survival of the fittest" model applies and justifies materialism and consumption. This is, upon critique, obviously false. The wealthy are NOT our fittest. They are indeed the most feeble, least fit representatives of our species, requiring the highest amount of material maintenance and producing the least with it. They are the most fragile as well, most likely to fail if their support is withdrawn. They are dependent, in fact, on the strength of the truly productive masses; without them they would have nothing. There is little, if nothing, admirable about the affluent; even if we admire their means we are more often awestruck by how little is accomplished with it.

If not "survival of the fittest", then what? A sickly destructive parasitism? It is hard for me to describe my feeling—the terms thief, cannibal, vampire come to mind—but I might even find some virtue in these. What then? The self-destructively violent? Is there anything wrong, even, with violence? I'm not sure I can argue that either. What I CAN offer with integrity is this: I affirm life. I observe that there are actions and attitudes—lifestyles as well—which contribute to and promote life and those that do not, both *personally* and *globally*. There may even be violence that promotes life and strengthens the species—as I said, I won't argue against that possibility. What I cannot even imagine as defensible, however, or attractive in any way, is a promotion of the unhealthy, non-viable, unattractive, and few—at the expense of the many—and I mean many in an interspecieal sense.

If one is to affirm life (and the only alternative I see is to jump off a bridge) one must affirm the welfare of the species as a whole and that within the system that supports it. Of course I have an understandable preference towards my species and its welfare over many others—for example; smallpox—and within the species I have an understandable preference towards me. I'm certain, as well, that if the Chinook salmon and the Spotted Owl could speak, they'd inform me that they feel the same way. But this preference does not preclude the fact that I have a vested interest in the protection of a sphere greater than my own—that the health of the ecosystem contributes to my health—and if it suffers, so will I. The environmental movement has not realized that it must be a humanitarian movement fundamentally to be effective. The environmental movement should move not to save the planet, but to save human beings. Why save human beings? Not because human beings are the most highly evolved species on the planet—that is most likely a creature far more functional that we, perhaps rats or seagulls. Not that human beings are the dominant species on the planet either—that title most likely goes to some form of soil bacteria or maybe ants. No, human beings are important because human beings are the most *self aware* creatures on the planet—and as so has the highest capacity for pain and suffering. I hate pain. *A self aware creature not only feels the pure animal pain of the wound but it also wonders why, and thus suffers twice...*

So then, with a return to sailing, I desire to live a lifestyle of skill: to live in integrity, character; not requiring much in terms of material maintenance or possessions save what directly contributes to my personal health <u>and not a step beyond.</u> Sailing, in its true form, expresses that. The scale of my consumption is a measure of my skill, and even more so, my more lightly encumbered boat sails further and faster. I want to be symbiotic in my relationships rather than parasitic—I do not wish to engage in violence unless it is necessary and constructive. I think that many of those who sail feel this way. As follows, the ecological stance of the true sailor is often cautious and measured but **intense.** We who sail have made the business of the wind, weather, and water our environment—we have a vested interest in its health and stability. We have a vested interest in it that is proportional, again, *to our level of investment...*

And so, I am an environmentalist primarily because if I live effectually I live minimally. I am an environmentalist primarily because I am a humanitarian. I am a humanitarian for no other reason, admittedly, than having the curse of some intelligence and the resultant imagination—if I see another person suffering, I like all intelligent people understand, symbolize, and thus *personalize that suffering.* A person with imagination cannot view pain without making it in some way their own. Of course, there is a rational fallacy in this—to assume I understand the pain of another is nonsense for certain—and I never do. When I see suffering I imagine what it would be like if *I* were in that position. But I'm not, and I might not be, because I'm different. Fallacy aside, having some sort of empathy does indeed make a person a nicer sort to be around, and I wish more people were like that. But they aren't. They certainly aren't.

Figure 8: Twenty-seven whale watch boats, a hundred thousand horse-power shaking our hull from afar, and two orcas running like hell.

5

RESPONSIBILITY

As we prepared to invade Iraq once more one heard terrific amounts of rhetoric—certainly from both the pro-war and the anti-war forces. It seemed remarkable, this time around, actually how little popular support there was for this new war and how little our government cared about that fact. This attack was necessary to maintain our standard of living—we must dominate the world oil markets to insure our cheap fuel—there could hardly be a more convenient scenario than to have a so-called "madman" in control of one of the world's largest remaining oil deposits. Imagine how difficult things would be if Iraq were controlled by an enlightened, benevolent, and anti-American government. Of course we'd have to go to war, regardless, but it is certainly convenient to keep those madmen around for when they're needed, such as today.

Still, for myself, as I claim to be a pacifist who is more than willing to bear arms to enforce that stance, I am made very uncomfortable by the anti-war propaganda. Certainly, I have no respect for the pro-war pro-oil people either, but since I recognize them as a bunch of evil cocksuckers I really don't expect anything out of them but mindless fascism, violence and hate. For the anti-war folks, however, I'd expect a bit more integrity. The lack of integrity that is shown is simply astounding.

It seems amazing to me when I see college students who are living on the dole either from the government or from relatively affluent American parents, or when I see educated professional people making the statement that they "don't support the war." that they ignore the very real fact that in many, many ways they very effectively *do*. They earn a good American wage, which is available to them primarily because of the unfair manner in which America conducts international business—they pay taxes to a government that subsidies big oil and provides more weapons to various groups than any other country in the world—a country that spends more money on armament *than the rest of the world combined*. These weapons do not come for free—it is indeed the American taxpayer that pays for them, and if America were less affluent, then certainly less weapons would be bought.

Now setting aside any political argument here, as it is unimportant to the conversation, and whether it is right, wrong, or insignificant to bomb a nation of oppressed people into oblivion in order to steal their natural resources—what is important to the conversation is the lack of integrity shown by those who claim to be, and in many ways are, the people claiming to care about the welfare of others. As I said, many people don't care and don't care to appear to care. Some people, however, proclaim to care but their actions are wholly ineffectual, or negatively effectual. If one pays taxes in this country, one supports war, one supports environmental destruction, one supports corporate kickbacks and graft, and one supports the moneyed elite that perpetuate the system. *This is not debatable.* One also, to some degree, supports public education—albeit within the context of capitalist fundamentalism—and one does support some meager social welfare programs. But one could teach and one could feed the poor, if one desired, directly, without the governments tainted involvement. We do not get to pick and choose where our tax dollars go—this much is certain. From any meaningful context, if one claims to "not support war" one must not support that which wages war.

Again, I have no interest in the actual social issues here. Perhaps as damaging, to my mind, as war itself are ethical and religious systems of thought that so effectively allow individuals to evade and ignore their basic responsibilities and the results of their actions. Very few people in this country have the right to say "I don't support war." What most people should say is more along the idea of "I don't like the idea of war, but I am unfortunately unwilling to make a personal sacrifice to help create a world in which the action of war is less necessary." But this makes for poor banners, and such an honest and personally demeaning statement would hardly be fun to espouse.

Of course, from our point of view, of our meaningless, nihilistic universe, in some sense the very real question arises: "Who cares whether we go to war or not?" And, indeed, who cares? The asking of this question, however, is just as much evasion of the real issue once again. The real question—the only meaningful question, is this: "Do I wish to be the sort of person who is willing to harm others in order to maintain my personal level of comfort?" This certainly is a much different sort of question, and the one we should ask. Again, in a meaningless nihilistic universe, if a person wants to be an axe murderer, there is really nothing one can say in terms of the "rightness" or the "wrongness" of that action. We have no god, we must remember this. Still, however, I am rather unlikely to choose for my friends people who do not wish to be benevolent people. I think most people feel that way. The great problem, and the great source of concern, is how effective we have become and concealing the fact that most people, indeed, are axe murderers by choice and temperament. There is no *qualitative* moral difference between, for example, in buying a shirt that is manufactured in labor camps by slaves and captured orphaned children or by personally capturing an orphaned child and making a slave of it and forcing it to make a shirt. Several thousand miles makes no difference in any moral sense I could conceive of. Most people might have no problem with the first scenario but do with the later—and might even attempt to make an argument attempting to confuse the issue. We cannot allow this. It is no improvement to be both an axe murderer *and a liar as well...*

Within most creeds, even those which make attempts at humanitarian benevolence, there is embedded an escape hatch—a clause or an action which allows the adherent to, in essence, escape one's personal responsibility. Religions, of course, or any that practice petitionary prayer, are the most heinous offenders in this sense. Prayer can only be seen as a *convenient alternative* to direct action—if one's brother is hungry—feed him, damn it!: he doesn't need a prayer. Environmentalism, as another example, has recycling as its surrogate—recycling aids nothing, but it is a *convenient alternative* to effectual direct action, in this case, which would be to not purchase products that have packaging that needs to be recycled.

Again to ask, why should we care? The reason is simple—we must, if we wish to *personally* create meaning for ourselves, having arbitrarily chosen to live, we must not then hide from our own existence. The issue in this discussion is not the conduct, but the integrity. When we allow ourselves the luxury of hiding from our accountability to ourselves, when we blind ourselves from the real effects of our choices and actions—we are no longer embracing life—we are no longer engaged in *affirmation.*

I make no claims about what form a person's life must take, or what they should value, or how they should live their life. What I want to communicate, however, is that in order to life effectually, a certain number questions must be asked, and only a very few possible answers to these questions are valid. While I do not suggest that everyone should live on a small sailboat in the manner I do so, *I personally do not see very many other options for an honest thinking person of average means*—and least in the society that I currently inhabit. I can however, make certain conclusive statements about what sorts of actions are *not* acceptable in a lifestyle that attempts to create meaning within the affirmation of existence. It is certain that a conventional, work-a-day lifestyle contributes nothing to health and a meaningful existence. It is certain that a lifestyle that lacks in the free time necessary for immersion into one's passions and the immediate experience of living will not be meaningful. It is certain that a narrow existence, devoid of the diversity of society and the world will not be meaningful. If we go ahead and accept the hypothesis that when we affirm life—with integrity we must affirm all life—the issue becomes more complicated yet, but still within the context of affirming life one must not be captivated by material goods, one can not be captivated by the quest for status, one cannot be captivated by the attempt to find fulfillment in children, in pets, in partners—one must find these within oneself, one must create meaning solely for oneself. This is not to deny the fundamental importance of human relationships, of course, but rather to say that one does not find one's value in relationships, but rather the context for one's existent value is established. It again is a matter of environment. One must choose that environment well.

It has become very clear to me those who see to effectually excel within their environment must adopt a certain form to do so, just like a sailboat or an airplane must be designed to fit their environment. As we have discussed, however, many people choose environments that they fit within—they do *not* choose environments that if they personally evolved to fit with would make them better people. And as we have said, this choice is simple cowardly escapism—an attempt to cloister oneself from life. We hopefully see now that in order to embrace life our responsibility must be to embrace *all* life—there is no rationally valid reason to pick and choose—the choice to live is, with integrity, an all or none proposition. The degree to which we are able to embrace this ideal is a measure of our strength.

It remarkable to me to see over the years those people who have had the courage to attempt the motif I suggest within this book, and the powerful formative effect that the symbolic lifestyle voyaging on a small sailboat has had upon them. The environment engendered within the motif is very powerful. The image of the sailboat is at once very kernalized and discrete, yet functions within a global context. The constraints are very well defined. As such, those that live within this symbol reflect this symbol. Anyone who sails a small boat takes good care of their health, for without good health one would not have the ability to sail these performance oriented craft. One becomes a material minimalist by default. There is simply not room to have much in terms of possession. One becomes very skilled at sailing, because there is no other option. It is important to note that in this case, health, frugality, and skill are not virtues—they are <u>*necessities*</u>. It is required to be this sort of person to function within the environment. One must be healthy, frugal, and skillful to be a sailor. The environment is raw and immediate enough that one cannot exercise the luxury of denial about one's health, skill, or ability to live in absence of material aids—to be lacking in any of these has an immediate and pronounced negative impact one one's life and provides a strong impulse to remedy. As well, and perhaps above all, the activity of sailing requires such an acute eye—it requires such and intimate involvement with one's world—one must perpetually be utterly aware of the cycles of season, of wind and tide—denial and unawareness are wholly incompatible with sailing. Awareness and involvement are not exclusive properties—when one learns to be aware of wind and tide an the forces that drive them, as subtle as they may be, one also has one's eyes opened to the dynamics which drive the winds and tides of human existence in general. The same senses that feel the approach of the sailing wind are the same senses that have the capacity to more fully relate in empathy one's fellow man. One cannot help but do so. The process is unavoidable.

And as such, I also find that those who sail almost without exception embrace the same magnanimous humanitarian values—and invariably feel a deep burden to share and aid one's fellow man. Why? I would also say that most sailors are more or less atheistic nihilists—this is the reality that they understood that drove them to sea in the first place. They are all intimately involved in the quest for meaning, as they recognize that they have none. Yet almost without exception these live what would be called environmentally wise lifestyles, most recognize the fundamental issue of overpopulation and the crime of bearing children in a starving world; most understand critically the nature and cycle of wealth and poverty and to the highest degree possible choose not to participate. Why then the consistent choice of humanitarian values? Why is this compassionate streak so pronounced among this group of people? Is it justified as an appropriate response to the environment, or is it embellishment and denial once again?

I reply that the answer is *both*. We are not infinitely intuitive—hardly—and so we must admit, as we discussed earlier that any projection of understand of our own feelings unto others is necessarily erroneous. It is difficult indeed to embrace the inherent alienation of the human mind that its fundamental unidirectional subjectivity creates. The reality of consciousness is isolation. We must embrace this reality free of denial as well, as soon as our strength that we have developed allows us to. Yet the chain of thought that irrationally has made the conscious being make the arbitrary choice to exist, must then embrace the totality of its existence, which is, ultimately, to embrace the totality of existence itself. This totality, we assume, irrationally but from a utilitarian position—for it is the only *effectual* assumption—seems to involve *other* beings, who have arbitrarily chosen existence as well…

But I think the final answer is much more mundane—as is fitting within the explanation so far. The sailor learns to sail well because without that skill, one's passages are difficult, uncomfortable, and dangerous. One learns to live compactly, because, without that skill—and make no mistake, it is a skill—one's craft is encumbered, sails poorly, and is a financial burden, which ultimately means one will be at a lack for time. One seeks strength and health because one must pull lines. This is simple. I believe the move to humanitarian and a projection of responsibility is equally simple. It is simply that one has made the choice to exist. Part of that existence will involve other human beings. If the existence of those other human beings is difficult and uncomfortable, interaction with those human beings will become difficult as well. With the immediacy of the life of the sailor—and the places the sailor visits—this difficulty can become of prime importance. The sailor recognizes a responsibility to help and teach because it is necessary to do so. There is no virtue in the action—humanitarianism does not here arise through rationality, it arises naturally as a response to the environment. The empathy that makes the aid effectual did not engender the action—it simply made the action possible and likely more useful. The inherent lack of denial within the lifestyle makes the actions more immediate and effective. The result?

Effectuality. .
Purpose is expressed in form…
Beauty is that which represents the ideal…
Passion is meaning…
Existence is not rational.

6

THE OAR CLUB PROJECT

The idea of the Oar Club was conceived by two drunken guys in adrift in the Straits of Georgia one summer night. The trip has been underway for several weeks, and had resulted in a large number of adventures. The day in question had been a tough beat to weather, and now a good deal of that way made good threatened to be lost by a change in tide. Bob Marley was playing, the deal had been made that Marley would play until we (I must admit) made port. 16 hours of Bob Marley later, Bob was still playing. I haven't listened to Bob Marley since.

Eriks, my crew, and a very fine fellow, I believe is responsible for the name, "The Oar Club—a Sailor's Club." The point was an inside joke, admittedly, and has nothing really to do with rowing but that sailing a pure sailing craft was at times a lot of hard work, and you for certain knew when you were in the Oar Club. It wasn't necessarily a good thing to be in the Oar Club, but when you were, you certainly were about to learn something. We chuckled at that very present reality for far too long, but the name stuck.

Eriks got involved with a girl when we got back, and pretty much gave up sailing. Alone I started the Oar Club, and produced the website, and started on my series of diatribes. At this point, I was the only person I knew who sailed a non-auxiliary reliant sailboat—I was feeling tired of trying to reinvent the wheel as a solo project and was very interested in finding other people who were working through the same problems. Five years now into the Oar Club project, and with the tens of thousands of individuals who have read this crazy material and have visited our web page at www.oarclub.org—with the hundreds of people who have participated in our work parties, have built sails with us, who have had the wild parties when we pull engines out of boats—who have crewed and learned to sail with us—with those who have made this their life and sailed their beautiful craft off across the horizon—the theme of the Oar Club has surpassed sailing. It isn't about small boats, necessarily, as it isn't about big boats, although we certainly have member boats from 12 to 60 feet. It isn't about inland or "blue water" sailing, as we have members who do both. Just as the Oar Club is hardly about rowing, it is about sailing—it is hardly about sailing, it is about *living*. It is about an attempt to put into effective practice the collection of ideas that are espoused in this book—the first task is an attempt to *demonstrate effectual living in spite of the irrationality of existence*. There is hardly a task more important to the survival of mankind than this. If the bulk of mankind looses the fear of the otherworldly but is not bold enough to make the step to personally responsible existence—the bulk of mankind will choose non-existence in some or the other form. This choice to non-existence most likely will involve a great deal of denial, of resentment, of then hatred, and ultimately violence. Mankind may not survive. Not that this means anything, but the experience is likely to be uncomfortable...

The second task is equally as important, and it is that that I hinted at the beginning of the book. When one seeks to create meaning—when one seeks to grow, to be strong, to live a life a passion and integrity one will immediately find oneself at odds with one's fellow man. We all feel the need to seek passion and meaning—we recognize that this is our task. The majority of people are too afraid, or emburdened, or crippled to participate in a effective attempt at growth. In spite of the inherent denial of conventional life—the transparence of consciousness does not allow one to lie to oneself *completely*. Eventually, at some point, at some level, we are aware of the falsehoods we must hold in order to keep our sanity intact. But when another can effectually demonstrate strength to do what one cannot—what other response can be expected but fear and thus hatred and resentment? This is hardly more illustrated by the symbol of the engineless sailboat. Most that call themselves sailors are neither skilled enough, nor strong enough, nor intelligent enough to learn to sail a pure sailing craft in an effectual manner. Those who cannot want to believe that the task itself is simply impossible, and leave the issue at that. But what might be impossible for some may be routine for others—these incapable certainly see the sharply handled craft sailing in an out of the harbor with ease and skill—what response can be expected but fear and resentment? And so grandiose schemes of denial are created—engineless boats are reckless, safety issues, etc. But whatever—we are here not to convert those who can't or won't, but rather to aid those that *can and will*. One of the most fundamentally important means of providing that aid it to provide a social forum for the very rarified society of those sailors—of those who have chosen this means as an acceptance of life—so that on those dark nights alone there are voices that can be heard from which we can glean support and affirmation This is necessary, as we are not ultimately strong. We will not be as successful alone in any endeavor as we would be with the aid of valuable friends. The way is hard indeed, the task of creating meaning for oneself, and I believe that it may well be beyond our individual capacity. Yet we must try, and try hard. We have learned it is useless to pretend that there is any other *effectual* option.

We teach celestial navigation. We are often asked, why, in this age of electronics, would one want to learn celestial navigation. The question, rationally, is valid. The idea that a sextant is any more reliable than quality solid state electronics is probably insupportable. It is true that electronic navigation aids may cease to work, but also is it true that the sky may be cloudy, that clocks may stop, that almanacs and trigonometric tables may get wet, that eyes may make bad readings and cold fingers may drop a fragile device. This is all true. One is best served, most rationally, in most cases, likely by a spare GPS unit in a sealed bag with a fresh set of batteries—a device that can be had new for a quarter of the price of a quality used marine sextant. If the satellites themselves cease to work, or are shut down, it is likely that staying at sea until they turn back on may be a very reasonable thing to do, as the resultant mayhem with a culture that is dependent on such devices may well be worth avoiding.

A sextant may be a useful backup device, it is an excellent piloting device, but for me, ultimately, the choice to use a sextant is *irrational.* It is a device that broadens my horizon and enriches my world. My position within the GPS is a sterile arbitrarily chosen grid coordinate and is inherently meaningless. My position within the eyepiece of the sextant is an angle relative to a star—my position is relative to the universe itself. The stars themselves, with their ancient and neumenous names, speaking of centuries of man's prior attempts to create meaning for himself—attempts that have failed and have all but been forgotten, *but not by me…*—these stars serve to guide my symbolic craft through a symbolic journey to a symbolic places. These symbols aid me in my construction of meaning, and my universe is greater for the act of understanding and embracing their presence. It is a beautiful act indeed, to relate time and place not by looking at the ground but rather at the infinite sky…is my universe different then because I look to the sky to find my place? I believe it is. My environment is different, and as I see it better and more beautiful, and I too, as I live effectually embracing that environment, must eventually achieve more my ideal as well. This is the task, to create meaning, to be fundamentally what one projects one should be, arbitrarily, irrationally, but with necessity…and it is the necessity of our task that makes the difference, is it not?

Remember, again, I'm the undertaker's kid. Life is stunningly short. When one considers that one blows the first twenty years of existence more or less unaware of what is going on, and one spends the last twenty years all too aware of one's poor health and failing body, one realizes that there's only a very few years—thirty on the outsides, where one stands a good chance of being viable and able to effectually embrace life. As I rock through this year towards the age of 40, still young, but fully aware that I'm half shot with my best years—that I stand on the pinnacle of by youth and vigor—it's all downhill in some degree for here on out. I think for most women, there's even *less* time, they seem to live longer but age faster—and that's tough.

This reality is very scary. It is very difficult to face. We attempt to hide from this reality by every means possible. The result of our denial—our attempt to evade the issue and to evade personal responsibility is that we attempt to let life decisions make themselves. The result is appalling and grotesque...most people actually *do effectually choose suicide, but their cowardice makes them choose very long term and painful methods of killing themselves.* Get a desk job, get a bad marriage, get a kid or three, get a dog, get fat, get diabetes, and rot away by the inch. It's like committing suicide with sandpaper.

We must grab and grasp and hang on like hell and fight—we must snatch every possible moment. There is nothing more precious than those clear starry nights, than sunrises and sunsets, of laughter among friends, of the desperate clasp of lovers—imagine the *crime against life* we commit when we let these opportunities pass us by. What madness causes us to do so? Because to recognize the urgency of the moment, and the necessity of embracing it is *terrifying—we admit the terrible temporal nature of existence.* Denial, denial. We hide from ourselves.

It is hard and raw and cold many times to live near reality and to embrace meaning, but that hard edge is what makes the blissful moments of passion possible—we cannot pick and choose our times to be involved with ourselves, we are involved with our own existence only as much as we are involved with all of it. It is unimaginable to me at this point to hypothesize what possible reason could be offered, within the context of meaningless, irrational existence, that one should *not* sail off into the sunset—that one should not seek the mysteries of the high peaks—that a man and a woman that care for each other should *not* embrace in that most basic human affirmation of other, if only for a moment—that we should not reach for all...what possible reason. What possible reason?

Still, I will admit, there comes a moment when it is not wise to have yet another beer. There do exist these practical issues. This much is true. But most often, unlike in my example, these practical concerns are trivial in nature compared with the practical *necessity* living within passion. Most of the time our desire to jump to the practical is escape, our attempt to validate our cowardice. We must see this. If there is a practical issue, the most fundamentally practical issue can only be our duty to living the current moment in the most effectual way possible. The current moment, rationally, is all we have—and to speak of practicality, to speak of sacrificing the responsibility of living the current moment for some future end can *never* be seen as reasonable.

So now I'm going to hand you the skills to seek the last viable frontier...

7

HOW TO SAIL

Now it becomes obvious that much is and has been said about sailing. A look through the bookshelves of any bookstore will demonstrate this fact. Our goal here is not to add to the pile of data, nor to provoke debate, but to rather preface the context so we can speak of sailing with our peculiar attitude—not of theory, but of practice.

I faced a bit of an ethical dilemma when being asked to write this book. There are, again, a lot of books out there about "sailing." I'm trying to do something a bit different—perhaps rather than compile a list of dum-dum skills, maybe to communicate an *attitude that carries the necessity of certain skills with it.* People have funny ideas about how they learn things, and generally an over-estimated idea of how well they do so. I remember a time back when I was in college when a "friend" I had came to me with a question. Now to preface let me say this was the sort of guy who was Mensa member but everybody else thought he was an idiot…he said that he had a date with a girl the coming Friday. He asked me if I'd teach him how to play the guitar. Now I was shocked, of course, as much by the request as by the fact that he had a date, but it illustrated a point very clearly. Playing a guitar is just a matter of knowing chords, right? Learn a couple of chords and that's really all there is to it. Learning Aikido is just a matter of learning a couple of moves, right? Learning sailing is just a matter of learning to tack, jibe, and scream "Ready About!"…

There is no substitute for spending time on the water. I could tell you how to sail in and out of a slip in great detail a thousand times—this will do nothing but warm armchairs. If I can convince you that you CAN actually do such a thing, and should, and effectively enough that you do so—then you'll learn to sail with no help from me at all. So then, I try to convey the need, and to point at things that one should certainly know, with the hope that the reader will take the message to heart…and the core I'm really just attempting to be a cheerleader of sorts…

So much of learning is realizing what one does not know, and what one must then learn...

We've discussed a little of this already. We will review. Sailing is simply motion—hopefully forward—generated by the forces of wind. Controlled sailing is the act of balancing all the forces acting upon a boat—not just wind but the forces that come from the boat itself moving through the water—both simple hydrodynamic lift as well as wave action. All forces acting upon the boat in total contribute to the boat's course and speed.

Again we examine the case of a boat sailing to weather. This is the case where wind blows across sails rather than to into them, where lift is generated rather than drive, and where the balance of all forces acting upon a boat become most critical and important. The principle is simple. Basically, of course, when a wind stream encounters an object, it separates and flows around it, re-connecting with itself on the downwind side at some distances and after generating a good deal of turbulence. If the shape happens to be an airfoil, basically meaning any asymmetrical shape where the flow on one side of the object must travel a greater distance than the airflow on the other side—lift is generated. This lift is simply a conservation of energy issue—Bernoulli's principle of high speed creating low pressure, low speed creating high pressure—thus the greater distance side requires a higher speed of the airflow, thus lower pressure, thus "suction," thus lift in that direction. The difficulty is that the amount of lift generated has a direct impact on the speed of the boat, and of course, due to the nature of "apparent wind," the speed of the boat has a direct impact on the amount of lift generated. The velocity made good to weather is the quantity we seek, and this is dependent on a great number of variables. We have discussed this so far.

Thus sailing, again, simple in theory, difficult in practice. Many problems arise in application that detract from the efficiency of this windward lift. First off, the sail is not a rigid object, and the shape of it itself is determined by a certain angle of attack to the airflow—likely less than ideal—which is required to keep the sail set. The sail has irregularities to it, and a surface that has some amount of friction to it, which causes turbulence and interrupted airflow, again destroying lift. The speed and density of the air itself is hardly constant, nor is it often a true laminar airflow—thus turbulence is introduced even before wind meets sail. The angle of attack of the sail to the wind, at least in any sort of seaway, is not constant either, and thus the sail must be oriented for "optimum" drive, not "ideal" efficiency. Thus a good deal of guesswork is involved—theory can be a effective guess, but it is still a guess, and the main trick to sailing any boat well, is to learn the boat and find what peculiar combination of sail and orientation is best.

Still there are certainly issues which are relatively constant. Sailing closer to the wind gets us up wind quicker than sailing further off the wind. Sailing on the wind, sails are trimmed, more or less, as inboard as possible without inducing stall. Stall? Stall occurs when the angle of attack to the airflow is too great, and the airstream on the high-speed side is in essence flung off the sail due to sheer inertia—resulting in turbulence and loss of drive. This occurs near the section of the sail with maximum camber, as one might expect, as here the centripetal acceleration is the greatest. Stall occurs quite often in sails, but its effect is often invisible and only shows up as reduced speed. Yet much can be learned by studying stall. Though we're not going into these in great detail, we will address the issue. A sailor in a pure sailing craft has a need for speed—he is always in a race against the elements—he races both with and against the tide, the wind, with storms and calms. There are good reference texts on this material if further study is desired. Rather than reading, however, I will always recommend sailing…

Airfoils once more: a digression.

High aspect airfoils are more prone to stall than low aspect airfoils from change in angle of incidence in airflow. Thus high aspect airfoils, though hypothetically more efficient, require more control of angle of attack to retain that efficiency

High aspect airfoils, again, while hypothetically more efficient on up wind courses, are markedly less efficient *for given area* than low aspect airfoils off the wind. The reason for this is a quantity called "concentration of geometric center." To visualize, picture two tables, both 100 square inches in area. One is more or less square, one is triangular. Imagine if one were to locate the center of area of both tables, and to spill a pint of beer there. Which table would the beer run off of most quickly? The triangular table, of course, as the distance from the center to the closest edge—the path of least resistance for the fluid to travel, is markedly shorter than on the square table. Thus high aspect airfoils induce much less drag off the wind as they simply contain and retain less air. And of course, this is exactly when you need drag.

Cold wet air is denser than hot dry air, and has much greater inertia. Thus is far more likely to break away from the sail, although it also generates more lift.

A full cut sail with a good deal of camber to it, though it generates more powerful lift, generates more centripetal acceleration and thus stalls sooner, generating potentially less lift, especially at speed. It certainly creates a good deal more drag and thus heel.

Flat sails stall less quickly, though they generate less lift. Still they are capable of carrying that lift to higher speed potential.

Flat sails are more closewinded than full, though they accelerate less quickly and may then generate a good deal of lee-way on some designs of hull before they get to speed.

The draft position of a sail has an effect on stall and lift as well. If the draft position is well forward, the sail stalls less easily and sets more readily, but generates proportionally less lift. If the draft is well aft, more of the sail generates lift but the sail overall is more prone to stall.

The slot effect: The interaction of the headsail and the mainsail. This is all critical and seldom understood. The purpose of the slot effect is not so much to speed up the air over the main, although it does this too, but as much as the trailing air off the inside of the headsail is redirected towards the after part of the main and prevents stall on the mainsail. Thus the sum effect of the two together is much greater than the two apart. How effective this re attachment of airflow can be is complicated by a number of factors—how deep the overlap of the headsail is relative to the main; how wide the slot is, whether the twist of the two match, whether the leech shapes match—but now we are getting into the art of trimming a sail for going to weather.

Efficiency aside, it simply takes more sail area to push heavier boats. This is especially the case when sailing off the wind. This sail area is likely to be less efficiently handled, for takes more skill to handle large sails smartly. Not that it is impossible, but it is important not underestimate how large of an obstacle this becomes.

The point?: That it isn't as simple as things might seem. One hears, especially from people who sell boats and boat products, that one thing is good, and another bad—etc. Again, it isn't nearly so simple. If one wants to design a sail, or a boat for that matter, that only does one thing—like sail around three yellow things in a bay on late summer afternoons, on flat water, and under 12 knots of air—it is a relatively simple matter to maximize for that scenario. But this is not the kind of sailing we are talking about in this book. We desire a boat, and sails, that operate at the highest level of efficiency over the broadest range of possible conditions. What kind of boat or sail is that? Well, that remains to be seen…I say this to temper the hype.

On to the practical.

Starting with the basic trim of the mainsail, there are in essence two things to watch for. The first is the amount the sail is sheeted in relative to the centerline of the boat, and the second is how much twist is in the sail. These are very much the same issue—if a sail has a great deal of twist it really means your are only sheeting in and using the bottom of it. If a sail has very little twist it means we are using most or all of it. Very interrelated concepts, but we will deal with them separately for purposes of explanation.

Setting up for a weather course, close hauled, if we were new to a boat we might sheet the main sheet in fully inboard, amidships, and then slowly ease the mainsheet until the luff of the mainsail just starts to flutter, and then we harden it up again out just so it stops. This is the starting position, and relatively close to where the sail should be for a weather course. The problem is twist. When a mainsail suffers from twist, the result is that the head falls off to leeward and will then lift and luff earlier than the rest of the sail. If this is corrected merely by sheeting the boom further inward, the bottom of the sail will be too far sheeted inboard for its own good and will stall too early. The key is some sort of vang or kicking strap which pulls the boom down, rather than in, and thus tightens the leech. Tightening the leech hauls the top of the sail inward in relation to the lower part of the sail, this allows the boom to be eased and thus much higher efficiency to be found throughout the sail.

Yet we can have too much of a good thing. If we tighten the leech excessively by too much downward pull—the leech becomes so tight that it hooks to weather. This makes the draft of the sail fuller, as the sail is more cup shaped now. This, as we've seen, might be good or bad. It might be good because a fuller sail is a more powerful sail and generates more lift. It also generates more heel. It also generates less speed—as the full shape retards airflow more—of course this is where we got our lift. So basically, for sailing in flat water—a cupped shape is likely not such a good idea, a flat shape makes more sense as the drag on the hull is at a minimum. In high winds, it doesn't make much sense either, as we are likely already fighting with heel and weather helm. In tight quarters handling, perhaps for tacking through a marina, the cup might be good, or might not—the cupped sail likely does not point as high as the flat one, but the cupped sail will generate drive more quickly and will be more responsive. So what does a person do? Learn to sail one's boat. Understand what makes an effect happen.

And yes, it may not be quite so simple yet. If the vang pulls down so that the entire boom comes down as a unit, with no bend, the tension in the sail will be primarily translated the leech, as we've said. But if the vanging action comes down into the middle of the boom, and the boom bends, a good deal of tension will be applied to the middle of the sail as well, flattening it as a unit. All the effects we've spoken of apply. Thus, the use of the vang isn't dogma either.

Knowing this, if one has a mainsheet that leads to the end of the boom—as many boats have—and a kicking strap on a boom-horseshoe that can be moved fore and aft and set up in a number of configurations, we can control things very readily if we understand what the effects will be.

So then, hauling a sail in trims it. Hauling it down removes twist. Depending on where the downward pressure is applied will have an effect on whether the sail is made more full or flattened by the action of the vang.

A mainsheet traveler, of course performs basically both of these functions in one, although a vang or a kickingstrap is significantly more powerful and versatile, as we have said. On smooth water and light air in most boats it makes sense to have the traveler well to weather. Yes, this tending angle on the boom allows twist and will cause the boom and lower part of the sail to be somewhat over-sheeted. This is true, but as the wind is light twist will not be extreme, the narrow entry will allow one to point higher, the slight hook to windward generated at the bottom of the sail is generally offset by greater speed to weather. As the wind speed increases, the effect of drag and stall will be felt, mostly through increased weather helm. Twist will increase, the boom will need to be eased and vang tension applied, or the traveler moved to leeward to counteract this effect. As wind speed increases further, a certain amount of twist can be allowed into the sail to feather the top and to diminish heel, at this one should be considering a reef but sometimes this isn't practical or the increased wind is perhaps local and temporary—at any rate the amount of drive from the bottom half of a large sail is different than the drive from the total of a reefed sail, though how so is dependant on the boat. Again, one will have to sail one's boat to determine which is most effective. The issue becomes pointed when there is a bit of a lumpy sea, the boat will be moving slower than it would be in smooth water—more power is demanded out of the sails rather than speed, a reefed sail which likely will be flatter and can be trimmed free of twist is often the best solution at this point.

Also, it can be noted that twist can flatten a sail. How so? Because one should note that the air flow moves across the sail in a straight line—if one eyes this straight line one will see that in a sail that has a good deal of twist, the middle section of the sail is often quite flat and free of much draft. Is this good or bad?

Depends on the sail. At any rate, if the sail has twist, to some degree the head and foot are not at optimum angles to the wind. We've discussed this. Yet perhaps if we sacrifice the head—which does little anyway, and the foot, which may be running in a great deal of turbulence, to optimize the middle—we may make a advantageous gain in *total* lift. Indeed, much of the time this is the case in heavy air. All the time? No. Depends a great deal on the boat, how it is sailed, and the conditions. Again, I will not tell you what is right, only to look for a possibility...

As for headsails, the situation is much the same but the solution is different. The issue again is how far sheeted in and how much twist. The control is different, as the question is how much sheet tension and how far forward or aft will be the sheet car lead? If one moves the car forward, obviously more tension is applied to the leech than the foot, and twist is removed—again powering up the sail. If the sheet car is moved aft, the leech is allowed to rise and more twist develops. How much is ideal? Depends on the boat and the sail. Again, in light air and flat water, the headsail is often trimmed for a leech closed by having the car well forward and the sheet thus further eased. As the wind builds, the sail gets the car moves aft until good shape can no longer be controlled, the top of the sail begins to fall off and helm balance becomes poor. At this point we are looking at a headsail change, and the whole process begins again.

How balanced is the helm? Any more than about 5 degrees of rudder is likely starting to slow the boat down...does it make sense then to carry the imbalance in the sails? It depends—some boats drive very well overcanvased and with atrocious weather helm—especially many older race boats of the 1940's and 1950's. Modern boats want to run more upright and the presence of a good deal of weather helm is often a problem. The only way to know is to make the change and observe the change in speed. Still, more than 5 degrees of rudder is a good place to start thinking about the issue.

The key to the slot effect between the headsail and the main is this: First, to make sure that the headsail is sheeted properly and then the main is sheeted to match. Since the mainsail is to some degree running in air off of the headsail this is the prudent way to go about it for many boats. Secondly, it is important to make sure that the headsail is not oversheeted as in relation to the main as this will choke the slot, and the airflow redirected off the headsail will blow directly into the main, sometimes driving it inside out with the appearance of luffing. This is not luffing however, although the appearance can easily confuse a beginner. This effect can also be caused by too much leech tension in the headsail—as we might expect. Just like in the main, if we apply too much tension to the leech, the headsail becomes cupped—if it is too cupped it drives air directly into the lee side of the main. Experiment to know what is correct—correct simply means fast. Last, it is important to match the twist in the headsail and the main so that the slot effect works from the bottom of the main to the top, not just the one place or another. This can be seen well from sighting up behind the mainsail and looking for a uniform camber. It is certainly readily apparent from other boats—and a little radio contact can be useful if one has a sailing friend who will play tag and watch for trim. Again, there is theory and there is practice—again, we are looking for the optimum, not the ideal—and what that may be on any given boat may be a bit of a surprise.

The last thing to consider—position of the draft in headsail or main. This is controlled basically by halyard tension. As wind speed increases, cloth stretches, the sail bellies, and the point of maximum camber moves aft. This causes the vector of lift to move aft as well, causing more heel and less lift. The stretch from the cloth can be removed to some degree by increasing the halyard tension, thus again pulling the bellied cloth up and down rather than aft. It is important to know how cloth stretches—as it is an important clue to how sails work. When a sail stretches, at least in a modern sail, very little of the change in shape comes from actual elongation of the fibers in the cloth. Most of the stretch comes along the bias of the sail, as the lay of the cloth changes shape. Thus, the application of halyard tension more than anything balances the pressure of the wind and pulls the shape of the cloth back into its original form. If, for example, the lay of the cloth makes for little diamond shapes between the weave—the force of the wind likely stretches this diamond shape side to side and flattens the diamond—thus the sail bellies. If we apply halyard tension to the top and bottom of this diamond, it is pulled back into its original shape, and the sail into the shape it was cut to have. As a rule of thumb, the halyard tension need only be tight enough to pull the sag out of the sail at any given wind speed. Thus in light air, only enough tension to remove the wrinkles is necessary—in heavy air, however a bit of Norwegian Steam might be called for.

Sag in the headstay or bend in the mast to leeward also cause a sail to belly and move aft, causing weather helm problems. This is an issue solved by proper rig tune and tension. A significant issue, it has a significant effect on boat speed—and is more complicated than one might think—there is a section on this issue located later in this book.

None of this makes any difference, by the way, whether one is sailing a modern sloop or a more archaic gaffer. The principles remain exactly the same as we are speaking of aerodynamic principles and how to put them to us. I will say, however, that the degrees to which they matter are different from boat to boat.

On a performance oriented boat like RENEGADE the sail trimming and fine control of the helm made as much as three-quarters of a knot of boat speed. On MACHA, however, you can trim your ass off and very little seems to happen—which of course is a product of the low aspect sails. Actually, on MACHA, you can pretty well ignore sail trim all together and it makes very little difference, with the exception of the gaff vang and the topsail. If you want to go faster on MACHA, you need to put on bigger sails. Which, of course, with the big sparred rig, is easy to do.

This is sailing to weather close hauled. Sailing on all other weather points of sail are in essence the same, but the interaction of slot becomes less pronounced, and to a good degree the control of twist becomes more. Still the principles remain exactly the same as long as wind is blowing across sails and not into them.

Sailing downwind is purely about wind blowing into sails. It is about generating drag. The key to speed and efficiency off the wind is dependent primarily on how much canvas one can carry—pure square footage. It is also controlled to a certain extent by helm balance, as some extreme sail combinations may cause such weather helm that speed is diminished—that is, just before a broach.

Of course there are tricks and techniques…but first I would suggest is that in sloop rigged boats there are seldom many good reasons to run directly dead down wind, wing and wing. There are many that view this a some sort of stunt of helmsmanship, and to some degree it is as it requires more attention and provides less feedback than any other point of sail. Yet in many conditions, it is an ineffective means to sail, and if there is any sea state, uncomfortable as well. It depends on the boat, and depends on the conditions, of course, but in many cases running broad is a faster course or at least no slower in terms of speed of advance than running dead down, the course itself is certain to be a more comfortable one, and sheet to tiller steering gear works very well—which it does not for a wing and wing course. At any rate, and on any course down wind, the key is to avoid a gibe—this is much easier to do if running broad than running dead down as well. Using a boom preventer is good practice, and at any rate can be used to vang the boom down, preventing chafe as well as flattening the sail and providing more area, but a gibe with a boom preventer still runs an appreciable chance of tearing a mainsail, and by no means calls for less attention at the helm.

Watch for chafe when sailing down wind. On most boat it is very likely that the main sail will chafe on the shrouds to some degree—make sure these surfaces are smooth. Again, vang the boom down acting as a gibe preventer as well as diminishing chafe.

Realize that in any kind of sea-way, a small boat will often roll badly sailing dead down wind. The beamier the boat is, generally the more pronounced this is. For this reason I almost never sail dead down wind, greatly preferring to tack back and forth from one broad reaching course to another. Again, the zigzag course seldom makes for any difference in the speed of advance because the course is sailed at a considerably higher speed—but in light conditions one may as well sail the most direct course and be done with it. Of course, at these times, roll is not an issue.

Many people have come to enjoy sailing down wind under a large headsail alone. Traditionally called "scudding," there is nothing new about it nor is there is anything wrong with this technique as long as the sail is built to withstand the strain. Unfortunately, it seldom is. Especially when the headsail is a roller-furling type, designed to carry and set in relatively light air, the act of carrying it full or partly rolled in any kind of wind is almost certain to ruin it in short order. Beware of this.

Rigs again. Low aspect rigs are much more effective down wind rigs. The reason for this is simple—down wind sailing is all about area presented to the wind. If one were to look at the basic triangle presented to the wind of the sail plan, it becomes evident very quickly that increasing the base of the triangle increases area much more quickly than adding height. Besides this, adding length through bowsprits and long booms adds sail area that isn't blanketed by an upwind sail, which tall rigs do not. Hence an argument against high aspect rigs, or multi-masted rigs. I see no reason, none, on any boat of less than 50 feet of length to need to break up the rig into a ketch or some other aberration that crushes boat performance. None. The ketch, especially, is a poor rig. In a day where many would turn up their noses at a gaff cutter for being slow on the wind (?!?!) and choose a marconi ketch would be well to learn that in the day when one raced against the other, the Universal rule gave only 1 percent handicap of a gaff cutter against a Bermudan sloop, and gave 9 percent to a Bermudan ketch against a gaff cutter...which is why, in this day and age of powerful engines, about the only time one sees a ketch under sail is at anchor.

Now on to even more practical matters—how to handle sail on a sailing boat, without the aid of crew or engine. Suppose one is sailing on one's way towards the islands and needs to make a headsail change? How is this done without the aid of a helmsman or an auto pilot?

Most boats will have a natural course to weather that they will steer with—nearly close-hauled and with the tiller lashed. We will get into this in great deal in a little bit—but for now a short explanation of why will suffice. When wind hits a sail it generates heel and lift. The heel, of course, is directed sideways rather than forward, and depending if the sail is up forward in the boat or aft in the boat, this sideways motion will tend to push either there stern of the boat downwind, or the bow down wind. This much is simple. The more important effect is this—lift. As lift is generated, it pulls the boat forward. But because heel is occurring, and because the sail then is not on the centerline of the boat, the area from which the forward drive is located is not on the centerline of the boat either. Thus lift causes a boat to want to turn to weather as well, and in direct proportion to its strength.

Most boats can take advantage of this to create a course equilibrium to weather. Generally speaking, the boom is let out a bit low of a close hauled course and the tiller is lashed slightly to weather to keep the helm down. The key is to find an equilibrium where the boat is pinching and luffing, and slowing working to weather. Most of the time this will be a stable enough course for a single-handed sailor to go forward and make a headsail change. Of course, in this case, the headsail is let flog, the main is appropriately sheeted, the tiller lashed, and the headsail change is made, in that order.

The reason this works is simple but a bit difficult to understand. The reason it works is this: if a boat is sailing and it for some reason falls off the wind a bit it will heel more—because the sails are now trimmed less efficiently. The sails are now too much sheeted in, are stalling, and generating very little drive, the boat slows and the predominant forces left are all acting to turn the boat to weather. If the boat turns to weather, the boat heels a little less, the slight application of rudder becomes predominant, and the boat falls off the wind. Somewhere in here is an equilibrium where the boat steers a steady course. Don't expect it to cross oceans, but the course will be stable enough to get a headsail change done.

If one has learned the tricks of sheet to tiller steering, a sheet to tiller gear set up off the main sheet will perform this task even better and allow some distance to be made effectively as the headsail change is occurring. That discussion is forthcoming.

On MACHA we don't do sail changes. We either put sails up or we take them down depending on how hard the wind is blowing. A very nice thing about the large main sail of the gaff rig indeed.

As for the task of putting in a reef, single-handed—this can be more of a scramble. Again the technique will depend a bit on the boat. Some boats under a close sheeted headsail and a lashed helm will hold a course much like they might under the main, other boats are very unstable under these circumstances and do not cooperate at all. Again, one will have to experiment. Sheet to tiller gear is of little use here as well, as the only sheet that can be used is the jib sheet, and this seldom seems to be effective without the interaction of the main. Still, in many cases a combination can be found of reasonable stability under a headsail alone where the boat naturally steers a close reach, which allows the boom to be sheeted out and at least enough time—perhaps with an occasional scramble back to the helm—to get a reef put in. The key, as in all these things is practiced hands operating with efficiency—there is no reason why a mainsail cannot be reefed on a small boat in a matter of seconds—assuming one is proficient. This proficiency can be tested at the dock, and should be, by attempting to put a reef in, blindfolded, with a group of buddies howling and throwing buckets of water. This exercise is simple compared to putting a reef in at sea, for the boat isn't pitching, yet it will certainly make one aware quickly of what problems are likely to present themselves.

MACHA, however is a little tougher for reefing. First of all, we aren't reefing until it's blowing at least the low twenties, as the topsail itself coming down was the first reef. Second of all, the mainsail is just really big. Fortunately, this boat as well is a coherent system. One simply heaves to, parks, and puts a reef in with the boat simply sitting quietly in the water. A little less quietly at sea, for sure, but not the disaster some might think.

The Practical Issue of Sailhandling:

Handling sails on a well rigged sloop of under thirty feet is child's play for any competent sailor. Above thirty feet the difficulty increases quickly and concessions must be made to keep gear manageable. Perhaps the biggest problem is headsails, which on sloop rigged boats must be changed relatively often to suit different conditions. As we are talking about non-motorized vessels, the luxury of simply rolling a one-size fits all sail and motoring through the inconvenience is not an option. The efficiency of the small sloop is such that one may forgive this effort, and skill can make it speedy—but as the size of a boat increases, it is much less easy to accept. At about 35 feet in length, most people will find the task of changing a genoa to a working jib and back several times in an afternoon—not an uncommon task in inland waters—completely intolerable.

Since we see by this point that a Sea-Stead boat is likely to be a heavier displacement boat than perhaps average—so that it can successfully carry its stores and gear—its sailing rig will be large. With a modern Bermudian sloop, this means a tall mast, which as size increases becomes much more costly and difficult to stay. And yet height gives very little—making the basic triangle taller adds little sail area and less *effective* sail area, as the top third to quarter of any triangular sail offers relatively little drive.

Figure 9: Two thousand square feet. You can't see the three head-sails aback behind the main, all powered and drawing. Yes, I'm single-hand-ing...

For a well crewed racing boat none of this may be a concern—but it is certainly a concern for us. We require a solution that allows ease of handling that does not involve simply sizing the rig size down or unduly affecting performance. A solution exists in the more modern evolutions of the gaff rig. The gaff rig sets a simply enormous amount of sail on its short, inexpensive mast—perhaps 30 percent more than an equivalent Bermudan rig. A gaff cutter, especially, is a powerful rig, with its multiple but small headsails provide an hefty drive for a large boat. While this rig gives up some hypothetical weather ability, it is unlikely that the heavy, full keel hull that suits the ocean voyager would be any more weatherly with a modern rig. Certainly MACHA has little difficulty keeping up with similar sized but modern rigged boats to weather—indeed most of the time we feel we're faster. Off the wind the gaff rig is certainly faster. In light air only the light displacement race boats keep up with the cloud of canvas we set on our spars.

Question: What about the junk rig?

Regardless of what proponents say, I currently only know of one junk rig vessel that successfully sails without engine assist. It is rigged with nothing more than blue PVC tarps on wooden battens, and polypropylene for running rigging. It was built on a beach north of the City of Vancouver totally out of salvage drift logs by a committed Luddite in his mid 70's exclusively with hand tools. About 40 feet in length, it was built in this manner in less than a year's time. Again, this is the *only* junk rigged boat I've ever seen sailed. It is not weatherly. It is not fast. It is, however, owned and sailed by a true deity of the waters. This is the reason for its success and reflects little on its design.

While a junk may be easy to handle, the rig itself is much less powerful than a gaff rig, and much much less efficient than either a Gaff or Bermudian sloop cutter on the wind. I am not an expert of junk rigs; my opinion is simply based on the fact that the one's I've seen have really made a poor showing of themselves—I've sailed over the top of them like they were at anchor—certainly with *multiple* knots of boat speed difference. If one has a fascination with the junk—pursue it. Just make certain that one can find a true working example of a successful *non-auxiliary* vessel as an example, and to carefully question the often rather shrill enlightened sorts that advocate the rig.

Remember, it is not unusual in this world to encounter a 3 knot current that one must beat against. An outflowing current and an offshore breeze is a distinct possibility in most any harbor entrance in the world. *It is no good talking about waiting for the right conditions*—there *are* places where the right conditions may not *ever* come. Imagine an attempt of sailing around a small island in one day, perhaps a course of 25 miles in length. Yes, one must take into account the wind and the tides but assuming that there is a 12 mile beat and a twelve mile run involved, with a 3 knot current changing on a 6 hour schedule—that boats that lack a critical threshold of performance will *never complete the course.* I wouldn't own a boat that didn't have the ability to readily make a 4 knot speed of advance—<u>speed of advance</u>, not just speed through the water—to weather in average conditions. By implication, then, small boats must be progressively higher performance vessels than larger ones to meet this bench mark. Remembering economy, at some point it's cheaper to own a larger low performance but faster boat.

Many older texts suggest heaving-to for sail evolutions. I do not think many modern boats have the proper balance or underbodies to do so readily. They may do so for survival purposes with serious attention paid to balance and perhaps involving a sea-anchor, but there's hardly a reason to set a sea-anchor to reef a main sail. My old boat, hove-to, still had a strong tendency to fore-reach at an appreciable speed no matter what I did. This is not necessarily a problem, and makes for a quick trick when making a sandwich, but I do not see the technique as being particularly useful for sail changes. Better, I think, is plan to make way and to continue to make way. On a larger, heavier boat such as MACHA I do heave to in order to reef the main—otherwise the drop of the topsails or a jib are easily handled underway. We have described how to do so.

We can also see that if we are sailing a boat, and not motorsailing, how much more we rely on our sails. On a motorsailing boat, or indeed many boats, the first reef that is taken is to strike the headsail—which many times is a roller-furling unit. This is well and convenient, but being left with a single sail would make the task of reefing a main much more difficult if the engine wasn't in use, as there would be no drive to keep course stability while the reef is being tucked in—and the only alternative is to lie a-hull and roll badly. This is certainly not the best seamanship nor the best conditions to tie in a tidy reef.

I personally do not see either roller-furling units nor full-batten mains as appropriate gear aboard a sailboat. There are certainly advantages of convenience to each, but the fact remains that on a sailboat one hasn't the luxury of motoring to weather to make sail changes. To large a large degree both full-batten mains and roller-furling demand this—there are times which it can become necessary to reef a mainsail that is partially drawing, while sailing downwind. I am doubtful this could be done to a full batten sail without damaging it, or having the cars jam, or some other catastrophe. I haven't the final word on this, some disagree, but be certain one considers the issues and the potential ramifications of each carefully.

VANG THE BOOM DOWN SECURELY AND TOP UP THE LIFTS when tying in a reef, it makes the project much more simple and gives a sailor something to hold onto as one works.

These problems in headsail changes and in reefing are typical—one finds stiff piston hanks that haven't been maintained—and in the wet and cold of a pitching foredeck this can be insurmountable. One can find that the slide gate on the mast is frozen as well—this can be catastrophic. One can certainly discover that one can be afflicted with dyslexia involving a simple reef knot, yet the reef knot must be applied exactly the same and with a protocol—I suggest always tied with one side slipped, the slip loop pointing up. If that moment occurs when a reef then needs to be taken OUT in the dark, it makes the job much simpler. There is very little as frustrating with having to deal with a mystery knot in the dark with frozen fingers. One is tempted to apply a knife, and this is often the only resort, but a poor solution this is…

And yes, a sailor always carries a knife, and yes, a knife with a point on it has no place aboard a boat. This was a safety issue 300 years ago, and the same issue remains. An edge is much less likely to inflict random damage than a point. To sails as well as to other people.

While we are on the subject of safety issues, I'll need to make a position clear. Safety gear is reasonable, so far as it goes, as long as one never makes the mistake of using it. Safety gear more often than not is found to be relied upon, and as such I see it as creating hazards of its own. Lifelines are perhaps a good example. Rare is the boat that has lifelines that would seriously be capable of keeping a full grown man aboard in a seaway. Putting an extra piece of string or netting on them solves nothing. Making them so absurdly rugged that they add several hundred pounds of top-burden doesn't make much sense either. It would be little effort to grab the typical life line stanchion and simply bodily tear it off a boat—they are simply not strong enough to be effective. They could be built that strong, I suppose, but on a small boat the heft of the hardware would be excessive. Not to suggest taking lifelines off a boat, necessarily, as their real purpose is to keep a slightly tipsy sailor on board his boat while in an anchorage, but also not to suggest that they are really any more than ornament as a piece of safety gear. The only solution for a small boat is a set of proper jackstays and with the crew in harnesses. Floatation aids, man-overboard markers and the such are only then encumbrance. The thing any sailor and crew should realize that to go over the side of a boat means **_certain death_**—some people magically escape, of course, but death indeed is the practical reality of the issue. It is an especially grim issue for the single-hander. When asked of man overboard drills, the Col. Blondie

Hasler replied that he simply instructed his crew to drown like a proper English gentleman. I've always though that was the best advice I had ever heard on the subject.

Docking and Close Quarters Boat Handling:

Docking and sail-handling in tight quarters makes a lot of people nervous. This shouldn't be the case, necessarily, but certainly it is the situation which can take a lack of skill—normally hidden in convenience and large amounts of space in which to be sloppy—and makes it apparent. Again, there are not really any good reasons for this attitude. A good sailboat, well handled, is nearly as maneuverable as a car in a parking lot is—many people are nervous sailing ten feet from a pier but not nervous about flying down the freeway sometimes inches from a careening semi-truck. The key, of course, is practice and experience, so the first step again is to get out on the boat and run through some drills in basic boat handling.

People speak of marinas that prohibit sailing inside the breakwater. There are such places, admittedly, but they are certainly few—and I go so far to say that the prohibition of sailing is a good indicator of a lot of unfriendliness and a good place to avoid. All the marinas I have ever entered save one have been supportive of sail. All I have encountered were absolutely positive and supportive of good boat handling practices, as well as were other boaters.

I think there is really very little of an excuse here.

I should point out, however, that I'm writing this focusing on moderate sized sailboats—perhaps 24 to 34 feet on deck. A lot of yachtsmen like to say with an indignant snort that their boat is bigger than that and because of that one couldn't possibly sail it in and out of a harbor. I remind you now I'm sailing a sparred 52 foot 15 tonner in and out of a marina. The big boat argument is nothing but absolute ignorant bullshit and deserves a bit of a retort. I've seen and personally sailed a 112 foot, 200 ton, square rigged brig in and out of a marina—I think that's likely a bit bigger than any boat we're talking about here. The size of the boat is *not* the key issue. Nor is the tightness of the harbors. Any look at existing pictures of traditional harbors in the day of sail will find images of enormous, heavily sparred vessels crammed in with reckless abandon—much, much tighter than *any* harbor one sees today. If anything, harbors are *less* crowded than they were a hundred years ago.

Anybody who proclaims to know anything about prudent seamanship or boat handling must admit that the primary and most fundamental attribute of a safe, well-handled boat is the ratio of crew strength to boat size—the brig in question had a trained, skilled 14 person crew. One cannot ignore the reality of the importance of crew strength. Bigger boats are not more difficult to sail as engineless craft providing that they are well crewed. In many ways, they are *easier* to sail. They stand up to a blow better. With their taller rigs, they are less often becalmed. They, being heavier, often achieve a better sail set in light air and a chop. They carry way and steerage further. The only thing more difficult about large boats is this: if one makes an error in boat handling, it is bound to be a large error, and one is bound to smash things in a large way. This can be troublesome, for certain.

Practically speaking, however, it is tough enough to find enough crew skill to handle a Sunfish let alone a Wondrous 50 in tight quarters—when the foredeck bum makes yet another dash to the mast to douse the main—as he fumbles through the halyards to find the correct one yet again—as you're coming dead down into a dock in a blow trying to explain to some dolt yet again what a waist spring line is—you're heading for disaster. Not to say it can't be done, it just probably requires a professional crew. It used to be that the fat cats with big boats knew this—they hired a professional crew to run the boat so the owner and his family and friends could actually sit back and have a good time. He sometimes bought them spiffy little caps and shirts to work in as well. People don't have that much taste anymore so the owner just yells and screams at his spouse…The trouble is that "blue-water cruiser" has come to mean simply "big" and the novice buys more than he can afford and more boat than he can handle. If he's new to the game, and married, more often than not the wife isn't so big on the idea but is willing (ahem) to give it one highly, highly critical try—and on the first sail the roller furling jams for about 5 minutes in fifteen knots of air and it scares the hell out of everybody and that's the death knell for Tonga.

On the flip side—I'd like to slap the guy at the wheel of his big abomination hollering stuff at his wife—who he's kept in some sort of box for the last thirty years, and now expects her to take a diving leap and roll off five feet of freeboard to a finger pier rocking in prop wash born of desperation. God! It's awful! What's worse, is she usually does make the jump—and you can hear those weak ankle-bones craze as she hits the dock, the shockwaves run through that body (that looks like 250 pounds of chewed bubbled gum) from the bottom of her heels to the top of her scalp. You can hear it over the roaring of the motor and the barking of the little white shit dog. No wonder women hate sailing and boats in general! I'd hate it too if it were like that. Jeez, as I just said, at least at one point in history if a man had such a little unit that he needed to compensate by buying a ridiculously large boat, he at least had the balls and respect for his woman that he hired a crew of young bucks to do the stunt work for her. But the petty bourgeoisie of today haven't got that level of dignity—so they abuse their women. Pisses me off. Nope. I won't lift a finger to help—I'll drive the boat for a fee if he'd like—but I have found that all I do is get yelled at too. I'm not his wife, and I'm not on the payroll, and he doesn't get to yell for free. Sorry that the world is like that, it isn't like that everywhere, but it is here and that's the way it is.

Back on subject—hedge your bet. Make sure you don't bite off more than you can chew. Have some good experiences. Start really, really small—like knowing how to get on and off the dock before one starts thinking of the South Pacific. This game takes nothing more than practice, but it does take a lot of that. Learn to sail inland really well. Offshore will be a piece of cake.

There is no virtue in running shorthanded. It is foolhardy. Unless you can carry all the sail you want, in the conditions you want to, as long as you want to—you've got too much boat on your hands—and you'll not be "sailing" it anywhere.

Part of the reason people want big boats (other than status again) is because bigger boats have more interior space. They do—but not if they're properly crewed. If one compares the practical interior room of a 28 foot boat with a single-hander aboard, to a 50 foot boat with a crew of six—I think one will agree with me that the 28 foot boat feels much more roomy...

Back to boat handling...

I think it is important that one of the way one demonstrates one's superior boat handling skill is to make sure one doesn't inconvenience other boaters in the display of it. What I mean by this is demanding right-of-way, or basically being in the way of other boaters on a mad rush out of the harbor. Other boaters of less skill will certainly be obstructions—just assume that this is part of the game. If one chooses good times to make entries and exits—this is seldom a problem. When the weather is difficult and so is the harbor entry, traffic inside the harbor is invariably light. In these cases, be sure one uses all the proper signals if necessary, and sails with assertion. There is no question that you have a right here, and so do what you will—personally I have never had it become a problem. The easiest solution is to leave before 8 and return after 7. You'll have the entire harbor to yourself.

Figure 10: Our old 40 foot slip. We're 52 overall. We sailed in and out of
this teaching sailing for a year.

Fortunately, most of the time that the sailing is really good, most people are too afraid to go out and the traffic is bound to be light. If one sails the tide rather than the cocktail hour, one will find that traffic is seldom a problem either.

When cruising, it is often very hard to know what lies behind the breakwater. In these cases it is irresponsible to sail in blind—so one must wait for conditions that are appropriate for a very careful approach, even if it means sculling inside in a flat calm—or sending in a dingy to investigate before entering. This may seem like an inconvenience but it is certainly a reasonable part of nautical tradition and practice—one should not feel inconvenienced at all.

You have to know that people have no understanding at all of what you're doing. This includes other "sailors." You also have to assume that most people are simply assholes and will jerk you just for fun, if there's no chance you'll catch them to make things straight. Freeway ethics, one might call it. We had an experience much like this the other day, trying to clear customs into Canada. Tiny little customs dock in a bad place for sailing in and out of. We ended up making at least a dozen attempts to get into the dock under sail—every time the dock cleared and we turned to come back in, another 30 foot powerboat appeared from nowhere, cut us off in the narrow channel and beat us to the dock. We'd gybe, head back out, and wait for another attempt. Finally we gave up and just headed to the anchorage, and I rowed in with the skiff to clear customs. Of course, once I get there I find the procedure is done by phone—I had no need to even try the dock. What a hassle!

Maxim: Do what is right for the boat FIRST. Worry about details later. Assuming I even needed to make that dock—to try would be hazardous, and was. I shouldn't have even bothered to try. As if Customs would be unable to board us in the anchorage...

Those cautions being raised, there are really only a few scenarios that one can face. Which are getting on and off a dock, or getting in and out of a slip. Practically, getting in and out of a slip is just getting on and off of a very short dock. For practicing these maneuvers, use the longest dock you can find to make the maneuver safe, but mark the dock off in a distance only as long as your slip. That way you learn to only use as much dock space as you need—and this will become critical.

Before you try anything, however, you'll need to know a couple of things about your boat. These are basic skills. First, at any given speed, how far will the boat carry way? Try to think in terms of boat-lengths rather than feet, as you'll always have a ready measuring stick. In other words, if you pull off the sail power, how far will the boat coast and maintain steerage? This varies quite a bit from boat to boat, keels make a difference here, but you need to know your boat very well. Some maneuvers are nothing more than just coasting into place. Learn to judge distance.

Secondly, you'll need to know what the turning radius of your boat is—also think again in terms of boat lengths. For many modern boats with powerful rudders, this is just over one boat length—older designs often require more room. Think, as well, that when one makes a turn that the action of the rudder is going to kill some speed—this can be useful to burn off excess speed or can be an inconvenience. Be aware of the possibilities.

Third, you'll need to know what the boat does when you initially APPLY sail power—some boats take off a little bit before the rudder gains steerage and often in a marina you haven't room for this surprise. Again, all of this can be practiced out in the open with no risk to anything—so take advantage of that possibility before you go and scratch paint.

So go and, put the boat through its paces. What I do when I teach people to sail is this: Take people out and throw a cushion overboard—sail circles around it—the tighter the better. Now, throw a second one over the side, and sail figure eights. Can't do it? Miss any tacks? That is unacceptable. Do this until it becomes positively boring. You need to be as comfortable sailing as you are driving your car—I assume you can drive your car.

After this is easy—which takes most people about an hour—sail up to a cushion, stop, and sail away again. Is this easy? It should be. It will teach you that some approaches make a lot more sense than others. This will teach you low speed control, how far the boat carries way, etc. Some boats are just not very comfortable with low speed handling. This is one of the curses of modern design. Since they design boats for a minimum of wetted surface area and control surface area, the amount of control the boat has is very heavily dependent on its speed. At low speed many of these designs are very difficult to keep under control—take this into consideration if you haven't purchased a boat yet.

After this, you might try moorings someplace. The difference between moorings and the cushions is that you've likely got obstacles to dodge while making your approach—so one learns to make clever approaches and begins to think about locating escape routes. You'll learn quickly that it is always nice to try to make your approaches to weather, if you can, and that down wind approaches are always more difficult and less forgiving.

TARGET
TO
WEATHER

BE SMART!

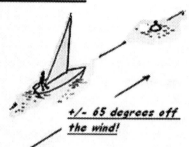

+/- 65 degrees off the wind!

Approach at a close reach. If you come in too, you may not be able to spill wind to slow down. If you come in too low, you'll not be able to round up and you'll miss your mark!

DON'T!

Don't try these manuvers under roller headsails! You'll not point high enough, you may not be able to tack, and you're prone to loose control especially at low speeds. USE THE MAINSAIL!

REMEMBER! You must have boat speed for control! Sail with confidence!

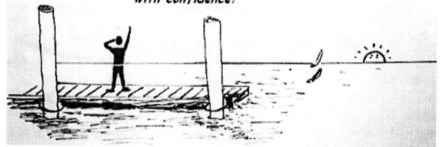

It is also helpful to find some place where the tide sets through the moorings—and learn a little about relative velocity. Having current present is not as difficult as many would have you think—but it is good to get used to the experience as there will be a few surprises for certain.

After approach to the moorings becomes easy, it is time to make weather approaches to a dock, stop, and sail away. The goal is docking, not touch and go landing. Unless a crewmember can easily step shore-side with a line in hand, it's a failure. If you are practicing single-handing, this dock person will need to be you. This will seem no trouble unless one panics.

Next; make weather approaches to the dock, and parallel park. Limit your working room between a couple of pilings, hopefully about a boat length and a half apart. You'll find that by carefully pinching and luffing you'll be able to slide in sideways. In other words, we're pointing so high that all we make is lee-way—but lee-way in the direction we want to go.

Now, sail to weather into a slip. Easy? Should be, and I'm sure it will be if you've done your practice.

Now let's start with down wind approaches. These are considerably more difficult. Obviously the trick is to keep the power down. How will you stop? There are only two ways—pure physical beef on the dock, or by surging a line around a cleat or a piling, strategically chosen. Practice your line handling and your composure. These maneuvers aren't difficult, but a failure will invariably mean a crash. Don't crash.

Not sure where you are going? Of course this means taking a sail by and checking it out. Not sure? Don't try.

MAKE SURE your spring line is strong enough, elastic enough (nylon) and irrevocably bent to your ship or you will have a disaster—again this is a skill requiring some agility but really quite easy as long as you do everything right.

**Be careful as many people suffer from spring line dyslexia!** Which is to say, that as they leave the forward moving vessel with a spring line will run forward, towards the bow, rather than back towards the stern. It happens again and again, and people find out it is hard to push a rope. A hand on the dock, all helpful and such, is very likely to screw you with their aid and make you look like an ass by turning nice boat handling into a crash. _**Take that line aft and to the first bit you can get a turn on.**_

Don't freak out and fall over the lifeline as you get off your boat. I've seen it happen. The worst I've seen happen, however, have been under power. A couple of times now I've seen a guy jump over the side of the boat onto the dock, the mooring line or something fouls on the throttle as he goes over the side and the boat just guns ahead…I've seen a boat go clear over the dock all the way to the forefoot this way. Very dramatic…crashes can happen—beware!

And I said SPRING LINE, right? This means led from amidships about where the center of lateral resistance is—if you clamp the brakes on too far forward the stern will flip out; too far aft the bow, although this is less dramatic. On a lot of boats, the sheet winch is pretty close.

OK, here we go.

Oh yes, for these drills—have a capable buddy on board so if you screw up or fall in the water your boat won't just sail off…And one other warning—people will see you coming in and offer a helping hand. Politely refuse. You need to learn to do this alone, and there is only one way to do that—alone. Besides, docking a boat with lines is a skill few people possess, even skill for small boats. You'll not take my advice on this and you'll see what happens. Invariably, if you let someone take your line, they'll take the bow line—and the first thing they will do is pull on it—generally perpendicular to the dock. Of course the immediate effect will be to swing to boat all out of shape, and if you're coming into a slip, the stern will swing out and you'll likely bump the boat beside you. Mark my words, they'll do this every time. Make sure your crew knows enough about line handling not to do this either. You don't need a lot of space to stop a small boat even at speed with a good spring line and cleat—a foot and a half? Don't panic, shoot for high efficiency motion.

DOWN-WIND!

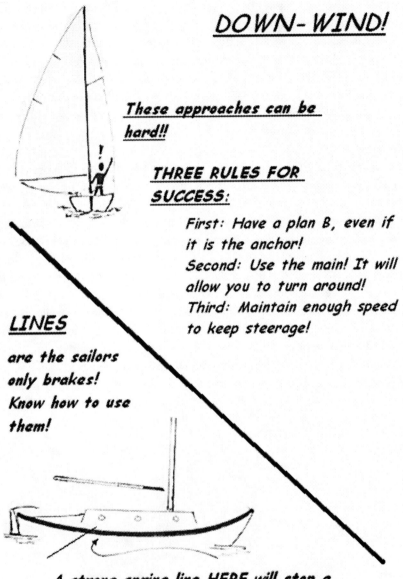

These approaches can be hard!!

THREE RULES FOR SUCCESS:

First: Have a plan B, even if it is the anchor!
Second: Use the main! It will allow you to turn around!
Third: Maintain enough speed to keep steerage!

LINES

are the sailors only brakes!
Know how to use them!

A strong spring line HERE will stop a boat parallel to the dock!

OK: We're coming into the marina slow, preferably under the main, reefed if need be—all we want is steerage. Why? A lot of guys think a headsail would be better—with the idea that you can spill it off the wind. No, that flogging headsail will still have plenty of drive off the wind. Besides, if you need to abort the maneuver the headsail will not round your boat up readily at low speeds to get yourself out of trouble. Don't make the mistake that all ASA instructors do either: don't try to sail in under a roller furling headsail thinking you can roll it up at the last minute, or roll it partially to control your speed. It doesn't work, and you'll lose way and forereach into something. Use the main, that's why it is called the main!

If the wind is really screaming—you'll probably going to only get one attempt under bare poles. Try to avoid this situation as maneuverability is obviously very limited.

So here we come. We want no more sail area than necessary to maintain steerage, again, right?

Approach the dock, slide up close, step ashore, and take a single turn around a dock cleat or a pile. Ease her to a halt by gradually applying tension in a single pulse—if you do it right, the boat will just scooch into her fenders and stop. If you don't she'll crash into something, of course.

With practice, you'll need about two boat lengths, not all of this needing to be dock space—as certainly your slip won't be that long. That length means a final approach and surging to a halt.

WATCH THE BOOM! If you've still got sail set, for it's really easy to whack it on a piling or a neighboring boat. If you have the boom sheeted amidships for a final dead downwind approach in moderate conditions, you'll find that that you can slow the boat quite significantly this way. The difficulty of course, is the threat of a gust from the side—certainly a possibility in a marina with a number of boat-sheds, etc., so be aware.

Be aware as well as the very significant blanketing effect that breakwaters and buildings have on wind speed, both upwind and downwind of them. Be aware that if it is blowing hard, that at low tide the apparent wind behind the breakwater will be much less than it is at high water. If you've got a difficult entrance, try to use this to your advantage.

By the way, here is the save all technique for how to get in to the impossibly tight spot, down wind, under sail. Come blazing into where you've got to go, round up, take a quick tack to where dead to weather of your chosen hole is. Drop the anchor. Dump the main sail, and pay back rode until you work yourself in. Just leave the hook on the bottom until you're ready to go; give a haul and sail off.

Now leaving a slip isn't much different, but one actually sees more crashes when people try this under sail than in docking. The reason for this is simple—as we've said, people do not anticipate the initial surge of motion of the boat before the keel bites and the rudder gains control. Again, high aspect rudder designs only make this worse as they are prone to stall at high angles of bite—one will see the boat, helmsman with the rudder hard over, just fore-reach into a piling. Be aware of this situation and again, know your boat.

One has basically just a couple of possibilities here as well. Bow in, and bow out, of course, and up wind and down wind exits.

The simplest, of course, is the bow out, down wind exit. You set your main, let slip your lines and sail out of the slip. (see the section on toggles) If you're going to have to make an immediate turn, of course set your main on the tack that facilitates that turn.

Bow out and upwind is hardly more complicated, except to say that it is generally best to let slip the lines, have your dockman give the boat a solid bob-sled running start to gain steerage, and sail off and away.

So certainly it makes a good deal of sense to keep the bow out in the slip, right? This is inconvenient, somewhat, as it isn't often reasonable to back into a slip under sail. This means at some point turning the boat around under oars or sails in mild conditions. This practice is certainly good prudent seamanship and eliminates a good deal of trouble.

Assuming we ignore this and we leave the boat in the slip bow in—then we've got difficulty. To get out of the slip is going to require oar power or line handling or something. No surprise this, and certainly traditional—this is how we go about it.

Let us say first that we are bow in, with the wind wanting to blow us out of the slip stern first. This may be an easy situation on some boats, on others difficult. If your boat will keep steerage making sternway this may be very little difficulty, even so much as you may be able to set and feather the main—or further keep it from setting my "scandalizing" by topping up the boom and letting the leech flog. If a nudge astern is given by the dockman, a gentle bobsled start, the boat can be let out and the helm put over so the bow is pointed towards exit, hopefully, a broad reach or close—the main sheeted in gently to apply sail-power and to discourage uncontrolled fore-reaching, the boat will sail away easily.

If the stern faces out and this happens to be upwind, there is not much to be done other than to row the boat out of the slip against it, or to haul it out by lines. If the wind is too much for oars—generally about 15 knots—and lines are needed, it is probably just best to turn to boat fully around, put it back in the slip by any means accessible, and make it a much easier, bow out, upwind exit.

When sailing in confined spaces avoid these common errors:

When tacking to weather in a narrow fairway, be sure to use the full width available. Many feel uncomfortable tacking mere feet from the transoms of other boat or spiting distance from a breakwater, but this is necessary and not danger-ous or reckless if one has control of one's boat. Use the full distance, maintain speed and steerage, else by pinching and tacking back and forth too short one will destroy speed and steerage, and one will loose control.

Trim the main for maximum maneuverability—this often means full sail with a slightly cupped leech on boats with cruising style underbodies.

Maintain steerage: Do not go so slow that you have poor rudder response time. Again, this varies boat to boat—again, large boats with large underbodies often retain control at very low speeds, faster boats often need more speed to retain control. Don't be so cautious that you create hazards.

Make all maneuvers clearly and with distinct intent. Realize that most boaters do not understand sail and that your actions will confuse them. Be explicit, this is basic courtesy to other boaters who need to know what you are doing. Use sound signals when appropriate. *Again, recognize that even so many boaters won't under-stand what you are doing, and it will be dependent on YOUR skill to avoid an issue*. Be prepared to settle up against a boat-shed, or pilings, or the transoms of another boat—gently and with skill, to avoid someone will less ability.

A boat with a lot of freeboard, high windage, little underbody, and a wide beam is really going to be a hassle to dock under sail.

Again, be very hesitant to accept help with your lines as it can often cause trouble.

Lastly, it will happen on occasion—although certainly rarely—that someone will gripe at you that your sailing maneuvers are reckless and dangerous. You'll immediate recognize the source of this complaint when you hear it, as it invari-ably comes from people of very marginal seamanlike ability and very little recog-nition of this fact—they assume that whatever must be dangerous or impossible for them must be dangerous and impossible for someone else too. The thing to do is to blow these people off. Say that you'd absolutely be in support of a policy that demanded a practical test of boat-handling ability of anyone on the water—this usually will shut them up. Don't let them worry you—these people hide in the shadows all day looking for something to complain about and you just gave them an opportunity to make their day meaningful. More often than not, rather than these, you'll meet people who are overwhelmingly appreciative of your obvious demonstration of all-too-rare ability.

Special concerns for large gaff rigged boats.

Handling a large sparred full keel vessel is very different than a modern moderately sized sloop. First, the turning radius of such a vessel will be twice to three times that of a fin or cutaway keeled boat. This often requires, in tight spaces, supplementing steering by backing headsails and oversheeting mainsails. The rudder simply does much less turning of the boat in harbor conditions. Another concern is the often very long boom. This makes sheeting out the main sail as a means of slowing often impossible without nailing a piling or some other obstruction. Fortunately there are good tricks for gaff rigged boats. Dropping the peak can very much depower the main, as can tricing the tack of a loose footed main. I see loose footed mains as *imperative* on all marina bound gaffers as it will be necessary to depower radically without dropping the sail entirely. A carefully scandalized mainsail actually sails backwards quite nicely, and makes a good trick for backing out of a slip—no driving shape at all—just a large sack of sailcloth fluttering near the leech of the sail.

If you've got a heaving line, and know how to use it, you can get a line to the dock in many conditions. If you can get that line to a competent hand—most all the troubles are over. Warping a big boat in and out of tight corners is time honored and as safe as any means of handling a boat. It is, however, a situation that needs a decisive skipper and a good crew or everyone will just pull like hell, often in random and opposite directions.

One needs to realize anyway that once one gets the Sea-Stead lifestyle underway, docks and marinas are going to become a thing of the past. They are simply prohibitively expensive. If one does need to get on or off a dock, which will happen on occasion, this can always be planned around the conditions. Even MACHA, at 32 thousand pounds, can be *rowed* in and out of the tightest marina in the silent calm of the morning, and if we've got that kind of problem facing us, it's simply what we do.

Special Techniques for the Impossible Situation:

These are the techniques for getting out of those places that everyone will tell you "you just can't possibly go" without an engine. Even if you've got the engine, you'd be well to be aware these. Relying on an engine is foolish, and it doesn't make it any less foolish to rely on someone else's engine either. You can't get a tow just anywhere, even if you needed it. Skill and knowledge must be the final line of defense!

Kedging:

Kedging, of course, is the technique of using anchors or a series of set anchors to drag oneself clear of a situation to tight or dangerous for one to sail. It works, of, course, and there isn't much to it except grunt. On a small boat, the effort involved is minimal, but on a larger boat some backbone is going to be required. Still, it is a technique that will save your boat, especially in lee shore situations, and if one has any doubt about getting clear it's good to give kedging a good thought.

You will find, however, that, unless your boat is set up to do so, kedging will be much more difficult than it needs to be. I think a sailing craft of any tonnage—and pretty much all of them anyhow—should have a central roller for the bower, and one on each forward quarter for kedge anchors—ideally with rollers too as it eliminates a good deal of chafe and makes the whole hauling effort easier. The bower, except on small boats, is likely to be too heavy to be rowed out very effectively unless it is on rope—which it shouldn't be—and under about 30 pounds. Better, I think, is to have a pair of anchors for kedging, on rope rodes, and be ready to use them. One can row a 33 pound Bruce with 40 feet of chain and 400 feet 5/8 rope rode to weather in up to about 20 knots of wind. This will get you a good way off the beach, and you could repeat a second time if you needed too, but you'll get pooped and less effective at some point.

To get started, and assuming the bower is well set, haul in on the main anchor until one is at about a 2 to 1 scope. Get in the skiff with the kedge hook and start rowing. You'll have to decide weather you'd like the rode in the skiff and to pay out as you go, or to have crew pay out rode on deck. I think the latter is generally better but it's a close call. Row out as far as you are able, taking care to do so in a direction that will allow you to pick up the bower as you ride up over it. Pitch the anchor over the side, and return to the yacht. Haul away, pick up the bower, haul away some more until you're on short cable once again. If you're clear, sail away. If not, you'll need to do it again, of course, but such is life.

Note, again, I said rollers on the *forward quarters* for the kedges, right? There is a reason for this. In tight quarters there will be one tack that will be favored more than another for sailing clear, right? Set up the kedge so that by laying to on the appropriate quarter the boat will naturally favor this tack. The roller for the bower won't have this bias and might make things a bit more difficult.

Practice this before you need to use it or you'll likely find that something is amiss somewhere—it is a simple technique, but nothing is ever as simple as it seems!

Casting:

Casting is an obscure technique that might just save your boat. It is used in much a similar situation—the need to leave a very tight spot, off of a lee shore, and to weather. It is a bit difficult to explain, so listen carefully.

Pay out the bower with as much rode as possible, with the boat falling back towards the beach. Whatever side of this exit has the most accessible space, plan to sail to weather on that tack. The amount of rode you pay out is limited by the width of the area you have in to sail. If you have 200 feet from the point at which the anchor lies on the bottom to an obstacle—say a reef or a cliff—which perpendicular from this point to the wind, pay out 190 feet of cable. You'll see why in a moment.

Sail to weather as hard as you can on this chosen tack, laying hard on the anchor cable. As you go to weather, the rode will stretch taut and force you through stays to the opposite tack. Sheet in hard and keep going. When you are directly head to weather of your anchor, round up hard, coast as far as possible, and the moment you loose way, drop another anchor. Fall back, pick up the first one, and repeat as many times as needed until you're clear of the trap.

The reason casting works:

1. At no point are you sailing without a fall back plan. If you screw up, or miss stays, or the wind heads you hard, you've still got an anchor on the bottom which will keep you off the beach.

2. You'll be able to point much higher than you normally will, as the boat will make no leeway whatsoever. The anchor rode is preventing leeway, not the keel.

3. You can really pinch and push your tacking to the limit, as you can't really miss stays. That taut rode will bring the head around regardless.

This allows you to sail much nearer the obstruction than would be prudent otherwise, as being caught in irons could be disastrous.

4. You can pull this trick off without launching the skiff. This may be better for a single hander. You can also, hypothetically, use this technique in winds that would be too strong to effectively row out cable in the smaller boat.

The technique has two disadvantages:

1. Of course the anchorage where you are must be clear of other boats, moorings, and the like that might foul the anchor rode as you swing on it.

2. You may be found in a situation where you cannot safely retrieve the last anchor you set. This means that this anchor will need to be sacrificed to save the ship. All in all, however, I doubt I'd care much in the moment.

Drudging:

Drudging is a bargeman's technique for getting a boat down current in a situation where there is not enough wind to maintain steerage. The Thames sailing barges carried a device called a "drudging iron" which was a heavy metal sled that was meant to skid along the bottom slowing the barge down as it drifted on the current. This was streamed off the bow and slowed the boat down enough, relative to the current that the rudder gained steerage. The barges would travel miles like this, down stream, head to current, and is one of the main reasons that they could get away with such relatively low performance rigs. I've found the same technique works on a small boat, and all that is needed is a shot of chain with no anchor attached. It takes little to slow the boat down and gain steerage, and with chain you can simply pay out more or less to control one's speed. You'll simply laugh, the first time you try this, at how *incredibly* well it works and just how much steerage and maneuverability it provides. These old guys thought of everything, didn't they? Of course they did, for there weren't any other options but thinking or going on the beach.

So this is how you sail a boat in an out of most anything. You'd have to be really in a pinch to find yourself in a spot that none of these skills would get you out of—and you'd have to ask as to what were you doing there in the first place.

Again, don't let your first attempt at these emergency techniques be in the middle of the emergency, or you run a fair chance of screwing up.

Last question, and a bit of a diatribe: Taking a tow?

So, what about taking a tow? This is a sticky subject for some people, and we'll attempt to deal with it in a sensible manner.

It is an attitude commonly held among the motor sailor crowd that "sailors" *cheat* by getting towed in an out of most every harbor in the world. If one asks about the Pardeys, in particular, you'd think by the crap you hear about them that they've been towed to more places than they've sailed. It is surprising to consider that a motor sailor who must power to make any passage has no problem calling a sailor without an engine on board a hypocrite for sailing up to a tight marina and accepting a tow inside. Well, if so, and an occasional tow makes you a hypocrite—I guess the Pardey's may well be hypocrites, just like Ferdinand Magellan, Columbus, and Drake were all hypocrites every time they launched the long boat. I guess, although I never took a mechanized tow in RENEGADE in the ten years and over 10000 miles of inland technical cruising—I did, twice, drag her out behind the kayak in places so narrow that I couldn't get the sweeps overboard. That means I'm a hypocrite as well. Last time we came back from Canada in MACHA we took a tow into the Customs dock—a place so tight we had to remove the bowsprit to get into—but that's another story…

Obviously, towing sailing boats with smaller pulling boats is a centuries old tradition, and a fair piece of seamanship. As well, I'll state categorically that if while attempting to prove something you unduly inconvenience or risk other people's boats you're making a better case of yourself as a jerk than as a sailor. Be sensible, don't be an ass, be a safe and prudent seaman above all else. This all being said, if you've got the skills you need to have, and that *everyone should have, engine or no,* you'll very rarely be in any need of assistance of any sort. Trust me—don't listen to Captain Piddlemarks. Once you've got the skill you need, you'll sail in and out of your marina and not give it a second thought. You'll do it time and time again. Don't listen to the crap people say. The Pardeys, I'm sure, as talented as they are, probably haven't gotten a tow more than one out of a hundred ports they visited. They also visited a hell of a lot of places that a tow wasn't available. So have I. So have the Carrs—not a lot of tows to be had there in Antarctica. So has Tom Cunliffe. So has John Guzzwell. So has John Letcher. So have the Hiscocks, in their engineless Wanderer. So did Peter Tangvald. So did Conor O'Brien. So did Joshua Slocum. If these people were reliant on towing, as some suggest—they'd all have died at sea…Baloney! Don't get depressed because somebody with a 60 horse motor and the three bladed screw *will* call you a hypocrite. Remember you're doing this all for yourself, not to impress Captain Piddlemarks, as nothing impresses him but himself. *Certainly, a sailor is only a sailor as much as he or she sails.* Definitely, having gotten one tow in the last dozen years *does indeed* mean that I'm not as good of a sailor as if I had not gotten a tow at all. Again, our goal is to grow and become more skillful—taking a tow gets us into the harbor but doesn't teach us a thing. *Take a tow before you get killed.* Take a tow before you kill someone else. Take a tow before you wreck the boat. Take a tow if you screw up and get in over your head, especially before you bash something and give "sailing" a bad name. Even if you *can* kedge out of a marina, or what ever, be a good sort if someone offers you a tow so all your kedging isn't some big pain in the ass for everyone else—take the damn tow, as it will make the tow-er pleased as punch and give him something to gloat about. All of this is OK, at times, and might even be necessary. But remember the goal, and who we're working for. Even if you're a terrible flunky, and need a tow half the times you go out—which would be very stupid indeed—you're a better sailor than someone who carries a big inboard with them and needs to use it every damn time. You're a safer sailor too. You'll learn faster, and learn more, and be vastly more independent. The key is, of course, not to rely on the availability of a tow—at this point you're simply motor sailing again. You're just relying on someone *else's* motor, which isn't any better. Only you can make this judgment.

Hell, *I've* even towed dead powerboats home.

I had an experience on MACHA this last summer. We needed to fill tanks and supplies in MACHA, so we anchored out, waited for a calm, and then sculled all 52 feet of her into a marina for an overnight stay. We try not to do this too often, but when we do, we sure make the jaws drop. As we arrived at the visitors dock—Captain Piddlemarks was there to greet us. He asked to help us with our lines, and I told him that we were fine, and Sparrow and I just snugged MACHA's 15 tones into the dock. This pissed him off a bit, as it usually does when you refuse someone's offer of help—but you'll find out that it's a safety issue to do so and you'll learn do that yourself. Anyway, he starts quizzing us about the boat, and of course he wants to know what happened to the motor and why it doesn't work. I reply, well, it works fine in the boat it's currently installed in, but we tore it out of *this* boat and sold it. This shocked him a bit, and once he got his breath back he began to lecture us on the safeties that an engine provides and all that—blah blah blah, as if I haven't heard this before. I said, finally, in a lull in his gale of advice, that I really enjoyed sailing and the challenge it provided, and if I had the engine it would be much less of a challenge and I wouldn't enjoy it nearly as much. This got him edgier yet (because of course he reads this as me saying that I'd be bored doing something that he counts as quite the adventure; quite so!) and he began at this point to explain to me that there's sailing, and there's mechanical propulsion, and that because I use a sculling oar, I'm a motor sailor just like every one else, and I'm not proving a thing. I said I really didn't much care about the proving part, and that I didn't claim to be doing any proving. But this didn't slow him down either.

"Yep," he says smugly, satisfied at his demonstration of intellectual rigor, "Son, there's just no difference between motoring and using an oar, as they're both mechanical propulsion."

"Well," I replied, "Actually, in practice, I think that there's one major difference."

"What's that?" he asks, snidely skeptical.

"Using an oar keeps your dick stiff." I answer.

His wife, a jolly sort, watching her husband's antics from the cockpit of their boat, at this point nearly rolls in laughter and calls out "That's it, Joe, I'm getting you an oar!"

So then, don't take any of this *too* seriously.

8

PASSAGEMAKING AND WEATHER

In order to make the best, fastest, most efficient passage from one hypothetical harbor to another through a hypothetical group of islands, a sailor would need to know:

The radio weather forecast, if available: If not, one must have the means to make a forecast oneself.

The time, and magnitude of the tide:

The hypothetical speed advance of the boat in such conditions:

And this is modified by the chosen course, involving these local effects:

The effects of vertical relief on the localized airflow:

The funneling effect of predominant wind conditions in appropriately oriented channels:

The amount of likely turbulence in the windflow, and the resultant velocity veer:

The frictional resistance met by the wind of all weather shores:

The frictional resistance met by the wind of all lee shores:

Whether frictional resistance will further induce veer:

Whether katabatic flow will be encountered:

The likely presence of inversions and when or if they will disperse:

Whether sea breeze generation will be part of the local forecast:

Times of sunrise and sunset, and the local turn of the tide.

Figure 11: MACHA at anchor waiting for a 990mb low to blow out of the
area early in the spring.

And this will need to be known of every possible moment of the day, in real time, modified by the boat's present position and:

Local strategy influenced by sea state:
Local strategy influenced by channel convergence:
Local strategy influenced by channel divergence:

Head spinning from all that? It certainly should be—and this of course is the reason that sailing is challenging and interesting, as opposed to motorsailing, which makes the knowledge of *everything* on my list completely inconsequential. How much difference does this knowledge make? An immense amount. Locally, we sponsor a race of 35 miles around a local island—a course complicated and that involves most all of these variables. The race rules are as thus—no engines, of course, at anytime during the weekend of the race, otherwise no handicaps. Handicaps never been needed as the course is fair, skill is far more important than the boat—and frankly we've found so few sailors who have the ability to complete the race, regardless of how "trick" or fast their boat might be. During the weekend of the race, the course can be sailed at any time the skipper of the boat chooses—but at the second the boat leaves the breakwater, the clock starts running and continues until the boat re-enters the harbor. The forecast of course is known to all, the tides indicate a good time to leave—and usually all the boats leave within a few hours of each other—often within less than an hour of each other. The results? It has been typical each year we have held the race that fully half of the fleet hasn't finished. There is generally one or two boats that make good time—I hold the course record at a little over 6 hours, a few boats will straggle in about 10 hours, and then a long last few diehards will make perhaps 16 hour times. Why? There are those who would say this is due to the pure luck of the fact of being in the right place at the right time—but since the same people have taken first, second, and third for years running, that is an unlikely explanation. No, I would say that a good deal of sailing IS the skill of being in the right place at the right time, and there is a good deal that one needs to know to be able to develop this skill.

Of course, this race never gets "called" because a good part of the fleet, though certainly not all, are engineless boats, and they're going to complete the race whether it's called or not. This changes things a bit too.

Stories abound concerning this race—generally involving someone being caught in a rip in a near calm and being stuck there for hours. The statement that is typically made is "wow, if we could have only made a hundred yards, we wouldn't have had any trouble." Of course one wouldn't—sailing, if one does it, can be mindless for a thousand miles and impossible for a hundred yards. We've discussed this: that is what makes sailing interesting, of course—those hard spots. If one has only sailed the convenient times, and puttered through those "hundred yards', one might sail 90% of the time for a lifetime but only learn 10% of what sailing is all about…

Again this book isn't the place to discuss all the aspects of meteorology that apply, except in the short form to raise the ISSUE of certain phenomenon, so the reader at least is aware of their existence and can begin to look for their effects. There are certainly other books of some detail that will deal with these issues in depth—the best ones I know of are in the appendix. Still much can be said that can be applied even the next time one sails.

Diatribe:

The single biggest difference between a good sailor and a bad sailor is this: assuming both are actually sailing—the good sailor will make a good passage in good time and the bad sailor will have to work much harder at it, if he gets there at all. Everyone starts out as a bad sailor. You will too—expect it. This means, initially, slower passage times, getting becalmed, missing harbors, rowing a lot, and having panic attacks—in essence all the things people equate with not having a motor. This much is true: again, *when one is getting started, one is bound to be a bad sailor.* It's going to be a bit rough. It's going to be an ego buster. Expect this, and stick with it. Don't give up, assuming it can't be done, or that believe that predicting and riding the weather is just a matter of luck of the draw. I'm here to tell you, with others, and centuries of tradition, that it *can* be done, and done comfortably and reliably. However, this is the one area of sailing knowledge where you're not going to be able to disguise the fact that there's a lack of understanding. You can't buy a gadget, no matter how rich you are, that will make the wind blow as you'd like. Make a bad call, and you're going to pay. Probably the worst of it is that you'll get to drift around all night in the dark—perhaps in the rain—it could be a bit hair-raising but this possibility is the source of the adventure we seek.

Can you get killed doing this? Can you make bad enough decisions that you'll wreck your boat? Of course you can! So don't ever get yourself in a set of circumstances that will allow this to happen even if you *do* screw up. This is the essence of seamanship itself! For most of you, then, even if you've got "years" of motor sailing under your belt, you've got very little business traveling very far afield until you've got your basic skills. I think for most people this means a season of sailing going no further than the limits of one's home bay. I've always told people this who come for classes—I think the average individual can learn most of boat handling in about a week of practice—but to learn to sail, which means riding the weather—that will take a year of dedicated, patient, aware practice. Can I quantify the skill? Yes: I'd say that unless you can call the existence of stable conditions accurately 90% of the time you need practice. As well I'd say in unstable or changing conditions you need to be able to predict the local change of events reliably within 30 minutes of their event. This means know when the wind is going to arrive, when it is going to die, when it is going to build, when it is going to shift, or when the rain will show up. I think, in inland waters at least, you must cultivate 30 minute resolution or less. You can, you can, you can. If you're serious, you will. If you take this in a Zen and sloppy manner, you won't. If you're not keeping a good log, you're not even trying.

Can you get killed doing this? Again, of course you can. Let us admit that this reality is what makes the adventure in sailing. There is no interest or adventure or reward in the predicable outcome. Even in playing "solitaire" one loses the majority of the time—if one always won, the game would be even dumber than it is. There is a chance that you'll "lose" sailing, and the yacht press drums those examples up every chance they get. The accounts of death and disaster make for good voyeuristic reading—they make our pastime seem more exciting and dangerous than it really is, which gives us a little tingle the next time the wind pipes up to a might 15 knots—they give some of us good excuse so stand around and sneer at the dumb bastards, who, unlike us in our high and mighty prudence, would never be caught in the same circumstances. Blah Blah Blah. I've got a young friend who, for stupid reasons, was into driving fast cars. He was all excited about the tingle it gave him, and the thrill. The thrill in going fast comes from the very reasonable fear that there is a fair chance that you're going to wipe out and bite it. If there was no risk in the activity—if no one ever wiped out and bit it—going fast in a car would be no thrill at all. Well, he wiped out and bit it, and spent 2 months in a coma. He went from being a robust 23 year old to a very enfeebled 24 year old with the power of a 75 year old man with Parkinson's. No hyperbole in that last statement at all. Well, that just sucks, for sure, but the fact is he provided the rest of us with a great service—*he kept the tingle in going fast for the rest of us.* We've got new reasons to be afraid—especially when you try to talk with him and hear him struggle…he's making a little progress but damn, it's hard.

Don't worry about it. Be careful, go slow, take baby steps. Have a fall-back plan and another too. You'll be just fine.

So then, let's discuss things a bit.

There are basically two kinds of wind—frontal and thermal. This is a gross oversimplification but will suffice for us now. Frontal wind is generated by (imagine) the motion of frontal systems and by the effect of differences in atmospheric pressure. Thermal wind is generated by the local heating of air and surfaces during the day—and has many different forms, of which simple "sea breeze" generation is typical. One can certainly have the effects of one or the other during the day, or both. Still, basically, for frontal effects one must have indication of a change in barometric pressure—and the magnitude of the change has a direct bearing on the magnitude of the effective wind. Thermal wind is dependant on change in temperature and a difference in temperature differential—and the greater this differential the greater the magnitude of the effect.

Heating of air causes air to rise. This effect is modified by temperature, humidity, and topography, but in all cases the rising of air causes a change in barometric pressure, generally relatively localized, and this is responsible for the generation of wind.

In either case, air flows horizontally from an area of high pressure to an area of lower pressure, assuming that both of these areas are of the same elevation. At the surface, wind speeds are generally the lowest, and the horizontal air flow—the wind—is effected greatly by the friction of the ground and slowed. The source altitude of windflow and the frictional attachment to the surface is very important—as it keys in effect of the earth's rotation. A surface wind has its direction is relatively unaffected by the rotation of the earth. At greater altitudes, however, the frictional effect of the surface is negligible. At these levels the airflow retains the rotational velocity of the of the surface of the earth at its point of origin and flows from that point with a COMBINED speed dependant on BOTH the pressure gradient AND the earth's location. Airflow at progressively higher altitudes is progressively skewed from its direct course from the high pressure to low pressure point by the Coriolis effect of the rotation of the earth. In the Northern Hemisphere this means that flow at high altitudes is increasingly deviated in a clockwise, or deflected towards the right, fashion—veered—as compared to the surface flow. The converse would be the case in the Southern Hemisphere. If for some reason pockets of this upper level airflow reaches the surface, the wind at the surface will be veered relative to the original direction of flow. This airflow will reach the surface for a number of reasons, pure turbulence, thermal effects, etc., but the effect remains the same and of immediate interest to the sailor: surface airflow will veer increasingly over time in a strong airflow that is relatively stable—if the airflow is UNSTABLE, the surface airflow will be mixed with occasional gusts of upper level airflow which will appear veered relative to the airflow at the surface. These observations give us important clues.

In the Northern Hemisphere, again, objects deviate to the right as they move due to the Coriolis effect. With this in mind we can see why high pressure systems spin clockwise and low pressure systems whirl counter-clockwise: as wind flows out from high center it turns right—and into a low it turns right as well. As one gets further away from a high the pressure, naturally, becomes less—and less further until it gets into a center of a low. If we draw lines at areas around these centers at arbitrary intervals of pressure, we call those lines isobars. You've seen them on weather charts—they look just like attitude terrain marks on a map. Upper level winds blow mostly parallel to the isobars, as they're maximally veered. Lower level winds get some local deflection off the surface of the earth and flow more or less perpendicular to the isobars. There are a couple of rules for interpreting the variance between upper and lower level wind directions, the Buys-Ballot law and others, but the best is Alan Watts' "crossed winds rules."

1. Stand with your back to the lower winds (not necessarily surface) and if the upper winds come from your left hand the weather will likely get worse.

2. Stand with your back to the lower winds (again, not necessarily surface) and if the upper winds come from your right hand the weather will likely get better.

   The reason one tries to look at lower level but not surface indications is because the surface wind is usually backed about 30 degrees over land and 10 degrees over water due to surface friction. So, taking this into account one can get a good estimate of true lower level wind flow.

3. Stand with your back to the lower wind and if there little difference in the upper level wind, don't expect much of a change any time soon.

With frontal systems, strong winds are associated with the *edges of high pressure systems*, and located with the *center of low pressure systems*. As these systems move across the surface, surface airflow encountering frictional resistance or topography is deflected, this deflection creates eddies and turbulence that brings upper level air to the surface. Calms on the other hand can be associated with very little barometric gradient, but usually are surface effects caused by inversions—these caused by vertical stability, vertical stability caused by the lack of significant thermal action. If the airflow over the inversion is very stable with little turbulence, calms are likely to occur and persist.

While observation of the actual behavior of the wind at present gives some indication of what is to come—observations at distance can be made by observing the formation of behavior of clouds. Clouds can tell us much about the weather—it can tell us if the weather forecast we may have received is holding true, as well can it tell us much about effects that might be occurring on more of a local scale. Clouds are certainly useful to the sailor in many ways: let's discuss them a bit.

Cloud formation, like wind, is influenced by one of two factors—thermal action or the presence of a front. Cloud formation on a local scale is generally caused by thermal action. As sunlight heats a surface, the air on that surface gets heated as well because of conduction. Thus that air expands and begins to rise. As the air rises, it generally expands as it encounters less pressure with altitude. As gasses expand, the law of conservation of energy dictates that they must cool, and cool they do—at a more or less uniform rate. This rate of cooling is known as the Adiabatic Lapse Rate—generally meaning a cooling of about 1 degree centigrade for every 100 meters of elevation gain.

As our column of rising air rises, it does so to seek a layer of equal density as relative to the surrounding air. How far this column of air is able to rise is dependant on how high that area of equal density might be in the surrounding air. If the gradient (also called lapse rate) of the surrounding air is less than the Adiabatic Lapse Rate, meaning that the air temperature decreases *less with altitude*, the heated air will rise only a short distance before it reaches air of like density and will rise no further. If an atmospheric inversion is present—meaning an ambient area of *negative lapse rate, an increase in temperature with altitude*—the rise of the column of air will cease at that elevation. If the lapse rate of the surrounding air is greater than the Adiabatic Lapse Rate, the column of heated air will rise and continue to rise as long as this remains the case. At some point the cooling of the air will force condensation to occur, this condensation will cause cloud cover to be formed—and this cloud cover indicative of this effect.

Otherwise cloud cover tells of the presence, motion, and proximity of a front. Even more, they tell what sort of front is approaching—whether a warm front or a cold front.

So then, what do we read in the skies?

Types of clouds:

Cirrus:

The whispy, feathery streaks of cloud that appear at high altitudes are called cirrus clouds. Comprised mostly of ice, they are not substantive enough to block much sunlight and are more or less transparent. They are associated with the approach of a warm front, and the action of the warm front as it climbs over and pushes back colder air at the surface.

"Mare's tail's" are a form of cirrus cloud.

The appearance of cirrus clouds themselves are an indication of the depth of the depression that brings them. The more regular and pervasive they are, the more likely bad weather is imminent. The more drawn and windblown cirrus clouds appear, the more upper-atmospheric wind is present.

How far off is the depression? A good guess is 10 to 15 hours.

Cirrostratus:

Cirrostratus is associated with a warm front or low-pressure systems more immediate presence—as it comes closer the cirrus becomes more pronounced and covers the entire sky in a thin screen. At this point it is known as cirrostratus. Cirrostratus is associated as well with sun dogs, halos around the sun and moon—and other effects of atmospheric refraction. Cirrostratus indicates that the front is quite close and getting closer. The halo makes certain. At this point, 5 to 10 hours remain until wind and rain arrive. Watch the barometer. As a general rule of thumb, falling barometers mean:

8-10 Millibars in 3 hours means a storm system is all but certain.

6-8 Millibars in 3 hours means a gale is likely—strong winds are certain.

3-6 Millibars in 3 hours mean some wind likely, not much probably, but keep an eye out.

Less than this means the depression is more bark than bite.

Cirrocumulus:

As the cirrus gets denser with the further approach of the warm front, small, individually distinct clouds begin to appear. This cirrocumulus cloud is now thick enough in places to block some sunlight and will cause a rippled appearance in the sky. This is the famous "mackerel sky" that sailors of old spoke of. It means, yet again, that the warm front is at one's doorstep.

Altostratus:

The next cloud that typically might appear as the warm front comes in is the altostatus. A gray, uniform sheet at a lower altitude—altostratus is dense enough to diffuse sunlight more or less completely. It indicates yet again the immediate presence of the warm front and rain that it brings with it. You've likely gotten both cirrocumulus and altostratus on each other's heels. If the total covers 75% or more of the sky, rain is probably no more than 4 hours out. You'll note that the general trend is toward lower and lower level cloud cover.

Stratus:

Stratus appears much the same as altostratus but is present at yet a lower altitude and is denser yet and usually darker. Sometimes stratus rolls in as a uniform sheet in the sky, sometimes as large patches of cloud with breaks of sun between them. If associated with wind, which it often may be, it is often broken up and is referred to by sailors as "scud"—scud often indicates the high likely-hood of a low pressure storm. By the time this is here, you've probably has a shower or two, and the wind has picked up. Expect 10 to 20 knots more wind than existed earlier.

Nimbostratus:

Nimbostratus means stratus that is associated with rain. It is the thick, dark, featureless cloud cover that brings rain or snow. It is typically associated, again, with rain, a rapid fall in barometric pressure, and indicates that the front is no longer approaching but has arrived. The thing for a sailor to watch for at this point is a directional veer in the wind, as it indicates the passage of this front and the hopeful improvement of weather behind. If the wind backs, it generally means that another low pressure system may be riding the coattails of this one and that one should not expect an immediate improvement. Remember Watts' rules!

The immediate improvement of weather associated with a veering wind and clearing skies occurs when the area of a low pressure system called the "warm sector" is present. The "warm sector" is the area of the low pressure system that lies behind the warm front as it advances and the cold front that follows it. It generally brings much clearer skies, sunshine, and the end of precipitation.

Altocumulus:

Altocumulus clouds are round, globular clouds at moderate altitude—"sheepswool" fluffy clouds with only moderate shading and density. They are generally associated with clear sky and fair weather. They are associated with the presence of the warm sector we just spoke of, but are also associated with thermal lifting of air and its resultant condensation. At any rate, they indicate the presence of instability in the mid-atmosphere, and with the resultant wind conditions, i.e., gusty.

Stratocumulus:

If the atmosphere has more stability than in the last case, altocumulus often forms together into large, long, parallel bands of cloud that cover all or most of the sky. It becomes lower, heavier, and denser than typical altocumulus. It may indicate the presence of large atmospheric inversions. If it is dark enough, it indicates rain. At any rate, it generally indicates little surface wind until it passes.

Cumulonimbus:

As the warm front is driven away by the invasion of the following cold front, large-scale vertical lifting is stimulated and this carries a good deal of cloud into the upper atmosphere. Cumulonimbus are the large, towering clouds we associate with thunderstorms, squalls, and the like. Their presence means the immediate presence of the cold front, perhaps within hours. One should expect the local squalls to pass, but the ambient wind to strengthen and veer—this means the cold front has arrived.

Cumulus:

As the cold front passes and the high-pressure system behind it enters the area, it often carries with it the large, heap clouds known at cumulus. Mid to low altitude clouds, they indicate atmospheric convection and a good deal of atmospheric instability. They appear and disappear as the moisture in them is condensed, absorbed, and dissipated in the eddies of convected wind aloft. This atmospheric instability is likely to meet the surface in the form of strong, gusty wind.

So then, what can we learn from this?

A sailor can expect a good deal of wind whenever the atmospheric pressure gradient is large. The motion in the barometer tells us this tale, and local effects do too. Sudden changes in wind velocity are good clues. Sudden changes in wind velocity and temperature are especially so. Sudden changes in wind velocity and temperature often cause sudden changes in cloud structure and cover and are good indications as well.

Indications of atmospheric instability also indicate wind. Remember that strong winds more often come *down* than *in*. Cumulus cloud, again, is a good indication of instability.

Atmospheric instability is enhanced by surface heating. Surface heating, of course, generates vertical airflow, and this generates turbulence, allowing stronger, mid-altitude winds to find the surface.

On the other hand, if there is very little pressure gradient, once cannot expect much wind (or sailing). If little variation in temperature occurs during the day, little sea-breeze generation is likely to occur either.

If one is experiencing socked in rain in the middle of a depression, it is unlikely that any significant wind will appear either.

If the atmospheric stability is very strong—or an inversion is present—little wind can be expected to find the surface.

?

Where is the system's center?

FOR LOWS: Face the wind and the storm system's center is likely 90 to 100 degrees to the right!

STABLE AIR

UNSTABLE AIR

WARM FRONTS

HALO?

CIRROSTRATUS

ALTOSTRATUS

NIMBO-STRATUS

HIGH PRESSURE

HALO?

STRATUS

HIGH PRESSURE

← about 100 miles →

← about 100 miles →

5 TO 15 MPH ADVANCE!

15 TO 20 HR TRANSIT!

15 TO 20 HR TRANSIT!

COLD FRONTS

20 TO 30 MPH ADVANCE!!

ALTOSTRATUS

NIMBO-STRATUS

HIGH PRESSURE

WIND

RAIN! WIND

CUMULO-NIMBUS!

HIGH PRESSURE

RAIN! WIND

WIND

Inversions are often typical of areas that have relatively warm air and cold water—as the water cools the surface air—causing a negative lapse rate—and thus the "inversion." This cold, relatively dense air is stable and lies on the surface of the water like a pool, the upper level air does not have the turbulence or density to sink through it and reach the surface—so calms persist. Conduction inversions such as the one described are often obvious when viewing smokestacks, as the smoke rises it does so vertically until it reaches a certain altitude where it suddenly sheers off.

These conditions are likely to persist if cloud cover is total, for it often takes surface heating to create the instability to drive inversions out.

Of course one can only sail when there is wind...

All of these large scale phenomena are altered by local effects, but fortunately in relatively predictable ways. Wind encountering topography will either be slowed or accelerated—it will be slowed most by obstacles with large amounts of friction—like a wooded hillside, and will be allowed to accelerate as it leaves land and travels out across water. A wind leaving land and traveling over water is modified depending on its stability characteristics. If the wind is unstable, the experienced surface wind will be most pronounced at the windward shore because this is where the greatest eddying action occurs. If the wind is relatively stable, the wind will leave the shoreline at approximately the height of the shoreline, so that the area immediately near the weather shore will be a blanketed calm.

As the wind approaches a shore to leeward, on the other hand, it tends to encounter the shore with a flow oriented to run over the obstacles immediate the shoreline. Depending on how stable the airflow is, a blanketed area will occur some distance from this shore as well.

Not only does airflow velocity change as it approaches or leaves a shoreline, but it also often changes direction. If the airflow leaves a shoreline at an angle oblique to the wind front the direction will change to more perpendicular to the shoreline. This effect, again, is more pronounced in stable flow than in unstable flow. If the airflow encounters a lee shore at an oblique angle, the windflow generally alters to travel parallel to it. Again, this effect is more pronounced in air that is stable than that which is turbulent.

Thus, in very stable airflow wind, such as that generated by sea breeze, it tends to channel itself and flow along shorelines, and in turbulent air it tends more likely to follow the directional tendency of the front that drives it.

So then, of immediate use to the sailor are these observations. First of all, knowing a basic forecast and what is to be expected, indicators tell stories of what is afoot. Winds that are backing, or shifting counterclockwise (in the Northern Hemisphere)—are threatening to die. Winds with gusts that are veering are likely to strengthen, or at any rate not die. There is also the very practical importance of the fact that when sailing to weather on a starboard tack, gusts will be lifts—and will aid the speed of the boat, while on the port tack gusts will be headers. This, as well, often reflects itself in wind waves and makes the starboard tack less choppy on the bow. Therefore, it is good practice for a Northern Hemisphere sailor to favor the starboard tack as his long board if he can, for this tack will give the greatest speed of advance. This is why gaff topsails are usually set to draw best on the starboard tack—and why steering oars were usually on the starboard ("steering board") side of early vessels.

If one is becalmed, little is going to change without a serious change in temperature, either of the air or the water. Most importantly, there needs to be a difference generated in the temperature above the water as opposed to the temperature above the land. One can certainly watch for this to occur. Cloud cover makes this unlikely, of course, and one can only hope for wind generated for the cooling of night.

Tall objects create blanketing effects, both to leeward and to weather as the air must lift from the surface to flow over them. In stable air, the blanket to leeward of an obstruction can be as far as thirty times the height of the obstruction. The blanket to weather of an obstruction in stable air can be as far as ten times the height of the obstruction. In unstable air, the blanket to leeward of an obstruction is shortened to perhaps five times its height, and a leeward blanket may not appear at all.

When sailing to weather in a channel where the wind is more or less following parallel to the shoreline, it is best to try to orient one's tacks to take advantage of the lifts generated at the ends of points along the shore. If one does not, the alternative is to be perpetually headed. If the channel is converging, this is pronounced, so sail close in, shore to shore. If the channel is diverging, so will the wind flow, so try to tack short in the middle of the channel to again avoid being headed.

Sea breeze generation is not going to happen without sun, and before it does, usually some sort of cloud cover will appear inland as its precursor. This cloud cover, especially over hilltops, indicates vertical movement of air due to heating and horizontal airflow is soon to follow.

If the frontal wind is parallel to the shoreline, sea breeze generation will generally be diminished, as the temperature differential is simply blown out of the area.

Hillsides facing the sun heat sooner than flat ground and generate sea breeze most quickly.

If in doubt, and facing a calm, the old adage is "seek the shore." This is good advice from a number of different counts. First, if there is current to be encountered, it is very likely to be less pronounced in shallow water. Secondly, any breeze to be had, especially a sea breeze, is likely to last just off shore the longest. Lastly, if all else fails, and one is becalmed, any shoreline becomes an anchorage, so simply drop the hook and have dinner…just be prepared to leave when the wind comes back up.

If we look at high altitude clouds, i.e., stratus—we can see that they stream in more or less the direction of the upper level flow. Mid-level clouds, however, form more in waves—rows or lines perpendicular to the weather system flow. Much can be learned from this. If one observes the direction of the surface flow, one can expect that the surface flow will be backed (relative to the mid-level flow, as indicated by the orientation of the cloud bands) to some degree because its speed is retarded by surface friction. How much depends on a number of factors—but between 15 and 30 degrees may be typical. Generally speaking, the bigger the difference in the upper level flow as observed in the cloud motion and the lower level flow as observed on the ground, the greater the wind speed or at least more gusty and turbulent the wind will be. If this expected visible backing is not present—it indicates that the atmospheric effect observed are more of a local nature—likely caused by thermal convection, and the passage of a depression or a front is not a important determinant in the present conditions.

When one sees upper level clouds crossing the sky in a different direction than the lower level clouds—the conditions that dictate the behavior of the upper level clouds will soon prevail over all.

The observed direction of the upper level flow will give you a good indication of where the center of either the high or low system lies relative to where you are. Due to the Coriolis force, again, wind is deflected to the right in the northern hemisphere. As wind flows *out* of high pressure areas, high pressure systems spin clockwise as they move. As wind flows *into* low pressure systems, it is deflected to the right as will, so low pressure systems rotate counter clockwise. Knowing this, by watching the progression of the direction of the wind as a system rolls by will give you an idea of direction, duration, and course of a given weather event.

Perhaps 15 to 20 hours is a reasonable period of time in many areas between the time one first starts to see a cold front eroding before the rain starts to show up.

Sea birds seem to have an uncanny sense of what the weather will bring—if they don't see fit to leave their roosts, neither should you...

A sudden change in odor of the breeze means change for certain—either a sudden drop in barometric pressure or just as change in direction. If the odor change is simply different, it likely means a change in direction—but a sudden change in the very intangible sense of "more intensely" organic or "fruity" perhaps means a sudden fall in barometric pressure. This, of course, could have a couple of effects. The reason for the odor is the fall in pressure will pull volatile organic compounds out of solution in plants or even water that was contained previously by the higher pressure. This effect can be marked—pay attention to it. It is in essence the signal of a drop in pressure miles upwind—in the case of a seabreeze it often means the wind is about to die. A really good hint for neatly entering the harbor in one's local bay.

Lastly, remember that change in tide generally involves a change in water temperature, and this may be just enough to encourage a change in the weather that is about to happen to make itself known. Calms often appear and disappear within a half-hour of the change of the tide, and since this can be predicted locally often with great precision, is an excellent indicator of good times to leave, or especially, be inside, a harbor. Be aware, however, that as one feels the first stirring of the breeze to not be carried away with this rapture—many times this has occurred to me in the dark hours of the morning and I harden up the sheets to take advantage of this new wind only to nearly have a collision with a floating log in the very change in tide that brought the wind...

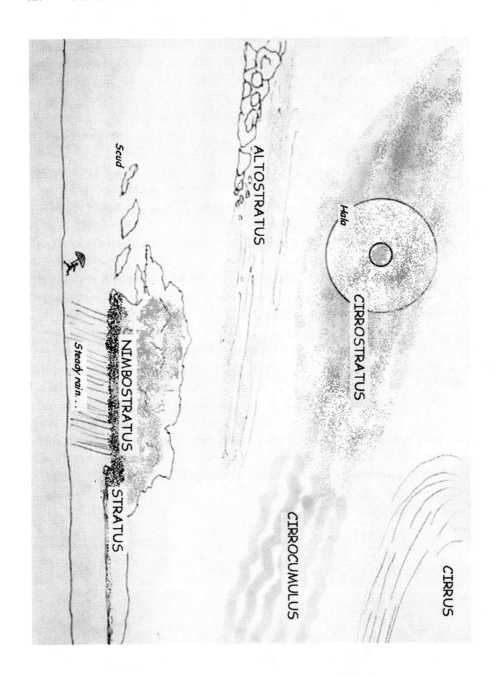

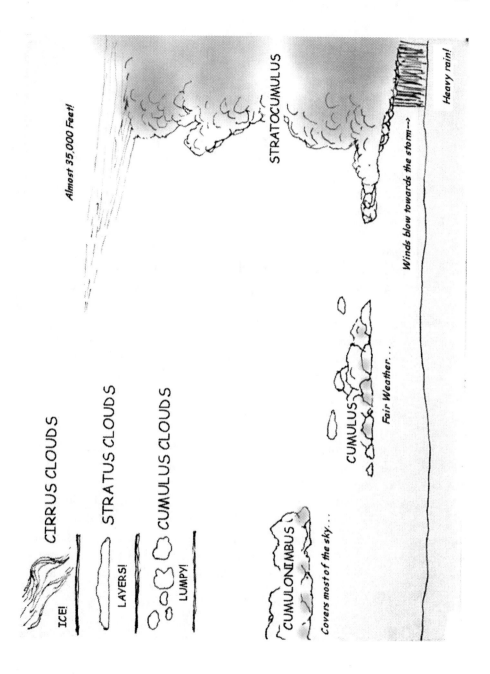

9

HEAVY WEATHER
TECHNIQUES

When one reads older sailing books one often hears of being "caught out" in a blow, and the subject is given a good deal of treatment. For good reason, as well, for fifty years ago even those yachts equipped with inboard engines has propulsion that was capable of little more than dealing with calms, and it was assumed that the "blow" would have to be dealt with under sail—requiring a good deal of seamanship. Today, this is seldom the case among cruising boats. Most have very substantial engine power and large propellers capable of providing control and steerage up to a full gale—some even more that this—and has made the seamanship involved in handling sail in difficult circumstances much less important. As such, the expectations of people and the strategies they apply to their boats has changed.

What a "blow" might be has a good deal to do with a boat and its crew. A solid, well-designed sailboat—even a small one—with a strong crew can make way to weather in force 7 relatively reliably, and as such—while these conditions may cause for a good deal of inconvenience, cause relatively little hazard. Truth be known, however, a true force 7 wind is a strong wind—and actually uncommon especially in the season that people desire to do their sailing. It is resultant of significant enough effects that it seldom will occur without prior forecast or warning. It would be difficult for a sailor, familiar with the signs of weather, to miss a gale's approach.

Figure 12: Nice little Sea-Stead Dinah Mo Hum sailing with MACHA in a cold 30 knots of air. Note everybody is having a good time. Some people call 30 knots heavy air.

Let me state flatly that seamanship is much better demonstrated by avoiding the gale than by weathering it—although the account of the former is much less interesting than the narrative of the latter. Yet again it is best to avoid the issue altogether. If one is to do some cruising, it is bound to happen that one will find oneself in a situation where one will have to deal with more wind than one would like, and it is wise to have the skills to do so.

There are in essence three places one can face heavy weather—in a harbor, tided to a study dock, in an anchorage of some security, or underway. Each carries its own hazards. Let us discuss these.

The primary hazard encountered by a sailor who is stormbound in a good safe harbor is overindulgence and the resultant headache. As such, the harbor is much to be preferred.

An anchorage is different. Upon entering an anchorage in a sailboat, one must make a careful decision about what one's strategy will be if conditions take a turn for the worst. This question is whether the anchorage is secure in a blow or not.

Some are, and some are not. The determining factors are the quality of the holding, the amount of wave action the anchorage will experience, and the number of other boats present. At any rate, it is not prudent for a sailboat to seek the obvious snug, in-close spot in the anchorage—it is wise to keep some sea room—unless one is preparing for a full-blown storm. One will not have a boat drag down on them if they anchor to weather—leaving the anchorage is kept a simple prospect as well. This may not be convenient, but it is prudent—and prudence is the key. Obviously in settled weather this is little of a concern, but boats will drag in as little as 20 knots of air and this could be a hassle. Pay attention, and always think ahead.

I have been forced to leave anchorages a number of times—an anchorage that would have been secure became irresponsibly crowded—the wind came up, and chaos ensued. It is an exciting event, to be sure, to hoist a main, sound a horn, and sail out of tight anchorage in the middle of the night under the light of a handheld spot-light—but I would often rather be underway to other places than deal with hours of being forced to watch other boats—all surging around on inadequate ground tackle, all on inadequate scope. As a sailboat, I have no recourse but to sail. To be entangled in another boat's rode and dragged ashore would more or less leave me helpless. Still, little harm would likely occur unless the conditions were really serious, but it is often simpler and easier to take advantage of the wind and be underway to one's next port. If conditions were likely to be that serious—I hope I would have been someplace else—and frankly, it is unlikely that the anchorage was in would have been crowded. Still, the point remains, there are good anchorages for a storm and *many that are not*. Be sure one chooses wisely.

If anchoring against disaster, and one has resolved to stay at all costs, setting two bow anchors is greatly more secure than one. Drag them both in against the load of a kedge and leave the kedge on deck, coiled and ready. Obviously the ambient load on each is halved, but more importantly the boat will swing less and less load will come in surges. It is unlikely to drag both anchors. As they swing less ground chafe will be lessened. Of course, it is important to have a good idea of what direction the wind will be coming from during the storm, but at any rate having two anchors set is a good idea for any boat that must rely on them. We on MACHA set two anchors at a matter of policy any time we have the possibility of 25 knots of wind or more and we're resolved to stay put. Yes, a bit of a hassle—but dragging is a far greater one. Watch for chafe! It is prudent to use a couple of rope snubbers to carry the load save the wear and tear on the anchor rode itself.

Being underway in a blow may become plenty wet, uncomfortable, and fatiguing—but as long as one can make way to weather there is little hazard. Baring this, as long as one has sea-room, there is little hazard. A sailor's strategy should take these two factors into account immediately. That is, to make as much way to weather as one can—in anticipation that one might not be able to later. As well, to choose a course that allows one room to run if one must.

Of course, this all describes being caught out in a "blow"—not being caught out in apocalypse. If that happens, you're simply out of luck and must hope for the best.

So then, being caught out in difficult conditions—it is good to consider:

How long the conditions will last:
How bad the conditions will get:
If there are harbors I can make in these conditions:
If there are not harbors, are there areas I can sail into to avoid some of the worst of it?
If there are any areas I must avoid because wind and tide may make them especially bad?

And hopefully there will be good answers to all of these.

Again there, is much said about being caught out in a "blow." There are techniques applicable to each type of boat, and the area one sails in. The point I want to emphasize, however, is this: the key is being prepared. If gear is unstowed, chaos will ensue. If one is unfamiliar with one's storm canvas—trouble will arise. If one hasn't adequate charts—one's options of places to hide will be greatly diminished—and running into an unknown bay would be foolhardy. At any rate, I'd say one had better be confident going yachting in inland waters in force 7 or 8 with a reasonable amount of comfort.

Although this book is written from the perspective of coastal or inland sailing—some deep sea techniques are still of use. Namely, that would be streaming warps. It will often become important to keep a boat's speed down, for as much to remain safe in a seaway and avoid broaching, as simply reducing a boats speed to avoid running off all of one's sea room. It is much simpler to keep a boat under control at low speeds than high—it is much easier to navigate at low speeds than high as well. There are conditions, however, that recommend making good time. Although running for harbor has probably sunk more boats than it has saved—I have done so, after making careful decisions, and am still here to tell about it.

Again, it is very tempting when facing the prospect of hours of slogging around in the wind and spray to want to get it all over with—but one must face this reality with discipline and honesty. Always choose the safe course. The times I ran for harbor I did so because it was the *safe* option...

However, I don't really believe running is nearly as safe as many people think. It doesn't take much of a breaking wave to broach a boat—some say as little as a quarter of one's waterline length. In inland waters, in force 8, against an opposing tide of two to three knots, with 10 or some miles of fetch—you will see breaking 5 footers on occasion, I guarantee you that. This is potentially dangerous and one had best pay attention.

Figure 13: The snug gaff rig really inspires confidence in heavy air.

Never ever, ever, *ever* forget about the presence of any lee shore. In large inland waters, of course, this is everywhere. It is the lee shore that was the terror of the past and it is certainly still a threat, although some modern boats have the capacity to make way to weather in conditions that older boats would have been forced to run.

Make sure you have good solid weather canvas, and that you have a rig and a *hull* that could take twenty hours of hard driving to weather. I don't believe a lot of boats are up to this kind of task. Take the boat out sailing sometime and deliberately over-canvas it—really lean on it hard. With someone else at the helm, go below and sniff around every bulkhead and chain-plate—try to find anything that creaks at all. If you find something, make a note, and beef it up. You need confidence in the boat. Nothing should budge. Fiberglass is cheap; add some where it's needed.

Remember as well that everything that is above the waterline that isn't sail area will be trying to drive you onto that lee shore, and you'll have to drive the boat just that much harder for every piece of windage your boat has. Keen on mast steps, multi-spreader rigs, radar, spray dodgers, etc.?

LEARN TO HEAVE TO! There can well come a time, even in inland waters where you're way too close to a beach, there's no anchorages, there's poor visibility, and the tide is opposed and the entrances to safer water dangerous. You've got no options and that point but to hunker down and minimize drift making as little leeway as possible or at the very least forereaching slowly in an advantageous direction—the boat should under it's own control and you can spend your effort keeping a good watch and practicing very catty navigation. Heaving to can be hard on modern lighter boats, but most will do it to a fashion well enough for inland waters—where a little bit of forereaching isn't necessarily dangerous. Practice. It will take a bit of fiddling to get it to work the first time. Techniques vary.

Lastly—don't overestimate your own ability and especially *stamina*. This experience is going to be tough…

10

LIGHT AIR TECHNIQUES

Often far more troublesome than storms is the necessity of the sailor to deal with calms. A calm can be as potentially as dangerous as a storm in areas with a good deal of ship traffic—barring this calms are certainly a good deal more pervasive and unpredictable. Still, a true Force 0 calm is uncommon, but a practical calm of Force 1 is not. A sailboat must be equipped to make way in these conditions. Most sailboats are not. If you're starting with some sort of production sailboat, you'll likely need to make some modifications to get a reasonable amount of sail area. There is no way to escape this. Large genoa jibs, spinnakers, etc., are the key. Large sails are always to some degree inconvenient, but when compared with long hours of rowing a heavy boat, most sailors will welcome their inconvenience.

There are many ways to equip a boat to carry more sail. Some sailors rig jib-boom arrangements or temporary bowsprits that carry special light air sails, or flying jibs. This increases the potential sail area greatly. Asymmetrical cruising spinnakers are excellent, as it is often especially difficult to maintain steerage off the wind. As large as possible and in as light as cloth as possible is the right choice for these conditions.

Tall masts are an aid, but they detract from performance in heavy air, and for many boats that cruise year round are probably not a good idea, especially when other options such as a jib-boom exist.

It may be often found that in light air, certain courses will not be able to be sailed, especially off the wind. If there is a good deal of chop or powerboat wakes, one might not be able to keep one's sails set on the wind. Try to find a course that one can sail—and sail it to maintain steerage. Head for a plausible anchorage, as everything becomes an anchorage in Force 0. Pay especial attention to traffic, and to current—as these become serious problems without steerage.

Figure 14: You must be prepared to keep good boat speed on in very
light air.

The effects of current become pronounced—so use current to aid one's apparent wind. If sailing with a tide against a wind, one might find that one can maintain reasonable steerage, but one might not be able to in the opposite direction. Sailing downwind with a tide makes it unlikely to maintain steerage—perhaps this isn't a problem and one can just drift—but again be highly aware of issues that can arise.

Boats with slick underbodies will fare much better in light air, as will any boat if it is lightly loaded. Do a nice job on the bottom paint and maintain it. All of the dingy sailor's tricks, such as heeling the boat to leeward to aid in sail set are just as functional on a large boat as a small one—so give it a try.

Boats with a good deal of form stability and a wide beam will have trouble keeping sails set if there is little wind and a chop. Narrow, ballast keel boats will fare better.

Often the key to sailing to weather is to get way on and keep it on—as long as one can keep speed on one will keep steerage. A single powerboat wake, however, can often stop one dead. It is entirely practical to break out an oar and get a knot back on again, where one may find that sailing is once again possible. Remember these concerns when faced with light air. Powerboat traffic, tide rips, and other phenomenon that disturb the surface of the water will greatly impede your boat speed, and the lighter your boat is, the more your way will be impeded—which is a drag, because the sole redeeming virtue of the really light boat is it's down wind light air performance. Sit still, and tell your crew to keep their butt planted on the leeward rail. An impatient friend will cost you a knot. If they remain fidgety, hand them the oar and let them work off some energy. Try to sail weather courses as the wind dies, avoid dead down wind. Think about all of this, never let the possibility leave your mind, and you'll be OK.

Patience and deliberate sailing is the key.

I think for most boats light air canvas of at least twice the square footage of the working sails is critical. More for heavy boats, less for light boats—not all of this needs to be able to be carried to weather but it does off the wind. That would mean perhaps 800 to 900 square feet on a typical 30 foot boat is an excellent start. MACHA can set nearly 2000 square feet of down wind canvas.

Again, don't necessarily be afraid of heavy boats being poor light air performers. Some are, for sure, but a heavy displacement boat with a fine, easily driven hull and adequate sail area can have very fine light air sailing ability. This is especially noticeable in conditions that are very light and intermittent—often a heavy boat will keep way in flat water for some time as the wind has totally stopped—a light boat will often not do this.

Light air sails are a fine place to take on some sail making projects. Building flying jibs is simple, easy, and inexpensive. Don't be fancy about building these sails—the look of them means little to their performance and they are easy to ruin by tearing them—they look ratty quick. I like to build flying jibs out of one ounce nylon. I miter cut them and induce no shape whatsoever in the seams. Make the foot and luff straight, and make the leech good and hollow. Cut the sail to the absolutely largest thing you thing you can possibly set on your boat. Make the luff even a bit long, as you can always add a Cunningham if you need to shorten it up. Tape the edges with light spinnaker tape and put a line of very low stretch synthetic line in the luff tape. You'll love it, and be surprised at how often you use it.

Often torn symmetrical spinnakers can be had at very low prices as the racers wreck them quickly. These, if they're large, can be recut into asymmetrical chutes easily as well. On a day with no wind tie the spinnaker up by its three corners to some trees in a park to see how it hangs into a set. Stretch a piece of low stretch line from the head and which corner will become the tack, and drape the spinnaker over it. Cloth pins can be used to tuck what is becoming the luff back and forth until a fair shape is achieved—mark this crease with an ink pin and take it home and cut it along this line. Tape it, sew the luff line in and you're good to go. A nice way to save some money!

11

EQUIPPING THE SEA-STEAD

Sails:

As difficult as it is to find a well proportioned boat—it is almost as difficult to find well proportioned sails. When one enters a sail loft and inquires of sails, the first question that comes from the sailmaker is this—is one racing or cruising? A nonsensical question when one considers it—are the demands of a sail for racing and cruising different? Does a cruiser want slow sails for some purpose? Practically speaking—there IS a difference between racing and cruising sails though there need not be—and wasn't thirty years ago. Today racing is only done in controlled circumstances and the range of conditions that a race boat encounters is quite narrow. Cruising today is generally done by those less than vital and less than experienced and sails are given more abuse and neglect than they might have thirty years ago when many sailors had habits acquired from the era of cotton. Thus cruising sails are often built too heavy and stiff with anticipation of this abuse. What one needs on an sailboat are highly versatile sails cut much like racing sails, but out of dacron rather than laminates so as to keep that versatility, built a bit heavier than a typical racing sail, but not built like a typical cruising sail. The shape should be optimal, as it is not the case in cruising sails typically—optimized sails require more attention at the helm and most cruisers are not willing to give that attention. There are lofts that will cut fast sails of dacron and not suggest full battens—that know what a fine entry and 50 percent draft chord means—but not many—and fewer yet that will listen when one asks for it. One can find these lofts, however if one looks.

I really think the best answer for the self-sufficient sailor is to build one's sails, either from kits or from scratch—although precut kits are generally very cost effective and simple. It will be necessary if one intends to do any sort of extended cruising to learn to do sail repair—it is easiest to learn to do this by making sails right off the bat. There is surprisingly little to making sails anymore, as the issue of good sail shape has been greatly simplified by the improvements in cloth. Modern cloth is so stable as opposed to cloth of even a few years ago that the magic and the judgements involved in making sails decades ago has been made largely inapplicable—handiwork is far more of a detail and no-one cares as much about the sail as the sailor whose life will depend on it.

A reasonably solid home machine is certainly capable of handling most sail-making tasks. Most home machines can handle cloth of up to about 9 ozs. in weight—or a heavy working jib for a thirty foot boat. With some modification of a heavier balance wheel, etc., some can take more, but actually a 9 oz sail is a pretty heavy one and it is unlikely that one will see heavier than that except for special circumstances. The sewing itself can be greatly aided by soaking the thread cone in dry silicone lubricant, as this lubricates the thread and the machine, and makes for much more even tension.

How to work the cloth through the machine? In sections, with the sail rolled up like a scroll. I use two sections of four inch SD PVC pipe with a slot ripped along the length as clamps to hold it together. The PVC clamps slide over the sail, and easily feed through the machine. It makes the delicate task of broad seaming easy.

Now comes the question of what kind of wardrobe do you want? Of course we often get some sort of sails when we purchase a boat, but at some point these will need replacing and it is useful to think of what we'd like. The mistake I see most people make is to invest in a good deal of ultra-heavy duty heavy weather sails. Now there is nothing wrong with storm sails, and if one has the need for them, there is no argument against them. Yet a storm trysail on a boat that hasn't yet been outside of its home bay is a little silly, and unneeded expense. More important that these, especially for the beginner who is learning on a straight sailing boat are good *light air sails.* A powerful genoa, a cruising spinnaker or gennaker, these are to be found much more often useful than the spitfire jib. Start there. For me, on RENEGADE, I carried two spinnakers, an enormous flying jib, a 175 genoa, a working headsail of a 110 that has a set of reef points in it to reef to a 90, a storm jib, a main with two sets of reef points in it. No need that I can see for a third, as at this point we're well into trysail territory and a hell of a lot of wind. No sense in destroying the upper half of the main. This works for me, although at times I drool for even yet a larger light air genoa—and will likely build it this spring. Remember, you'll need to make way in Force 1 from here on out or you'll get to row. MACHA has a simpler sail suit due to the rig. We set a staysail, jib, and yankee; main, topsail, and spinnaker. We carry a storm trysail for the bad times, but haven't yet used it.

As to the hazards associated with spinnakers—yes, every concern is valid. They are big, powerful sails, and can really screw up if mishandled. Most of the spinnaker handling advice comes from the racing set which generally has more and more energetic hands on board than a cruising boat might. Cruisers call for different handling techniques.

The easiest way to use a spinnaker, in my opinion, is much like a rocket engine. Point the boat in the direction you want to go and light it off. I set up the pole and both sheets before I make the hoist: I never tack it, I douse it and set it again on the opposite tack. This greatly tames things. If you swing it in behind the mainsail it will deflate and is easier yet.

Another thing I've done is install a couple of chocks on the foredeck that I can lay the pole to act as a bowsprit—much like one sees on the high dollar race sleds. I rigged a downhaul on it to keep it from lifting. I often set the chute out on this—about six feet in front of the boat—basically like one does an asymmetrical spinnaker. This is my save-all light air technique, they used to call this sort of thing a jib-boom on old traditional boats. I can set another light flying jib on it over the genoa in light air as well. Gosh, it works good, but it means for a helacious lot of sail area and it could potentially get really out of hand. Yet the things one will do to not have to row...

You haven't sailed yet unless you've carried your spinnaker over your big lapper in good conditions. Good God! That's moving!

While we're on it, my favorite spinnaker trick in light air is to simply take one sheet to the cleat on the foredeck and the other to the cleat on the quarter—forget poles and all, and just blow the thing out there like a kite. This is really nice when there's a bunch of powerboats madly tearing around, and a pretty good roll running. You can a lot of times get that thing to set way out in front of the boat so it doesn't chafe on anything. Surprising how well this works—but you'll start to think about the jib-boom pole system I just described. You wouldn't think it would set but it does, as long as you're running broad on the wind. Dead down it doesn't—but I almost never run dead down wind anyway. Take the main down too, or its flopping around will chafe your nerves.

Oars:

Oars and sailboats are a natural combination—sailing vessels with oars go back almost as far as recorded history. No surprise that we should find them useful; the surprise is that they aren't required gear on *every* boat—engine or no. What other piece of gear is ready to be pressed into service as: 1) propulsion 2) spare spar 3) shoring member 4) extra or emergency rudder 5) fending pole 6) depth finder 7) exercise equipment? Think your boat is too large to be moved by sweeps? You've got delusions of grandeur—the US Brig Niagara carries sweeps, 40 footers, and we'll bet your yacht comes in a tad less than 300 ton...

What is the rudder but a specialized oar? You've already got one—get at least a spare...

Practically speaking, a 8000 pound boat can be rowed by one healthy person at about a knot and a half. If you've got crew to spare, you might row at two knots for brief periods of twenty minutes or so—which can often be enough to sneak you into a bay that you would have drifted by otherwise. One handed rowing or sculling can move a boat along at a knot for hours on end—not saying it's fun, but it will keep you in the middle of a channel as you ride a tide or move you out of a shipping lane if you've been stranded there. A good pull with a pair of sweeps will get your boat out of a harbor with ease in wind up to about 15 knots—more than that and you'd have trouble pulling dead into it—but that's where the seamanship comes in—leave before the wind comes up like sailors did (do). You'll also find that with a combination of rowing and sailing you can work through some amazingly tight courses.

You've got a couple of choices about oars—you can go with sweeps or plan to scull. It depends on the boat which is more effective. Sweeps offer the advantages of being shorter, more effective at turning the boat, more powerful with higher speed potential—if you break one you've still got another—and you can use them to back up and as brakes to slow yourself down. Sculling, some say, is less work. I personally advocate sweeps but it's a preference issue. On MACHA sweeps wouldn't be a very serious proposition due their size, so we've got a single 16 foot sculling oar.

Figure 15: MACHA's sculling oar.

You've got other choices as to make. I had ash sweeps on RENEGADE. They make great aluminum and carbon fiber oars for drift boats that are very nice and not crazy expensive. You can get them as one piece jobs or break down varieties. I've used them, and I think they are very fine. These would make for good choices if you'll need to stow them below deck. If you look for wooden oars you're going to find that they are very expensive in useful lengths. You may well end up making them. You'll probably have to build your sculling oar as they need to fit the boat well. I build mine. The loom, or shaft, is cut out of a clear fir 4x4 which cost me eighty dollars, and the blade is nice piece of very hard strange fir I had laying around. I put a bend in the lower half of 1 inch per foot of length. The purpose of the bend is to get the sculling or to intersect the water at a useful angle (more vertical) and to give it a natural tendency to roll at the end of a stroke. I think greased thole pins are much better than an oar lock for sculling oars, but you see both. Use a lanyard at the inner end to keep the handle end down. I like the inner height of a big sculling oar to be just a bit less than chin high, so I can lock both hands over the top and work hard side to side. There's more skill in this sculling business than you think at first—so plan a bit of learning time.

You might have heard formulas for sizing oars to your boat. They're nonsense, so don't visit the wooden boat forum then go out and order an oar. Generally, your sweeps will end up being in the neighborhood of 1.5 times your beam, but this will depend on the height of your freeboard, how tall you are, how you plan to face as you row, and where you're going to stow them. Get a chunk of PVC pipe as a fake oar and see what's comfy—chop it off to that length and see where you can stow it—then order that size. Otherwise you're looking for trouble. A sculling oar is going to be a good bit longer than a sweep—basically as long as you can deal with—not a trivial issue.

A number of engineless boat people have made oar locks that fit into the top of their winches so consider that possibility if your winches have deep sockets. The winches are often placed about right.

I think standing up facing forward is a good way to row. A lot of work boats were and are rowed in that manner but with oars long enough to cross in front of you—giving a good deal more leverage.

When rowing a heavy boat, remember that nothing is going to happen quickly. You can pull to beat hell and the boat is still going to move relatively slowly. Think thrust, not speed. You'll find that short, alternating strokes will often get way on and off quicker than others, as they provide continuous thrust, not bursts, so try that. Remember that in a sailboat, you're always sailing whether you've got oars out or no—you'll find that sailing sideways into a slip with one oar pumping to keep the boat from rounding up or falling off is really no trouble. Don't be casual about dropping an oar over the side to slow yourself at speed as it will very nearly rip you right out of the cockpit—you'll gain a new appreciation for sail power and the thrust it generates.

Lastly—I advocate ALWAYS having the oars out and ready on entering and exiting marinas—but not for the reason you might think. I have learned that when people see you enter a marina under sail—they assume you've got the engine running and are "just practicing" or some such—and will power right over the top of you in most inconsiderate ways—especially this one: pass you because you're slow, then stop in front of you to ready mooring lines and fenders. This happens all the time. BUT, when you've got those sweeps out and dipping—whether you're using them or not, they get noticed and they're a very effective daymark saying "I've got no engine." People will then respect that (or be worried) and might actually display some seamanship and courtesy.

Self-steering gear:

Steering a boat for hours and hours, shorthanded or alone becomes incredibly tedious—and it doesn't take long for a sailor to begin to think of ways to eliminate the task. Popularly, two solutions present themselves, autopilots and windvanes. Both are expensive and complex—both unattractive to my eye at least—the autopilot noisy, complicated, and has excessive power demands for my boat; the windvane, costly, heavy, and more moving parts than I want to need to maintain. My solution? To teach my self the ancient art of natural self steering.

For me, I tried fiddling with natural course stability—this didn't work. I tried a dedicated steering sail—this worked but was clumsy. I even built a windvane—a horizontal axis vane, this worked as well but again was irritating to look at and didn't steer the kind of course I wanted it too. Finally, I spent a good deal of time studying sheet to tiller set ups—learned that skill, and this is what I have used solely ever since.

One needs some sort of self-steering gear—vanes are indeed tempting, but you owe it to yourself before you got out and buy one that you give sheet to tiller steering a good hard try.

I'll walk through this real slow—the concept is simple but counterintuitive, and frankly disproves a good deal of what we've been told about boats and course stability. Listen carefully: sheet to tiller steering works—it works as well or better than a vane, there is no kinda working about it. It is utterly reliable if applied properly. It cannot fail. Yet, if applied incorrectly, it doesn't work at all. Learning sheet to tiller steering was one of the most interesting and rewarding projects that I've ever encountered—certainly it was the project that has taught me more about sailing than anything else I've ever done. To develop a good, workable, sheet to tiller system DEMANDS that one actually understands what one's boat does and why—a truism perhaps, but I don't know of any other aspect of sailing that makes that demand so insistently. One can sail and make good passages with proficiency without understanding—I'm afraid I discovered I'd done that. Even if one has no need for sheet to tiller steering I recommend any sailor dabble with it simply to learn. It is an absolutely fascinating study.

There are a couple of misconceptions about what sheet to tiller steering is. Sheet to tiller steering is NOT simply tying the helm off to something while sailing to weather. As we will see—one hardly even needs to do that. It is also NOT something that "pretty much" holds a course. Unless the system holds a course as well or BETTER than a helmsman, it isn't a system. Third—a sheet to tiller system isn't a "system"—it is a skill—one that can be transported to most any boat and cobbled together out of most any parts. It is worthwhile to have a nice bag of gear—the quality of one's pieces make a very substantial improvement to the "tightness" of the course steered—but I recommend practicing with junky blocks so one learns WHY good blocks and low stretch line work better here.

Lastly, sheet to tiller system isn't and doesn't have much to do with natural course stability—that is, the much exaggerated ability of some boats to hold a course with no feedback to the helm. We will see why.

Let's once again talk about sailing. As far as sheet to tiller steering is concerned there are really only two courses—upwind and downwind. Let's keep upwind in our minds first because it is the simplest and requires the least help from the a self steering system. After we talk about upwind systems, run back through the mantras and think about downwind.

A) On any point of sail—upwind or downwind—as the boat turns to weather APPARENT WIND INCREASES. Let this be your first mantra. Many people, even those who have sailed a lifetime, do not understand this basic principle. Many confuse this statement with luffing—I am not talking about luffing nor to I have any interest in designing a system to luff. What I am talking about is that when due to change in course or shift in wind direction, as the boat turns to weather, apparent wind increases. This is due to the basic fact that boat speed remains relatively constant due to momentum. Obviously, again, if the sails stall, the boat slows down and apparent wind diminishes—but before the stall occurs—again APPARENT WIND INCREASES.

The converse is also true. As the boat turns off the wind APPARENT WIND DECREASES. No problems yet, right?

B) As heel increases—a boat—ANY BOAT—has a tendency to turn to weather. Heel is the also the PRIMARY force that turns a boat to weather. We've all been sold a bunch of bad information this business and been told a lot about asymmetry of hull bottoms and the like. Sure, there is a difference between boats. Some boats heel a lot, some not too much. Some do have lumpy bottoms. Still, all of that isn't nearly as important as the fact that as a boat heels—the center of effort—the hypothetical center of all forces acting on the boat gets swung way over the side (of the center of resistance, I suppose) and this makes the boat want to turn. It is no different than having a car with one driving axle that sticks way out to one side—that car would want to turn like crazy.

OK: This is why many boats will pretty much sail to weather with the helm lashed in steady conditions—they all have pretty much natural stability. As a boat falls off the wind and the sheets aren't trimmed, much drive turns to drag and the boat heels more, this heeling makes the boat turned back to weather. If there is a little bit of rudder angle applied making the boat always want to turn off the wind just a little bit—then somewhere an equilibrium is reached and a course is more or less held. No big deal, and most any boat will do it. Big heavy boats full keel boats do it best—but this isn't much help in the end—they only do it easily because they don't heel too much and are often very undercanvased. Driven hard, they round up just like anything else. Again, forget rigs and keels. They don't have anything to do with sheet to tiller self steering.

Some boats will also go along to weather a bit with the helm free and kind of bump and luff to weather in an inefficient manner. Well, this is also natural stability but not too useful. You're noodling along so slow that you're far past maintaining drive, and slowing down. This can as well build a kind of sloppy equilibrium but not a too useful one. I hear someone saying that their boat does better than that—but if it does—you've got a bit of a self-steering system already. Usually that is weight in the rudder, that as the boat heels it tips off to the looward side—thus applying a bit of helm correction. Nifty, I suppose, but inefficient and unnecessary.

Off the wind, now, you've got no natural help from anything. If the boat carried perfectly level helm in perfectly even wind—you might stay relatively put for a bit. But the second the boat gets off course at all the problem flies out of hand. Suppose you turn just a bit to weather. Apparent wind increases—this time creating both more drag and drive—the boat heels too much and you round up even more. The converse, of course, happens if you turn off the wind further. Without applying some correction at the helm—the boat just won't hold a course.

Here's another protest I'm going to hear—probably from someone in a gaff-rigged ketch—who boasts of—like Slocum on Spray—being able to sail off the wind with the helm untended. I don't doubt that in many conditions you might—and we can in MACHA as well, at least as far as a broad reach—but this is due primarily to the whopping inefficiencies of the rig and the extra ones you pile on to make the course stability happen. With a ketch one can over-sheet the jib and sheet out the mizzen and achieve something like course stability down wind—as the boat rounds up the jib drags like crazy being oversheeted, the mizzen stalls, the main poops along somewhere in the middle—the center of effort (CE) moves forward and the boat generally wallows off the wind a bit, assuming that there isn't much heel on. If the boat falls off the wind, the jib is blanketed, the main a bit too, but the mizzen is nearly broadside and pulling like crazy in its turn—the CE is way, way aft and the boat rounds up. This kinda works—but at what cost? Wallow wallow wallow. A sheet to tiller system and all sails could draw…having some inherent course stability in a boat is nice, for sure, but a little of care and effort are definitely worth some boat speed.

Some might think as well that the trick to getting a boat to steer itself off the wind is to get the CE way out forward. This would be true—if the CE was level with the waterline, but it is not—and any change in course will cause a change in heel—boom, she's gone. A guy can fiddle with a couple of models to prove this to himself if he feels the need. Build a little boat with a stick for a mast—tie a string up at the top and see if you can pull it straight towards you. Play with a couple of keels if you'd like. Move the stick around. Build a heavy one and a light one too. You're going to find that some might work a bit better than others, but unless you're really careful all will yaw all over the place.

So then, the solution: You need to create a system that applies more helm as apparent wind increases—so that if the boat rounds up—the tiller moves to weather and the boat falls off. This is how it works on any point of sail. Simplicity itself.

The obvious beginning: as apparent wind increases, so do the loads on the sheets—thus the sheets are a good place to start to look for something like a meaningful signal that can be applied to the helm. Any control line might work—but the sheets are handy.

The problem: making the signal from the sheets proportional to the signal from—pay attention—HEEL. You are balancing sheet load against heel. Make sure that is understood.

You'll see that somehow there must be a line tied to the end of a tiller, that runs through a little block somehow affixed to one fall of the main sheet pulling a bend in it. The end of this same line goes over to the rail and is made fast somehow—I use a jam cleat. The tiller would be pulled to weather then, doing nothing, so this must be balanced with elastic. Surgical tubing is effective, so are stainless springs—whatever gives the correct tension. You have to vary the amount of bend in the sheet, the amount of purchase in the control line, the stiffness of the elastic, the length of the elastic, etc. for each given boat. Again, you are trying to find a load that varies proportionally to the amount of weather helm the boat has as it progressively heels. You just have to fiddle with it until you figure it out.

You will figure it out. You will find a system that will steer the boat through a range of wind that equates about to a headsail change or a reef—whatever that works out to for your boat. This makes sense, of course, because you are talking a range of HEEL from very little to way too much. One doesn't need to go beyond this amount of range.

Again, there is no kinda working about it. Unless it works, it doesn't. Keep at it. It will work.

Figure 16: Simple self-steering: This is the system that I use ninety percent of the time. Note control line and elastic (hard to see) on tiller pin.
The elastic balances the pull of the control line, which is led from a turning block to the mainsheet, which bends a little jog in it. As the mainsheet load increases, this jog is pulled out and the helm is drawn to
weather, putting the bow down, which balances the weather helm
present in gusts. There are many ways to rig this achieving the same
effect, some are better for certain conditions than others, but the principle always remains the same. The large line running through the tiller is
useful for limiting the range of motion of the tiller, which is sometimes
necessary in a seaway.

PROBLEMS AND WHAT PROBABLY CAUSES THEM

A: Boat keeps rounding up no matter what you do.

You haven't enough power in the control line. Try putting more bend in
the mainsheet by pulling the control line through the jam cleat (or whatever)
on the rail.

You might have the elastic improperly adjusted. The end of the elastic will always be VERY near center totally relaxed.

B: Boat keeps falling off no matter what you do:

You've probably got too much power in the control line. Back off a little bit. Again, the elastic might be adjusted with the helm in the wrong place.

C: Boat just vaguely wanders around.

You've got a lot of friction, most likely. Either in the rudder post or in the sheet blocks, control blocks, etc. The loads coming off the sheets aren't big enough to overcome the friction. This may cause wide oscillation as well.

Eliminate all the friction you can find and try again. If it still doesn't work, power up the entire system by using a stiffer elastic and putting more bend in the sheet.

D: Things work for a while and then the boat just goes off on a fugue.

This is the most irritating problem—but the most interesting one as well. It is also pretty tough to guess the solution without a clue.

You are going to have to translate power into signal. This is done by using a fool's purchase somewhere in the system—in essence making tiller motion out of load in the sheets. I find that a 2 to 1 fool's purchase works for me most of the time—but I'm certain a bigger boat would need much more reduction in power and much more signal strength.

The sheets have got more power than you need by an awful lot. The change in the load as the apparent wind varies is pronounced, but it doesn't look like much—in other words, a sheet can shed quite a bit of load and not move much—that lack of movement is what you need to compensate for by using the fool's purchase and MAGNIFYING that motion.

The answer ISN'T powering up the whole system as it might be to overcome friction. A guy might think that, but it is unlikely that this is the case.

E: Things work, but the boat doesn't handle much in terms of variance in wind speed.

Fiddle with different stiffnesses of elastic. Try as well different lengths. I'd say if the boat won't handle light air but is OK in moderate—the elastic is too stiff. I'd say if the boat is OK in moderate but as the wind builds the boat continues to fall off the wind—I'd say the elastic is too light or perhaps too

LONG. You want the elasticity to peak up as the hull induced weather helm does. I don't think the elastic should be any longer than the motion of the tiller would be normally in a course correction. Again, one just has to fiddle until one learns what works.

As a rule of thumb, you're going to need to use stiffer elastic as you encounter heavier sea-states. Off the wind needs stiffer than on the wind.

Elastic really does more to adjust the POWER of the system than anything else. The stiffness of the elastic regulates the power of the system. The length of the elastic regulates the speed at which the elastic power becomes greater with elongation. For example, a short piece hardens up quick a long piece does so less quickly. Try to find an ideal length.

What about wind vanes: why a vane if sheet to tiller works so well?

Good question! You don't need one, but there are things that sheet to tiller steering just won't do. One will discover that sheet to tiller will not handle certain sail configurations some of the time. One will certainly find that it will not sail through sail changes without resetting the system, nor will it sail through putting a reef in the main. It certainly will not sail the boat under bare poles in storm conditions either. Of course the reason is obvious—sheet to tiller relies on the input of the sails for its signal, and when this is interfered with the system will be upset. In some ways, while the use of the sails is natural and eloquent, it is also inconvenient.

So then, since sailing often involves sail changes and evolutions, it would be more convenient if the signal that supplied direction to the helm drew from a different source. It would be also useful if the signal was wholly dependent on wind direction and not as much on wind speed, so that a wider range of conditions could be tolerated without needing to adjust anything. Again, it would really be nice if one could put a reef in the main while being underway and the boat would simply sail along as if a helmsman was present—this is what we are really hoping for. And a windvane will do that, and many different (although fundamentally similar) designs have been created that do just that.

So what's wrong with the commercial vanes?

Nothing, really, except that they are very expensive and rely on proprietary parts to make sure when something breaks that you'll be compelled to remain a customer, and they can bleed you for a couple of hundred more dollars for a special little widget. As well, the manufacturers themselves are very closed-mouthed about why their vanes work—again they want to make sure you remain a customer and don't build a vane yourself—which you could indeed do if you knew some key ratios and proportions.

But consider the reality of the fact. The commercial vanes, by and large, are relatively well engineered and heavily built. They like to suggest the fact that they are up to the task that they are designed for and are nigh on to bulletproof. This again is good marketing, but doesn't necessarily make sense. As we will discover, if a vane is used correctly and suffers no freak damaging incident, the loads that the vane are subject to aren't really all that large. But if a freak incident occurs, like running over a log or getting backed into a pier, the loads that they can experience can easily break *any* vane. So perhaps it makes more sense to build a vane that is easily repaired with tools and materials that are likely aboard any boat, rather than try to prevent the inevitable by overbuilding the device.

Another thing that is lacking in commercial vanes, obviously, is that they are customized and idealized for any given boat. They are, more or less, one-size-fits-all products. And as such, they *must be less effective than a vane that is specifically designed for a certain boat.* Each boat has different handling characteristics, and has different stability needs. An ideal vane should reflect those needs by being somewhat adjustable. Key rotational ratios are the vane to control ratio and the amount the vane dampens input by actuating. The last is a near to invisible ghost in the machine—but very important to yaw dampening.

What makes a windvane successful and what hurts a windvane's performance?

Let's assume that the ratios and proportions of the steering oar are correct, that the vane is adequately sized, and the gear ratio is appropriate. What can make the vane work better and what hurts its performance?

Inertia:

The heavier the vane is built, especially the vane and linkage of the mechanism, the less effective the vane will be in light air and the more prone to over-steering the vane will be. The reason is simple; it takes more power, which inevitably means more lift generated by a proportionally larger course error, for the vane to start moving and to apply a correction. The reverse is true as well—if the vane is moving to apply a correction, it is almost certain to apply too much of a correction, for the inertia of the vane will certainly carry it past the point of generating lift and will contribute to a weaving, oscillating course.

Friction:

Friction has much the same effect as inertia—it requires more lift, meaning more course error, to initiate a course correction—thus the vane will be less sensitive in light air and will tend to over-steer. The causes of friction are many—but cheap bearings, overbuilding and the use of overly heavy bearings certainly will contribute to the cause.

Backlash:

Every linkage has some degree of play it in, and this play contributes to poor course keeping. If the vane must move a couple of degrees just to load the linkage up so that it begins to apply a correction in the appropriate direction, it is easy to see why this will contribute to over-steering again. Good bearings and well thought out linkage goes a long way to fix this issue, but also emphasizes that a minimum of moving parts is also desirable, as the less links that exist the less places for backlash to exist. Simple designs that are perhaps less effective, theoretically, than more complicated vanes with more parts, may in actuality be more effective simply because they, in reality, manifest less backlash, friction, and inertia.

The boat itself:

The boat itself likely will contribute strongly to the effectiveness of the self steering, as will how effectively the boat is sailed. While most modern vanes have the power and capacity to steer even the most unbalanced boat more or less effectively with very little attention paid to smart sail handling or to carrying sail configurations that aid the vane rather than hurting it—most will certainly do so less effectively. And the vane—which is steering—will likely be the recipient of the blame. Some boats are just pigs and require *anticipation of the need to apply a course error*—no vane can be expected to effectively do this. Of course such boats are ill-suited to the purposes of cruising anyhow, but it is surprising how many such designs one sees.

Wheel steering will also contribute to poor course stability, for the reasons of friction, inertia, and backlash once again. Any wheel steering mechanism will certainly have more of these negative qualities than a tiller mechanism, and should give a boat owner cause for thought.

If the vane mechanism is mounted behind spray dodgers, radar arches, etc., etc., as seems to be currently the vogue, the vane will be blanketed from the true wind by these high windage accessories and the performance of the vane will suffer as a result. It is most important that the vane runs in clean air that is unaffected by the trim of the sails nor the boat itself.

If the pendulum oar itself runs in dirty water that is highly disturbed, it will generate less lift than one that runs in clean water. If the boat in question has a large propeller aperture burdened by a large screw, the drag and turbulence caused by these accessories will be very significant, harming the effectiveness of the rudder and as well as the windvane itself. In this case, the vane mechanism will need to be built larger and more powerful, which inevitably harms its performance—it is always best to keep drag at a minimum.

Figure 17: RENEGADE's home-built wind vane taking me home in the light air of the evening. I've built a couple of wind vanes for various boats, and they all worked. It's not impossible, but perhaps harder and more expensive than you might think. If you're interested, contact us on the Oar Club web page for plans.

Ground Tackle and Techniques:

A lot of people have a tough time with the hook. It doesn't need to be so. I'm not really sure that a lot of what gets flipped around in the yacht press is very good information to someone who is cruising in some of the "fringe" ports. Seldom are bottoms ideal, seldom is the depth convenient, and RARELY does one get an opportunity to swing on the publicized 5 to 1 scope. I feel lucky to get a 3 to 1 much of the time. Way too much traffic! Way too many other boats!

There are many different varieties of anchors—we've seen the types. I suppose they're all good, more or less. There really isn't a lot of difference between them when one looks—so why the different types? Because they're HEAVY—the attempts in engineering behind anchors is not so much to make an anchor just hold better, but rather to hold as well but *weigh much less* than some other type. That is a valid concern, for certain, but things are not that simple.

If one looks at a modern, alloy anchor—the specifications for holding are impressive indeed. And, again, if the matter were only that simple. Light weight anchors—all light weight anchors—have a fundamental problem. This problem is not with their holding power, it is with the ability of one getting them SET. The seabed maybe is covered with eelgrass or something else—or may be harder than one thinks, etc. There is no way around the problem of a tough bottom except for the initial bite, and this initial bite comes primarily from weight. So, if one wants simple anchoring, get a big heavy hook that looks like it would bite quick and life will be easier. I think there might be a place for a lightweight alloy hook, but not to get away with a *lighter* hook, but rather to get way with a *larger one*. Because of the alloy's light weight it allows me to carry something with awe-inspiring holding power that I wouldn't otherwise—especially in sand. This might be the answer to that desperate and final situation that might just keep me off a beach in a storm. Unlikely, but just maybe…maybe in some distant bay I would need something to kedge me *off* a beach.

As well, we need to realize that most anchors that fail catastrophically DON"T pull out or drag, they BREAK. Imagine that. I then, look askance at anchors that are tricky and funky looking and have lots of moving parts.

What do I use? On RENEGADE I had a pair of 10KG Bruces each on 30 ft of 5/16 chain—300 feet of 5/8 nylon line on that. These have almost never failed to set, nor have the dragged, including the time I rowed one of them out into the bay and stress tested it with my 1971 Bronco, in low range 4 wheel drive and 4.20 gears. If that thing sets—that's it folks. You not break it before you pull it out; if it comes loose it will set again with alacrity. I really trust the Bruce—but among well made anchors it is really just a matter of preference. On MACHA, we've got three 20 KG Bruces and one 50 pound Fisherman. The bower is on 5/16 high-test chain. We find this works nicely. We've got the gear and independent rollers on the bow to set them all at once if we need to. We never have, which is fine. It can be a bit of a grunt dragging all that steel back aboard.

How much rode does one need? Well, it depends on where you sail. I'd always carry at least 1000 feet. I've been forced to use it all, but I sail in an area where things are often really deep. How much do you need?

If I'm forced to use REALLY short scope—2 to 1 or less—I shackle a 20 lb. mushroom to the head of the chain. Makes for a pretty heavy get up but greatly helps keeping the chain down. The wind has to really howl before I move that around much.

I had at one time another Bruce, a smaller one, which was much more difficult to set. I don't think it makes any sense to own little anchors. They just don't have enough mass to get a good bite and you end up fiddling with them a lot. We've all seen the Friday Night Danforth Show and know what that's all about.

REMEMBER—the two virtues of a good anchorage:

It is protected from hazards under all conditions—this includes other boats that are going to drag. Not too many anchorages are safe from that point of view. In compromise, try to pick your neighbors well. Stay away from boats that are obviously unprepared for a blow—also boats with extreme top-hamper and windage, i.e., powerboats.

It is an anchorage that you can get out of if you need to—meaning when other boats begin to drag, if you simply want to leave to take advantage of a front. As we've said, sailing is the art of riding wind around. Often conditions that can make an anchorage unsafe—say 30 knots of air—can make for spectacular passagemaking conditions, especially in inland waters. The sailor is prepared to take advantage of these conditions and remains ready to set sail and leave…

A lot of times, in moderate weather, you're far safer on a totally exposed beach than in an anchorage.

On Setting an Anchor under Sail:

In the Sea-Stead lifestyle you're going to spend a lot of time at anchor so you had better be good and comfortable with it. You must know when it is set and when it is not. Generally, I think it is good to set an anchor at some speed of travel. This is different than what you normally see. Mostly, among the motor sailor set, what you see are people who motor up, plop the anchor, and back up. You've read about boats doing that sort of thing under sail—but there are many books like that where guys gas about traditional sailing techniques and (they read them somewhere) don't know beans about them. While on a large vessel of say 60 feet or so might be able to drop a hook and back under sail reasonably, or a square rigger might—a small sailing yacht isn't likely to generate enough power backing to even pull the chain shot straight let alone set the hook. Even on MACHA it can be difficult unless it is quite windy. We can often backwind the main and a headsail and controllably fall off at an angle, bouncing the anchor in as we go, but this sort of maneuver RENEGADE would never do. On RENEGADE, I liked to set the hook sailing at a couple of knots and surge the anchor in good and hard. Often times, under the main alone I'd come into a harbor with the rode flaked out on the foredeck ready to run. If it's tight or tricky, I'll lead the chain shot back to the cockpit, but not too often did this prove necessary. If I'm going to anchor, in say, 30 feet, I'll have that ready to go and as I approach where I want to set I'll drop the hook over the side and hold it at about 6 fathoms—keep sailing; as soon as I feel it bump the first time I'll let the whole works go. It pays out with alacrity, I head to the foredeck and as I reach that 4 to 1, I'll take a turn around the bow cleat and surge the boat to a stop. That rode will go taut, the boat will spin around and there I be, set and head to wind. Very slick and fast, and unnerving to everyone else in the anchorage. Don't be panicky about this—three knots is fast but not too fast, as long as one knows how to handle lines there shouldn't be a problem, as on a boat of five tones or less you'll pull the speed off rapidly. . Likely, even if the hook fouls our fails to set it will still pretty much stop the boat, but not with hard firm surge, so take note, haul the hook aboard, sail out to weather and give it another go. No big deal, you likely just got a big haul of kelp—still, that will spin the boat around. You won't make the beach in any event.

You can do this to weather, as well, if you feel the need. When the rode fetches up you can spin around and try to screw it in the other direction as well. I think a Bruce sets easier with a semi-rotary pull than a straight linear pull anyhow. I can't really validate that but if you look at the flukes you can see why it might. Not a big problem, again, as long as the hook is reasonably heavy.

It is hard to get the feel for a set hook until one has done a bit of anchoring—so I usually suggest a different technique for a novice or myself if I'm expecting a heck of a blow and really want to be certain about my holding.

Sail up to where you want to swing from and drop your primary hook. Do this under the main alone, especially if by oneself, to keep the foredeck clear and so when you let go of the tiller and have the mainsheet sheeted in as far as it will go, your boat will round up and stall nice and easy. Your boat won't do that? Sell it; it's a dog.

Make sure the anchor hits the bottom first and you pay the chain back in a straight line as the boat starts to get sternway. This is the trick, making sure you haven't got wraps around things. If you just dump it in a pile it is quite likely that things will foul up. Better let things tug a bit, you'll start wiggling the hook in. If the wind is really roaring you might just go ahead and accidentally set it. That's OK. We'll confirm the set.

Let's say you feel it starting to grab. Go ahead and pay out a lot of rode in highly antisocial fashion. You aren't going to swing like this so don't sweat it. Pay out to about an 8 to 1. You'll see why in a moment. Don't know how much rode you've paid out? A clever hint—stitch roman numerals on your rode at one fathom intervals. Then you'll know.

At an 8 to 1? Drop the little kedge over the stern, and haul on the bow. Bring our self back up to a 4 to 1. Now you've got a 4 to 1 on both, right?

Take the kedge rode to a sheet winch and haul it bar taut.

Have a beer and watch it for about 15 minutes. Does it stay taut? Of course, pay attention to the question of the tide coming in or out an whether this may screw with your experiment.

Does it slowly, slowly go slack? You're dragging, and if you would have tried this with an engine you never would have known, would you? Feel smug. If you need to, haul the kedge and try again. You'll get a bottom sample when you do; if all you get is a big blob of kelp you'll learn something as well. Move.

Now you've got options. Put the main away while you think about it, as you're going nowhere.

I do, a lot of times, leave both of them down, and I take care to set myself pointing into the direction of wave or wind action. A boat rides very nice like this, but if I've likely got a pretty good current running at some point I might not. Depends. It is often a good idea to keep the bow pointed into the direction of incoming powerboat wakes. Sometimes it's nice to pull the kedge and get a couple of chowder clams. At any rate, this technique allows a sailor to really feel a set, and he will sleep better for it. I really recommend making a habit of it, at least until one is comfortable with the anchoring game.

Again, an anchor's hold is primarily determined by its angle of bite to the bottom. This of course is the purpose of scope but can be greatly increased by a heavy chain rode. As I said, if one seldom needs a heavy chain rode but on occasion needs that short scope, a 20 pound or so mushroom anchor can be shackled to the head of the chain rode to act as a sentinel and will greatly increase the holding power of the ground tackle. This is especially useful in an anchorage that is experiencing a good deal of surge, or if one is anchored on a weather shore being set into deeper water.

In areas of deep water and steep shorelines, stern ties are often used. An anchor is let out into deep water and a line is taken ashore to haul the stern toward the beach. The tending angle of the anchor is reasonable even though invariably on quite short scope, because the angle of the bottom is so great. Again, it is this angle that is all important. Unfortunately, steeply sloping bottoms are often rocky and not the best holding, I personally do not ever feel particularly comfortable with a stern tie although in some areas it is indeed the only option—if the anchor were to drag or come loose from its holding among the rocks in a blow one would be on the beach in seconds.

Do what you can to make the anchor ride quiet or life will be hard for you, as you'll not sleep well. On boats with bowsprits and chain rodes you've got a good source of bone-jarring noise that makes a windy night all the more uncomfortable. You can fix this problem by attaching a short, heavy lanyard to the bobstay chain plate with a chain hook on the end—and attach this to your rode. Ease away chain until the rode rides on this lanyard, and haul the lazy bight back away from the bow. This will be all but silent and you'll ride nicely. People do much the same thing with lanyards at the end of bowsprits, but I don't think bowsprits are really made to take the jerking that an anchor rode can produce and I think riding on the chain plate is likely a safer idea.

Notes on sailing off the anchor:

Sailing off hook can be one of the most difficult feats of seamanship that a sailor has to face. One will notice that if one reads the yacht press, even older texts, there is very little discussion off how to pull this maneuver off. Of course, in a small maneuverable boat, in mild conditions, sailing an anchor out is no trouble at all. In heavy air, it can be a serious grunt getting the tackle aboard, but steerage can be had nearly immediately and there is little to fear. In a larger boat, however, getting an anchor aboard controllably and sailing through the gauntlet of boats that crowded in after you arrived can be a very difficult and daunting task. Hence the reason for very little discussion—I'm certain that very few sailors have every performed this maneuver in difficult crowded conditions in boats of any tonnage. And, since they haven't, they don't have a clue as how to pull it off. You'll hear a bit of glib advice here and there—but if you try their tricks in a tight spot you'll bash something.

Let's assume the basic problem. You've got an onshore breeze that is building and the anchorage is becoming untenable. You may have an inflowing current of some velocity. You don't have room between yourself and the beach to make a turn once the anchor is picked. You may have other boats or obstructions that make one or the other tack impossible. What then?

The main problem with larger boats is that once the size and displacement of the anchor is such that it can't be dealt with quickly by hand, the actual breaking out of the anchor is a much more tenuous event. The anchor is likely to be buried heavily, and as one grinds away at the anchor windlass the breakout is likely to be sudden and surprising but will provide next to no feedback, because the weight of the chain rode makes the pressure seem vaguely constant. Unless one is really paying a great deal of attention, it is very easy to miss. It is critical that one learns to always count the number of feet of rode that has been payed out as well as brought aboard, or the surprise will be even more punishing. As large boats do not get underway quickly, the authority of the rudder will be negligible for a number of seconds as the hull gathers way. If the anchor breaks out unexpectedly on the wrong tack—if the bowman remains un-aware of this—disaster may result. The powerful rig will gather headway, of course in the wrong direction, the rudder will be slow to respond, and the dragging anchor will greatly impede any steerage even when it starts to develop. On must not, at any cost, allow this situation to arise.

All boats handle differently enough under sail to make this procedure a bit irregular in discussion, but the steps to break an anchor out (to weather, of course, as leaving down wind is no trouble) are.

1.   Haul away to short cable—slightly less than a two to 1 scope.

2.   Back a staysail to force the bow unto the undesired tack.

3.   Sail up on the rode, being very careful not to break it out—right, and tack once one is abreast of the anchor itself. Tack smartly, and trim sails to reach back towards the anchor, on the now desired exit tack as the boat reaches back.

4.   Haul like all hell. As once comes across the anchor, power up the rig and belay cable. You'll jerk the anchor clear of the bottom and sail clear. Maneuver for open water and fish the anchor aboard.

You'll need to practice. There are no two ways about it.

There is a technique as a save all for getting an anchor aboard in very tight quarters where one might not even be able to handle the one above. In order be prepared to execute this, you'll need to have a rope trip line on a float or aboard attached to the shank of the anchor. Once again haul away to short cable. Take the trip line aft, outside the shrouds, perhaps to the sheet winch. Haul away on the sheet winch. As you do so, you'll notice that the boat will lie as to a bridle, now, balancing off the bow rode and the trip line. In this manner, you can force a chosen exit tack under control, much as one can as when leaving a mooring, with the main sheeted well out and flogging. Shorten away on both and creep up on the anchor, while maintaining this attitude to the wind. To break loose, harden away on the main sheet while hauling the trip line aft at the cockpit. This should pick the anchor free. It will still be hanging under the boat, but as it hangs well aft it will impede steerage much less than if it were hanging off the bow. As one is clear of the anchorage, fish aboard as normal. You'll find this trick might well save your butt some day, especially if you're singlehanded.

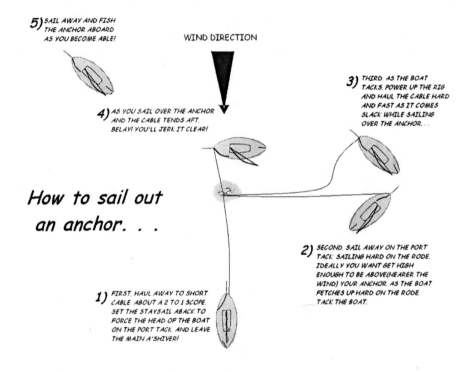

5) SAIL AWAY AND FISH THE ANCHOR ABOARD AS YOU BECOME ABLE!

WIND DIRECTION

3) THIRD, AS THE BOAT TACKS, POWER UP THE RIG AND HAUL THE CABLE HARD AND FAST AS IT COMES SLACK WHILE SAILING OVER THE ANCHOR. . .

4) AS YOU SAIL OVER THE ANCHOR AND THE CABLE TENDS AFT, BELAY! YOU'LL JERK IT CLEAR!

How to sail out an anchor. . .

2) SECOND, SAIL AWAY ON THE PORT TACK, SAILING HARD ON THE RODE. IDEALLY YOU WANT GET HIGH ENOUGH TO BE ABOVE(NEARER THE WIND) YOUR ANCHOR, AS THE BOAT FETCHES UP HARD ON THE RODE, TACK THE BOAT.

1) FIRST, HAUL AWAY TO SHORT CABLE ABOUT A 2 TO 1 SCOPE. SET THE STAYSAIL ABACK TO FORCE THE HEAD OF THE BOAT ON THE PORT TACK, AND LEAVE THE MAIN A'SHIVER!

Ground tackle details: In first picture note foredeck with large windlass and three bow roller fairleads. The second picture shows our 50 pound fisherman anchor stowed nicely on the channels. Above shows the bow pennant hanging from the bobstay chain plate. At the end is a chain hook. The chain hook above takes no load but clears a bight of chain away from the bobstay to make us ride silently. Note the heavy UHMW chafe block to protect the hull in the vicinity of the roller. These rollers are a nice design, notice the opening and locking bail.

The Ship's Boat:

As much as one might enjoy sailing, there comes a time when one needs to get ashore. Unless one is minimalist enough to want to swim—one will need a tender of some sort. One small boats the presence of the dingy is a certain inconvenience—and more than an inconvenience is the typical way many people are seen to deal with them, which is a certain hazard.

Let me say that in many cases one might get away with towing a tender, but one does sacrifice a certain amount of speed to the action—perhaps a half a knot? This might not seem like much to one who has the option of motoring into the harbor as the wind dies, but for one *without* that option it seems like a lot to give up, especially when faced with long hours of drifting or rowing. On RENE-GADE, I have towed a dingy in the past, but after having one capsize in a tide rip and create quite a hassle I quit—one a small boat it becomes a serious problem right quick. I have seen dinghies capsized by powerboat wakes as well. There are places where the instant unexpected presence of a sea-anchor could spell disaster for the yacht.

Some people tow inflatables too, which have less likelihood of catastrophic capsize—but the drag and associated speed loss is yet more pronounced. If you've got a dreadnaught like MACHA that was designed to tow things much bigger than a dingy you might not care much, but still it costs us a good bit of speed in moderate air. The drag doesn't count for much at low speeds, nor at high speeds once the dingy is planning, but at three to four knots it's pretty pronounced.

Some people carry inflatables on the foredeck—making the foredeck unusable. I suppose if well secured on a powerboat this may be reasonable—but a sailboat needs the foredeck for sailing. I think it looks lubberly and likely impairs weather performance.

I did, for years, carry an inflatable on RENEGADE—but I inflated it and stowed it at each usage. This was inconvenient but not as much as one might think, as long as one has a large enough air pump to make the task relatively quick. One can get very large air pumps—as these are used to inflate the large river rafts—that will inflate a small dingy in short order. The deflated inflatable is quite a large bulky package, however, and I can see that on many boats this could be difficult to stow. On an engineless sailboat, however, the old engine compartment often has a great deal of space for this sort of object.

I wasn't happy with the inflatable, but it sufficed. It rowed poorly, for certain, but it was manageable. I wasn't about to put an outboard on the inflatable when the yacht didn't carry an engine. It was clumsy and wet, but I had my hard-shell experience and was done with that. Still, I was certainly looking for a different option.

That option came in the form of a pair of inflatable kayaks. These new inflatable kayaks are not the pool toys one might imagine—they are serious, going places kinds of boats. There are different styles and makes that vary in quality, but they are, by and large, less expensive than the typical yacht inflatable, and to my eye, more durable. They are certainly more fun to paddle around in, and useful, actually for exploring an anchorage. They are not fast like a real sea-kayak is, of course, but they are faster than one would think. I have a pair of singles since a single inflates quickly—five minutes?—most of the time I only need one for rowing out a stern tie or a quick trip ashore. If I need to haul gear, I inflate both—and tow the second one as a barge. If one has crew, it is nice to have a pair of boats for coming and going. They fold into relatively compact bundles—and if the shore was questionable, they could be deflated and carried inland for safekeeping. The thought of having a tender stolen while ashore always hangs in the back of my mind…

If to be used for rowing out an anchor, what I do is ready the anchor and its chain shot in stops and hang it underneath the kayak. I row out, the nylon rode paying out as I go. When I am where I want to go, I slip the stops and the anchor goes to the bottom. Not a problem, and can be accomplished in conditions that I'd feel endangered in a hard-shell pram.

The inflatable kayaks are EXTREAMLY seaworthy—I would say one in an inflatable kayak and a survival suit could withstand fearsome conditions relatively unscathed—perhaps even surf landings and the like. None of the other options are really providing this ability.

Again, all things are a compromise on a small boat—but I would certainly encourage one to look into inflatable kayaks—there is not much wrong with *this* option.

But now that we're on MACHA we're back to the inflatable dingy again. We felt the need for a larger boat as we've often got crew and supplies in a larger way—also rowing out anchors which are considerably heavier than on RENEGADE. We've a 12 foot, "inflatable hard bottom" style boat, and we like it quite well. The hard vee bottom rows well, although they still have those crappy little oars it seems a manageable system.

A hardwired, installed, electric air pump is quite the luxury! We can blow our 12 foot inflatable in about 5 minutes! This makes stowage much less the hassle.

Figure 19: Inflatable kayaks.

Tough question: an outboard?

Well, *here we go*. After all the preaching I've offered up so far about the evils of motors I'm going to discuss the possibility of this tool. There is no question whatsoever that a small outboard motor on an inflatable is a very convenient option. Such boats get around quickly, are seaworthy, carry a good amount of gear with ease. The reality of crowded and increasingly developed harbors mean that the sailing yacht is forced to anchor further and further from access for safety and maneuverability. Many anchorages have no beach access at all anymore, as right-of-way is a forgotten idea and shore access may be miles from where the "mother ship" is anchored. I have gotten by without, to a certain amount of satisfaction, but the difficulty increases by the year.

A case example. We need to fill water tanks, all 150 gallons worth. We've got a half mile row to, and another back, from the hose bib on the dock with our jerry cans. So, how many days will this take me to fill my tanks? Don't snicker! This was the only port in the area that had clean water—what a bitch!

So why not an outboard motor? Well, for all the reasons we have discussed. Toting gasoline is a real hazard. If you've got it aboard, you've got most the dangers of the auxiliary back in your lap again. They are dirty, noisy, polluters for certain. They are dangerous machines. But, one *can* store gasoline safely. The use of the outboard itself, of course, in any given situation *is* optional—one might elect to not use them in pristine environments and not worry about it in developed harbors where the damage is already done. A small one takes up little space and doesn't weigh much. It is unquestionably useful. All of these observations are valid. This is a reasonable stance.

But, what about the dirty little question—is a sailboat that carries an outboard engine equipped dingy a sailboat, at least by my definition, anymore? A lot of snot nosed folks will say it is not. Many people who protest the idea and viability of straight sailing vessels will take great pride in pointing out that you *could* use the outboard for propulsion, and so, you're not a sailor anymore. On the other hand, I've had the same snot nosed folks state that there's really no difference between a motor and a oar as they're both mechanical propulsion—and if you use either it's just the same thing—so by using my sculling oar I'm a hypocrite and just a much a motor sailor as they are. No shit, I've really heard this a *couple* of times.

To some degree, I guess, philosophically, this might make some bizarre sense, but if this argument has any validity, and the mere *possibility* of having a motor at one's beck and call makes one not a sailor—then sailing, I'm afraid, is *dead as a stone*. We've *all* got the ability to motor whether we admit or no—one call to "vessel assist" and I'm motoring wherever I want to go. Just like having an inboard engine to get me out of a pinch, one call for help achieves the same end—motoring to safety. Not a bad option, actually, I've considered, for towing insurance packages are often really inexpensive. Why not? Get bored, get tired, get sick of making headsail changes—just make a call for a tow and motor on home. So, since I could *potentially* make the call, even though I *never* have, some will say that I'm motorsailing *just like everyone else*.

Sure, as I've said and as I think any reasonable person would agree—you're only a "sailor" as much as you sail. Again, that says you've got to care about this fact—but if you *do* care, integrity demands that you acknowledge it. Clearly, a boat without any mechanical propulsion whatsoever is a sailboat and the person who goes places in it is a sailor, by strict definition. As well, clearly, a person who owns a boat that is dependent on mechanical propulsion and is as well dependent personally on this mechanical propulsion to go places is not a sailor—or at least hasn't earned the right, by definition, to wear that title. Again, you don't need to care. All I'm saying is that reasonable people think you've actually got to do what you say you do in order to wear the badge and thus rightly enjoy the privilege of respect, if any, that comes with it. Most people call claiming to do or be something that your aren't, or haven't done—most people call that lying.

In any case, I guess, in some abstract way, ethically it might make some difference whether the motor were attached to my boat or not, or in another boat, or my hand were on it, or if I used it, or needed to. Bullshit. I wouldn't worry about the issue. I admit, it's a shame, that if on a 16 ton sailboat a two horsepower outboard gives somebody some ammunition to shoot at one's ethics, to carry even that. But, Captain Piddlemarks will offer his opinion on your integrity whether you want to hear it or not. I guess if I cared that much about what other people thought I'd worry about this. I don't. I don't think you should either, but if you feel the need to go prove something to yourself or to other people—you'd better not carry one.

So, then, is it "cheating" to carry the outboard? Well, the answer is yes, of course, if it is indeed cheating, *and* you care, *and* you state you do otherwise. If so, and the outboard is used as a auxiliary, and one's skills are not developed enough that one could function without it—of course, one is *not* sailing. If you care about this, well, then care. Personally, I care. Remember, that one of our purposes in choosing sailing over motor sailing is that it is an activity that is *obviously* a higher good: it is more challenging, enriching, aesthetic, and rewarding. It will make better people of us than will motor-sailing. I would personally feel the use of an outboard as propulsion on MACHA would reflect very poorly on my boat handling skills, and I would see the need to use the outboard thus as a mark of incompetence. Still, this is inherently a practical concern. Again, as well, to each at their ability. I'd still say that relying on an outboard with its much less effective propulsion is a quicker path to sailing proficiency than a inboard motor could be. And an oar, if Piddlemarks is right, if that's cheating too, even more so.

When we first launched MACHA we decided to carry an outboard for the inflatable. We did for several reasons. First, we had a new boat, an engineless boat, with which we had no experience in tight quarters handling. We thought the dingy might be able to be used to tow us in conditions we felt, at this point, incapable of sailing. As well, Sparrow was still a very green sailing hand anyway—and this was a lot of boat for me to effectively single hand. Also we (I) simply wanted to be sure we (she) had a good time—this was a permanent departure for us and the difficulties of the change in lifestyle were large enough without the added physical hardships of toiling with shore runs. I enjoy fishing, forage foods are always a large part of our food supply, and the outboard motor makes this greatly more effective. So, then, straight up, we carried an outboard. We figured we'd sell it when we eliminated the need. We tried, a time or two, to tow and push MACHA with the skiff, and found it effective enough. Certainly not anything that would be of any use in conditions other than very flat water and very light wind—it a truly dangerous maneuver in anything other than a calm to ship the outboard over the side of MACHA in into the boat, but one *can* use the inflatable to push the large boat. It is possible. It is damn inconvenient, however, and this is positive deterrent to doing so. It isn't going to save you from anything you sailed yourself into. An outboard on a tow boat might sneak you a couple of miles in a flat calm, which isn't nothing, but don't count on it for assisting you more than that.

The fact is, however, in our *first month* of cruising that new boat we sailed 550 miles and visited 17 ports throughout the San Juan and Gulf Islands. The percentage of time that we used the outboard for propulsion for MACHA ended up being a flat zero. We never used it. I used the sculling oar a couple of times, *because it is always rigged and thus convenient,* but I doubt there was twenty minutes of rowing done in the whole month. Thus, what does one say? All along, we've got to admit, if we're cheating at this game, they only people we're cheating is ourselves. So are we cheating? Are we nuts to care?

Again, you're only a sailor as much as you sail.

You will likely find, at this point, that if your marina requires you to have liability insurance, it will also require you to have an engine. Beware of this hazard. Some marinas will require some sort of token engine of permanent moorage customers. They may not care if it works or what it is, but they'll need to check the box on their little contract. None of this applies to transients, so if you're on the move, as you want to be, don't let it bother you. Still, you may be forced to carry such a thing as complete token gesture, even if you don't use it. If you're from the US, outboards are cheaper for us than in many places around the world and you might consider carrying one simply as something to sell along the way. They're easy to sell and will be worth much more than you paid for it elsewhere.

I think, *if one is careful*, an outboard can be a very useful tool aboard a Sea-Stead. Just make good and sure you aren't reliant on it—if it breaks, sinks, or gets stolen you don't want to be in trouble over it. Don't lie to yourself about your skills. The outboard *will* allow you to cheat yourself—be sure you have the discipline to not to cheat yourself. I think it is a terrible mistake for any first time sailor to carry one as I don't believe *anyone* has this level of discipline. Sail for a season or two without, and then go ahead and indulge if you feel the need. You'll find it isn't a sensible proposition for passage making. It will drag a big boat out of a tight harbor in conditions that you wouldn't like to row in, but that's about all you'll get out of it. Be careful about that damned motor and don't get your hand chopped off. I think they're really dangerous for hauling out anchors and lines and I would only row in these maneuvers. Please don't use it anywhere where you don't need to. If you actually succeed in getting somewhere truly pristine, put it away and keep the oil out of the water, OK?

Lastly, the *only* time I've ever had a problem that required a tow in 12 years of engineless sailing was the last time we came back from cruising Canada. We sailed in, dropped an anchor in Bellingham Bay—which is illegal anyhow, and as it was blowing and the high powerboat season of July was in full force on a Sunday morning. We called Customs. Oh boy, here we go. Now we're required to sail into the harbor, at low tide, at 10:30, no plus or minus on the time, with a harbor *completely* full of boats, and 20 knots dead astern. Hell. I towed MACHA in—it would have been irresponsible to do otherwise. The Customs goon came, checked our passports, asked us how we made our living, and left, but not before I asked a couple of questions of him. First and foremost, I made the case that they required us to make a maneuver that was unsafe—unsafe even under tow—and something I would never have done without being compelled to. I've sailed in and out of the same spot before—but I wouldn't try it with the conditions at the time—but they were sticky about the time. So, I asked, whose liability is it if they make me do something that I can't do? He squirmed, and finally admitted that it is *their* liability, and it's a fact. I think it might be important to bring that up with Customs at the very start. If I can get them to admit that, hell, I'll sail in and out of anywhere any time if it's on their tab. What they will do, of course, if you pull this stunt, is send the Coast Guard out to board you—but whatever, that would have been *easier* for us anyway. As we get boarded every once in a while anyhow, it's hardly a threat anymore.

Foulies:

As a sailor is on occasion required to carry on after the sun and the fun has faded from the sailing—it is important to have really good foul weather gear. Foul weather gear isn't a style issue, nor is it a status statement. In the conditions one needs foul weather gear, it is pretty unlikely that one will have any spectators.

The men who fish for a living in the Gulf of Alaska deal with some of the lousiest weather on the planet—and it isn't a mystery what kind of gear they wear. The requirement isn't just that it be warm and waterproof, but it be durable as well. Foul weather gear with a big tear in it isn't very effective, and if one is actively moving around on a boat it is often easy to wear holes in things quickly.

I advocate the ultra-heavy duty PVC coated fish-boat kind of raingear. There is a difference between brands so it pays to shop. Look for unlined jackets with neoprene cuffs—and good solid, roomy bibs. The urethane coated nylon jackets are initially more stylish and comfortable, but the urethane coating wears quickly. Don't make the mistake of buying lined foulies, as if they get wet, which they will, they are very hard to dry out while underway—the PVC types are pretty much impregnable inside and out, and if one takes a wave down the back of the neck one can go below and change.

Think the same way about foul weather boots. They need to be waterproof, roomy enough to get warm socks inside of, and capable of being dried out.

I think the best underway gear is heavy duty, expedition weight polypropylene long underwear under the foulies. It makes for quick and easy changes and stays dry—quickly protective on deck and quickly comfortable below.

Get a good pair of gloves, but in spite of what the racing people do, never handle lines while wearing them! A terrible bad habit, that…

If the weather is REALLY bad, a quality Type V work suit is the best thing going. Most of these are not too waterproof so wear your foulies over the top of it. This is plenty warm for most any conditions—wear it, you'll enjoy the sailing much more. There is no reason to be cold.

Figure 20: They do make you look obnoxiously salty, though...

The Handy-Billy:

Every sailboat needs a handy-billy, that large set of blocks used for doing tasks that couldn't be done otherwise. Suppose one needs to get oneself aloft in a bosun's chair to the top of the mast—the handy-billy will do that. Suppose one needs to break a foul anchor loose—the handy-billy will be a huge aid. Any time one needs some very serious grunt—the handy-billy is the key.

I like a couple of fiddle blocks, or a fiddle and a single with a becket for a handy-billy. These should be large blocks—big enough you feel totally comfortable hanging from them. As well, since a good deal of line is going to pass through them—and the only line you've got that is that length is the anchor rode—be sure they're big enough to take that sort of line freely. That will mean blocks with *at least* a 5/8ths of an inch swallow. They won't be cheap, but they don't need to be high speed racing blocks, so go for heavy duty and not trick. A fish boat marine store will likely be your best source.

So, when you really need power, the handy-billy goes to the load and the fall goes to a sheet winch...with only a 3 to 1 rigged to advantage almost a ton of pulling power comes pretty easily that way. You can pull hell off the cross with this set-up, so be careful. Make sure everything is up to that kind of load if you're really laying on it—know your knots, stay out of the line of possible recoil...

Critical and minimal systems for the Sea-Stead:

Bilge pumps	A minimum of two bilge pump systems. I believe that you should have a bilge pump accessible from the cockpit and one from down below. I also believe that it is useless to install a bilge pump that hasn't the capacity to keep up with a *missing* through hull. This means at least 20 gallons a minute, and a pump that can withstand frantic pumping without you tearing it off a bulkhead. As well, a portable snorkler is useful. You'll need it for the dingy anyhow.
Bucket	For deck wash, fishing, tool box, and yes, emergency head. On work boats it is common to issue "barf buckets" to crew as they come on board, with the idea that one carries them with them everywhere one goes. Just because you're sick doesn't mean you're not working—so wear them around your neck on a string if you have to. I always write "smile, Jesus loves you" on the bottom inside for when I need inspiration.
Fire extinguishers	One near the galley and one near the forepeak.
Foulies	We use exclusively Grunden's rain gear. The Mustang type V suits are better than others.
Navigation Gear	I'll list this in some order of utility necessity, as the costs grow and at some place you've got to quit. Compass Hand bearing compass: I really like orienteering style compasses over marine ones, like the classic Silva Ranger. You'll find them much cheaper and they double as chart tools. Dividers Straight edge Rotary Protractor—such as Compute-a-Course. It will piss you off as to how much these cost, but they are quick. Lead Line. You've got to have one. Almost no one does any more but people are insane. Cheap GPS: far more cost effective than a sextant.

Critical and minimal systems for the Sea-Stead: (Continued)

Navigation Gear, continued	Barometer: Calibrate it! Depth Sounder: a tremendous labor saver, but now you've installed a electrical system to power this. Nice GPS: Since you've got it, you may as well install one of these. Furuno sets are by far and the way nicest electronics I know of. Still far cheaper than even a new plastic sextant. VHF radio: Nice for weather forecasts. Sextant: Here we are. I wouldn't buy anything cheaper than an Astra IIIB. I've owned one of those and they're really good units. The plastic ones, even with their shoddy reputation, are overrated as far as I'm concerned. Unless you can get one for just about free, I wouldn't bother. Remember, you're using this as a Piloting tool until you also have… Chronometer: a good watch is fine. So are a dozen cheap ones. It might surprise you until you think about it but many analog watches are hard to read within a minute, which you need to be able to do. SSB Receiver: You'll use it more than you think.
Running and Interior lights	Oil *and* electric. Oil running lights are only legal if you have no electrical system at all.
Universally gimbaled cook-stove	A one burner type like the old Sea-Swing. If you've only got one fuel, go with kerosene, as it's cheaper in the long run. The propane stoves are convenient, but the canisters are expensive.
Wood stove	Or otherwise such as oil with a good flue for survival in the North. You must have something to dry the boat out, so don't consider the cheap little propane things, or think you get by with the clay pot tricks. If you can't buy a wood stove, which is possible, it will be inexpensive to have one welded up at a welding shop to fit the space you have.

12

THE SKILLS OF A SAILOR

Navigation and Chart work:

The ability to do good chart work is seen less and less all the time. Modern electronics have made many of the skills of the navigator obsolete. I think this is really rather sad, as navigational ability was one of the many small things that separated the sailor from the lubber—but many of these skills are still valuable and at the very least should be understood.

I have and do use a GPS unit. It is a tool and an immensely valuable one too. People who accuse me of being a "purist", whatever that means, often wonder why I do. I don't find it surprising at all—navigation has always used tools—if I were going to be a "purist" I'd have to eschew lead lines too. I think that is a little silly, and would be a good way to end up on the beach. I never argue that one should be primitive—else wise I'd be sailing a dugout canoe. No, only that one's gear should never be a *mask* for the lack of skill—nor should the gear get in the way of the experience. I don't think the question about whether a sailor should use celestial navigation or a GPS unit makes any sense—a sailor should use *both*. Trust neither, use one to confirm the other. Again, we must be practical!

Following this line of thought, I don't, however, have any interest in a chart plotter. The reason for this is that the chart plotter does away with charts—and charts, when chart work is done on them, and notes are made, become very valuable references to local knowledge of where one has been and what one has experienced. To keep these notes on a chart—to make them YOUR charts—to keep a log; these activities greatly increase the amount of knowledge on gains on any passage—the mind learns and remembers by writing down better than anything else—so do so. You'll be well rewarded.

Beside this, the batteries don't go dead on charts. That would indeed be a problem.

I have no interest in writing a text on navigation. This is one thing that the bookshelves are littered with. They are all good and complete, although many are pretty thick and in a lot of ways the techniques described are more useful for piloting a fleet of destroyers than a small boat. What I want to do here, however, is to describe some techniques that I think are quick, practical, and useful for the small boat. To, once again, convey an attitude...

The first would be to establish some sort of navigational protocol. This is a set of data that is always entered every time a chart problem is worked, and every time a log entry is made. A good deal of the time the information entered will just be a generic entry, but none-the-less the act of writing things down means you've thought about it. This in itself is valuable. If you're the type that is writing down conditions, tide, speed of advance, etc., every hour on the hour—you're unlikely to get to surprised by a "sudden change in conditions." This is hardly an inconvenience, it is good seamanship, and truthfully once one is set up to do so it's pretty quick.

Still, one must choose one's personal navigational language. The first thing to choose is whether or not one is going to think in degrees magnetic or not. I think there is hardly a question to it—do all your work in degrees magnetic. The compass obviously thinks in magnetic, the GPS if you use it can generally be set to think in degrees magnetic—your bearings and ranges are going to be in magnetic. About the only time that one is going to encounter a reading that is not explicitly in degrees magnetic is when dealing with the azimuths of celestial bodies—if one chooses to get involved in celestial navigation—but this is easy enough to remember in context because one is really measuring something else altogether...

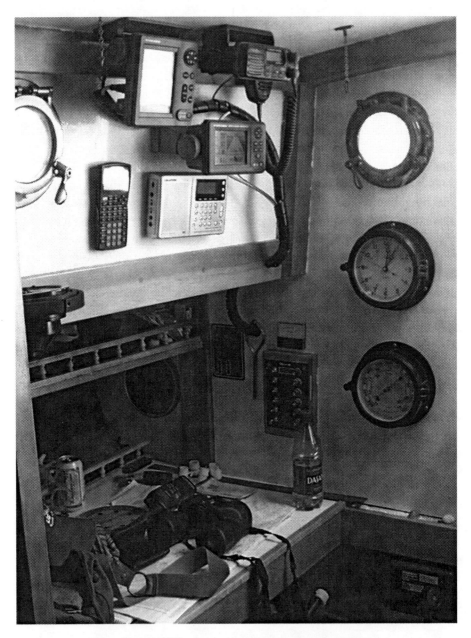

Figure 21: MACHA's chart table in its typical state of disarray.

So then a little chart protocol example. I might write on the chart—

1400—195—5.5

That means to me, 1400 hours, I'm making 195 degrees magnetic, and I'm making 5.5 knots. As these are on the chart, these values are all REAL values off the chart. Meaning, regardless of what I've steered, 195 is what I've found to have made, and 5.5 knots is what I've found to have covered over ground in the last hour. If the spot on the chart is a guess that comes off of dead reckoning or is more or less a guess—mark it as a little x. If it is a better position than that, really a fix, mark it as a little point with a circle around it.

The log, however, is different, and contains a lot more information:

1400			Lat:	48-44.9	
CO: 180	CS:180	CMG:195	Lon	122-55.5	
SPEED:6.0	VMG:5.5	SOA:5.5			
Observations:	NNE 15 B rising Ebb				

So what have we here? We have the time again, we have the latitude and longitude found off the chart. We have a "course ordered", a "course steered" and a "course made good," which a lot of the time, are not the same thing. The course ordered is what you asked for, if you're not on the helm—some people are perpetually high or low of the mark—it's nice to know. Course steered is what they think they've actually steered—you'll ask, but a lot of the time you can get an admission that they think they were a bit off. Course made good is what actually happened, you got that off the chart. Now you might know if you need to make a correction for the next hour on a couple of different details.

Speed is what you're making through the water, off a chip log or a guess. Velocity made good is what you've actually made over ground—this comes off the chart. Speed of advance is what you're making towards where you want to go—this is the number that gives you an estimated time of arrival and sometimes a bit of a sigh. Of course we're measuring our speed in knots—which is nautical miles per hour, right? And we know that a nautical mile is not a measure of linear distance, right? A nautical mile is one arch minute of a degree of latitude? That way we're not looking for a mileage scale somewhere on the chart, we're picking it up right off the latitude on the side. This becomes really important when you learn celestial navigation…

Observations? This is a bit of a mish-mash and anything you think important. Obviously, what the wind is doing is important, so here it is—the barometer is rising, in my personal shorthand, and we're still on the ebb.

How did you find your position on the chart to begin with? Well, usually, I just look at the GPS. Pretty stupid easy, eh? Of course it is, that's why they built it. There are good tricks, of course, that don't rely on the electronics which are certainly good to know. The first is how to do basic hand bearings. No real trick to this as long as one takes a couple of readings and chooses good objects to take bearings off of in the first place. It is hard to read a hand bearing compass too accurately as a good deal of them are swimmy, though, so know all positions are "likely" positions. Once one has done that, we could check the depth of the water possibly and see if that agrees—this is pretty simple too. If one has a sextant on board, all sorts of neat tricks can be performed and usually with much greater accuracy. By turning a sextant on its side, you can measure the angle between two objects on the horizon, and knowing the bearing to one—you've got a fix just like that and likely a good one as the sextant is mighty accurate. If you can get someone to install a compass like the kind they put in binoculars into the scope on your sextant you can do this all in one operation—very cool, very fast and accurate. If you like fiddling with trigonometry in a seaway, the sextant will read altitudes of objects as well—there are all sorts of tables in Bowditch that will find you where you are.

The trick to navigation is—work neat, work deliberately, do the same thing every time, do it a lot. One gets very attuned to what is going on—even so that one hardly needs to do it anymore—yet this is just the time one must insist on discipline. Consider it a ritual of going to sea, and the likelihood of finding yourself on a reef is much diminished.

One needs to become proficient especially because in sailing a real sailboat, sometimes things don't work out as planned and sometimes one isn't in the harbor at happy hour. Navigation at night makes a lot of people nervous—but I don't think this is very well founded. Navigation at night, in good visibility, at least—is easier for me than in the day time. Navigational lights and aids are much easier for me to see at night, and their watch much easier to recognize than in the day time, when they all seem to appear as fuzzy black dots. It think the reason people think night navigation is difficult is that they ASSUME they know where they are during the day, whether they do or not, and at night it becomes obvious that they don't. In the fog, in the rain, at night—one becomes really pleased with that GPS unit. Traditionally, one must admit, there are times where one just cannot see a thing, and in those conditions traditional boats traditionally ran into things. Navigating by sound and smell are possible, but iffy, and I don't like rely-ing on that sort of thing at all. Learn to do these things—pay attention and think—use all the aids you have available, but let the first line of defense being knowing what you are doing.

Lastly, spend a good deal of time learning to recognize running lights of other vessels. There is no way to do it other than to practice—all of a sudden your eyes will learn the trick and it will never be a problem every again—you'll practically see the boat underneath the lights. Still, unless one does this it is pretty confus-ing, and just another potential source of terror to add to a midnight adventure already filled with worry...

Speaking of traffic, one of the things people often refer to when advocating an engine is to get out of the way of shipping traffic. This is true, I suppose, but what are were you doing in the traffic lanes to begin with? Why is it that one needs to be there? The shipping lanes are only a little over a mile wide, in a flat calm one could row out of them in twenty minutes—at speed one crosses them in no time at all. Pay attention to the weather! If one is likely to be becalmed—don't be anywhere near the shipping lanes. In the dark, don't be anywhere near the shipping lanes. In poor visibility of any kind, don't be anywhere near the ship-ping lanes. I make a policy of sailing well outside and in frankly shallow water—you're not going to meet a ship there. If you're becalmed, simply anchor. In the worst weather, and in many places one can find oneself in a row of crab pots that will guide nicely in the absence of any other aid. You'll not meet a freighter here either. Traffic is a hazard like any other that any passage must be planned to avoid.

A quick note about "right of way." Of course a sailing vessel has right of way. A rowing vessel is SOMETIMES referred to as a non-powered vessel and SOME-TIMES a powered vessel so it becomes much more awkward. I guess you have right of way when you dip the oars in and not when they're out. I think it is wise, if it can be done—to always enter marinas, etc., with the oars out and ready if for no other reason than they're very effective marks—that is they clearly communi-cate that you are NOT a powerboat. People often assume that if you sail into a marina you're just practicing—and you've got the motor running. But people are boneheads.

So knowing you've got the right of way, but right of way having no teeth at all and never being enforced—a sailor is put into a bit of a spot. The main difficulty is the many cases of maritime law that insist that if ANY fault is shared in a mis-hap, then the fault is a fifty-fifty split. This means it is important that you do not share the blame, and are always flawless in your seamanship. Unfortunately, this law also states that if one DOES have the right of way—and one yields it—one shares blame. The privileged vessel MUST STAND ON—this is just as important as the other vessel's duty to yield.

So you're screwed either way. I think it is good practice to use sound signals whenever reasonable—although a lot of people just think you're honking a horn and get pissy—yet one must be certain that one does what is correct. In a of lot cases, however, when dealing with traffic of the yachty sort, the best thing to do is just avoid it—if this means waiting an hour or two for the smoke to clear (literally) on a busy evening, so be it.

Back to navigation once more:. It isn't so much important how one plots one's positions and works one's fixes as long as one *does*. On a real sailboat, one must play the navigator in a matter much like one on ocean racer—the key is always to make the best time and sail the most efficient way possible. One cannot be casual about it—cruising in a sailboat is very much like racing, actually. One is always in a race against the turn of the tide, a change in the weather, a storm or a calm. One has to complete one's passages on a certain time schedule much of the time. It is very easy, if one is sloppy in one's navigation, to sail extra distances, to ignore leeway and to have to regain distance to weather than one simply threw out—to not pay attention to the strength and duration of the tidal flow: this all costs time and distance. It makes the likelihood of facing inconvenient circumstances just that more certain. Have a strategy for the passage, sail that strategy, pay attention to how well it is all working out. If you don't, you'll end up drifting around in the dark more often than you'd like, and you'll spend some tiresome hours. If you do—you'll make good time and get a good deal of satisfaction of a job well done.

Lastly, if you feel the need to spend a lot of money on navigational gear, get the absolute best pair of binoculars you can afford. Don't buy them on name, pick them up and look through them, and find the ones that you can see the best through. I think it is awfully hard to beat Fujinon's high-quality line. If you can try them in the dark, you'll really separate the good ones from the bad ones. There is a very big difference in binoculars, and the quality is more or less dependent on price. This is one piece of hardware that is really worth saving money for.

A Word on Knots:

Very few sailing books would be complete without a bit to be said on knots. And I will say only a small amount, because after the publication of Clifford Ashley's

"Ashley Book of Knots" all other knot books become a bit silly. The "Ashley Book of Knots" is one of those very few books that ranks with Bowditch as a mandatory source text to have aboard any boat—so I'll refer to it assuming you'll get a copy. Yet, there is a lot of bad information surrounding knots, and I'll try to clarify some of this.

I've fiddled with knots a bit. I'm an experienced rigger, with most of my knowledge involving ships rigged in the late 1700. These ships were entirely fiber rigs, with no wire in them, and knots were the structures that held them together. There are many, many knots to be known, but few of them are any much use to a modern sailor, and fewer yet are much use in modern synthetic line. Still, there are a number that should be demanded of any sailor, but it is not only important to know them—but to also know *where to use them*. Knowing why to use them where one does is critical as well. In this section I am more interested in the why and where than the "how to tie."

I don't think there is any magic to knots except to say this: on any one ship there should only be one knot to be used in each purpose. There is no virtue in the "can't tie a knot, tie a lot" school of securing lines. This is a safety issue as well as a convenience, and also a very effective screen as to the quality of one's potential crew. I really do believe, if one has crew that can't remember to put the right number of turns on a cleat, they've got no business being on a sailboat—unless, of course, they're really good looking...

The Cleat: Tying to a cleat is a knot—and tied improperly it is a problem. The first thing to remember is that the loaded line intersects the base of the cleat at an angle, and thus takes its first turn around the after part of the base of the cleat. This much is critical. After this, we have options. If the cleat is large, and a heavy load is to be expected, a full turn around the cleat before crossing turns are made is prudent. Most cleats on small boats are not this large, so a half turn us usually made and then crossing turns begin. That is what I do, half-turn around the base, a crossing turn and a reversed locking turn. Neat and compact. Again, whatever one does is fine, as long as it is appropriate, useful, expeditious, and consistent—and never, ever, jams under load. Having to take a half dozen turns off a cleat to release a line is sloppy and dangerous.

It seems odd to me that often people who feel that a locking turn on a cleat is dangerous have no trouble with clove hitches. A single crossing turn on a cleat with a locking turn is just a clove hitch.

The Bowline: Called the king of knots; I'd say it is a knave at best. It is a useful knot but its use is much overrated. A good utility knot for sheets, of course, it has the great disadvantage of not being able to be untied while under load—not a problem? We'll see. It is reasonably secure but not as secure as some and by no means as secure as an eye splice. A bowline can be tied four ways in stranded line, two ways in braid line—all having slightly different holding properties. I refer you to Ashley's.

When used to secure sheets at the clew of a headsail, they can be tied as to hang up on the shrouds on every tack or to slide over the shrouds. Investigate.

The Clove Hitch: This and its kin would certainly take my vote as the most important knot. Secure, symmetrical, difficult to jam, quick to tie—much closer to the king of knots than any other I can think of. It does, however, have one important but little known property, seldom referred to, that can be readily demonstrated by tying a clove hitch around a winch. Tied one way, it holds, the other, it rolls out freely. Investigate. A clove hitch does not hold on any object that is free to turn.

The Rolling Hitch: This is a clove hitch with an extra turn. I refer you to Ashley's. If the extra hitch is tied so it rides on another, it is called a Midshipman's hitch and is especially secure. Since most all knots tied in synthetic line are less secure than those tied in natural fiber, it is often wise to go for the most secure of the lot.

The Buntline Hitch: This is the most secure hitch I know—and becomes a knife knot under load. It is very compact, strong and secure, and is an excellent upper termination for halyards or any end of a line which much hold a shackle, etc., as it is completely secure yet will not get drawn into a block like a eye splice might. It is again, an application of the clove hitch. I once again, refer you to Ashley's.

The Round Turn and two Half Hitches: This is the best way to secure to an object where heavy loads are to be expected and anticipation of the need to release under load exists. Surprisingly, it is the very close relative of the buntline hitch, and again, another application of the clove hitch. Ashley's once again.

The Square Knot or Reef Knot: For only one purpose, tying in reefs. The proper way to tie is right over left, left over right, with one side slipped and the slip facing UP.

The Round Seizing: a structural binding that will hold nearly kind of knot or turn together with great security. Again, "The Ashley Book of Knots" describes this knot and its many applications.

Any knot seized is a good knot.

Eye splices: In braid or in three strand, many varieties exist.

My Favorite Bend: Two eye splices with galvanized thimbles and a solid shackle with the screw moused. Nothing is as secure.

Lastly, a few knots to know for the odd application. All to be found in Ashley's. The carrick bend and its permutations, some favorite stopper knot, the sheet bend, some sort of loop in the bight knot—I prefer the butterfly knot—the constrictor knot, the prussik knot, the venerable marline hitch, and lastly the Tom Fool Knot—which is perhaps the one true traditional knot of the sailor, and the one that appears on the cover of Ashley's, and for good reason...

Again, a sailor needs a good, non-folding, non pointed knife in a sheath and a well shaped, nicely tapered marlinespike...

Rigging:

While we're at it, let's take a look at rigs. There's a lot of nonsense out there about rigs too, but see, rigs are commercial—one can buy a rig and bolt it on thinking its going to work wonders. A bit like the big carburetors the hot rod kids get worked up about. It's a good place to throw money so it does get a lot of hype. You can't get a straight answer in this game but I'm going to try. A sailor who doesn't rely on an engine DOES really rely on a rig, for certain, so the question arises...It is good to have confidence in the stick...

We spoke a while back about rig tune for sail shape. We're going to get into that now. This will conversation will be a bit drawn out but it needs to be to answer some questions.

So, what's the right way to rig a boat?

There is no right answer to the answer of what to use for rigging other than this one—if you are going to race, buy rod. That's all there is to it. Your rig will weigh just that much less and the guy with the lightest and most expensive rig will win, at least in the kind of racing people do today. There you have it.

Now if you're going to cruise a sailboat, you've got a lot of questions to ask. What makes a boat sail nicely? What is going to make your rig break? We'll talk about breaking first. The most likely answer is fatigue. Second is corrosion, at least in northern climates. If one goes really hot and salty, these might reverse, but these are your two bugaboos. The traditional way of dealing with both of these problems is simply make all of the pieces meatier so there is just more to rot away, in essence, and this is a legitimate approach as long as one isn't crazy about it. One can easily overbuild a rig, and that isn't necessarily admirable or smart. Have a designated weak link somewhere, please, and try to make it convenient. In the event that you rolled things over or something else like that, you don't want the strength of the rig to exceed that of the hull. It is pretty easy to do that. Wouldn't you rather (if you must choose) break a wire, turnbuckle, flange, etc. or rip out a chain plate as well as a reasonably sized piece of fiberglass? This thought, when dwelt on, brings up that proverbial sinking feeling...

As far as that goes—do your research and do a lot of it. I've rigged boats: I sail my own rig—yeah, I can throw around the formulas too. If you're going to re-rig your boat—do it yourself. You need to know what's up anyway, and this is the way to learn. Let me state this, however, as a bit of a preface: This is one of those areas of engineering where the envelope of error may exceed the designed parameters by quite a lot—so often a guy ends up guessing. And the guy who is often qualified to make the best guess is the guy that knows his boat—he ought to know it. I guess I wouldn't trust anyone who calls themselves a rigger (or any other supposed boat expert) who doesn't spend *at least* as much time on the water *in their own boat* as they do fixing other peoples stuff. You'll see why after hiring a few, then you'll henceforth do all your work yourself. Beware! There are lots of glossy books that sell products—just because one might have a name that's spelled funny and know a magic trick in string or two doesn't mean they necessarily will do a nicer job than you...

Do you want to know if someone is an, ahem, "Master Rigger" or not? The test is very simple. Take a look at the running rig of the boat. See it at rest and underway. Count the number of blocks and fittings and ask if it can be reduced or not. Look for areas of chafe: A truly masterfully rigged vessel will have none.

Options for the standing rig?

A) Swaged rig: Forget it. Cheap garbage. That was easy, wasn't it?

B) Stayloks, Norseman fittings, etc. These are the best options for modern wire.

The only real argument against them—and it isn't a good one—is price. It takes next to no skill to build stays with these, and they are hefty. Still, I am nervous about them used at the bottom of stays, where they fill up full of crud and corrosion no matter what one does. Still, a good option if one breaks them down and swaps out the wire every five years—the Stayloks perhaps every ten.

C) Spliced ends: in 7x7 or 7X19 wire.

This is not a bad option on some boats, but don't do it because you think it's going to be cheaper; *not necessarily so.* By the time one has fitted out the mast with custom hardware, bought the jumbo turnbuckles and jumbo thimbles one needs for this construction—one is easily into the price range of Stayloks. Splices are strong, but regardless of the magic values one hears attached to them I don't think it is wise to rate splices at any more than 80% of a wire's breaking strength. Splices in 7x19 are stronger than in 7x7 because the increase in number of strands make for more bearing surface—thus more friction.

I don't think splicing 1x19 is a good idea, although one can. One cannot help but fatigue wire in the process. If I were determined to use 1x19 I'd use a mechanical terminal. Besides, a 1x19 splice is a big lumpy thing and I think they look tacky.

By the way—there are rigging sorts who rave about splices and being something special—but pure hype unless there's a good reason. The good reason that usually exists is that the rigger is getting a good hourly rate—and it takes a lot more time to turn in a splice than screw on a Staylok...

So, for the accounting. What did I do on my RENEGADE? 7x7 stainless wire with Stayloks on the top and splices on the bottom. The Stayloks up high are much less likely to corrode and anyway they're hanging upside down so they won't fill up like a bucket. Splices on the bottom where, as my weak link, they're readily inspected. The splice is covered with a leather boot that can be slid up the wire to give things a check over and an occasional washout with a blast of penetrating oil. Some high dollar riggers will tell you to serve stainless—don't: that's stupid. You can't keep the water out. Make sure you don't keep it in. On MACHA, we use ½ inch IWRC crane rated stainless steel on the lowers, with big commercial thimbled swages on the bottom and soft eyes around the mast at the hounds at the top, secured with cable clips. The head stays are 3/8 inch wire. The topmast preventers are ¼ inch 1x19 stainless. It's a very nice rig, and hardly wiggles. Part of this is due to the *steel* mast, which is extremely strong and rigid, much more so than aluminum or wood. I wouldn't have any other sort of mast in this kind of boat. If you're curious about steel masts, get a copy of Skene's Elements of Yacht designs and work out a few compression scenarios and required mast sections in aluminum, steel, and wood. You'll be surprised at how well steel compares, if you don't mind a round section, and keeping the paint good.

By the way, you're starting to hear stuff among the cruising set about the virtues of galvanized wire again—*be very wary of this hype*. Sure, galvanized wire is great; it specs out great. Then it rusts, and it's not so great. Now sure, I've too seen the ancient galvanized rigs. Yes, they can last a long time but be sure you know what you're looking at. First, all of the old galvanized rigs that I've seen were huge and heavily zinced, not the case on small wire, in fact, you're more likely to beat all the zinc off the wire in turning in a splice than keep it. Secondly, the service was huge and heavy and maintained by a crew of moneys that threw gobs of tar around with abandon in the pre-OSHA days. Want to play Jack Tar? I've done plenty of that and let me say that it is only romantic for about 15 minutes and makes a hell of a mess. Service, to work, must be really really good or it's positively detrimental.

But, if you must, don't hire anyone to do it, *do it yourself*. Here's why. Service is really easy to apply, except where it's critical, that is, over the splice itself, where, once again, you've likely ruined the galvanization anyway. No one will care as much as you and here it is really important. The crux is the crotch, of course, and the one at the top, where the water is going to zip right around the thimble and in. Don't use pine tar to slush the works—though people will recommend it—which was originally used not so much for its water keeping ability as its *preservative* quality in hemp. The old service was hemp, eh—you didn't want it to rot. Pine tar is just creosote anyhow, more or less—a little known fact is that it actually absorbs water. No, instead, paint the wire heavily with zinc chromate and then slather it in something like an asphalt shingle adhesive. That will seal it up pretty well. Don't use marline; use nylon net twine which will last a long time once it soaks up that black goo and is kept black.

What a hassle! Yes, of course it's ugly. Now, twice a year, climb, inspect, black down, and repair service. Be up there painting all the obnoxious galvanized hardware. After 5 years, see how much money you've thrown away and next time buy stainless. Don't worry about it. Wire is cheap!

Here's the last question and I confess I don't really know how to answer it, because it is very complicated. Anyone who can answer it in a snap doesn't understand the question—a bit like the fellow I once knew that remarked that he had read that Einstein had made the comment that he found the flow of electricity in wires absolutely baffling and couldn't possibly understand it—while this fellow said there wasn't much more to it that just hooking the white wire to one side and the black to the other…The question? How does elasticity affect rig performance? Does the elasticity in the wire make as much difference as touted?

Well, yes and no. Obviously one couldn't build much of a rig out of bungee cord—so we can say elasticity does matter. But how about this for a interesting observation: even 7x19 wire, the stretchiest wire one might use on a rig has a modulus that often exceeds the functional rigidity of the hull. On many boats, when one sees the sag in that headstay, a good part of that is *coming from the hull folding up*, not just stretch in the wire. A scary thought—but demonstrable to anyone with a laser level who is inclined to set the thing up inside and go for a sail. The higher aspect rig one has, the more strain comes on the hull, and the more it flexes and cycles. By the way, fiberglass doesn't really fatigue, it erodes, which is to say, that as it flexes the little glass fibers get broken up and slowly the hull gets weaker. The more it flexes, the more this happens, so it isn't really good to flex a hull all the time; or at least it is good to keep it to a minimum.

Back to the question. With as light as most modern boats are built—you can sit below decks and watch people walk around through the deck above—how many of them can even justify 1x19 wire? Are the hulls just too flimsy to keep significant headstay tension? Is this why many of them go to weather like such dogs in any sort of wind? Had a big high dollar race in my home bay about a while back and it brought down two rigs. Lost five main sails. There are those that said it was blowing 35 knots (I'm not sure that's a justification) but I'd personally be surprised if it broke an honest 30 all day. These were all new boats—they had no excuses other than wimpy gear. What is the real reason that boat designers are evolving towards higher and higher aspect rigs—to compensate for the really crummy rig tension control? Pure fashion? I will not deny that high aspect, light rigs DO make sense in some places—flat water, light air pointing. My 35 year old RENEGADE, with its ultra low aspect ultra heavy rig and modified full keel, now tacks through 75 degrees in good conditions. I can still make 90 degrees under a storm jib and a reefed main in 35 knots of wind. Very few modern boats could do this—it is frankly rare that I find a boat that points higher. You may not believe this—fine, but when you see me rip by on the weather side you will. I must say, this is perfectly good performance, and any boat designer that is worth his pay knows it. In fact, among high tech, modern boats, I know of no stock displacement hull of the same waterline length that will keep up. I say this not so much out of pride but out of wonder—I would expect modern boats to be *much faster* than they demonstrate themselves to be. Ever sail against a Concordia Yawl?

Those suckers go fast, and really point pretty well, and a good modern fancy glass one with a racing interior would only be faster. This is an old, old boat, by design standards. MACHA is old even compared to the Concordia. Yet with her big gaff main boarded in and headsails hardened up she'll bash to weather unrelentlessly—seas be damned!—until you finally just can't take any more punishment. And she'll be making a real 45 degrees off the wind as well. What more do you want?

So before you spend the money on some fancy rig beef up the hull until you are sure that the chain plates aren't moving around. A good deal of your inability to keep the mast in column may be from that. All you need is about a quarter of an inch in deflection to notice, and most boats will give you that and more. A couple of full-length stringers would be a big help. After things are rigid, then start thinking about beefy wire. This is a worthwhile project, and you'll be amazed at how much better the boat handles.

Back on track, stretchy, floppy wire *will* affect sail shape to a certain degree, and if this is uncontrollable, performance suffers. If you do decide to change to stretchier wire for some of the interesting engineering reasons—mostly to use spices and have a more fatigue resistant rig—here is how this will likely affect your sailing performance. First, if you for some reason have a high aspect rig—don't, it's not a coherent system. If you have a low aspect rig, and you go this route, you won't see much of a change in your light air performance—you're not generating enough force to create sag. As the wind builds, you will, and you'll get sag in your headstay that may hurt your sheeting angle, as well as move the draft aft, make the shape baggy, and create a good deal of weather helm. For this reason, I don't recommend stretchy wire for a headstay or a backstay, but there might be good reasons for it athwartships. Some will say that in gusty conditions the elasticity in the shrouds takes a bit of the snap off and one gets a better ride in a chop—besides the heavier weight up there takes the motion off a bit too—which means one's sails stay set better and one might seem faster in these conditions. I'm not sure. I personally lean more towards a rod rig mentality all the time as long as it's well engineered. Experiment:

So whatever rig you end up with—assuming it remains a sloop and you don't freak out and put a junk rig on it—this is how you tune it. A marconi rig is a creature of tension; if the rig isn't tuned properly, which generally means loose or unevenly, you actually increase loads, not decrease them.

Start with the upper shrouds, and snug them up to about a ten percent load. You can either do this with a gauge, which is the best way, or by snugging them up until you can just strum an note into them. That's pretty close. Still, I recommend the gauge, as it is very difficult to work a really nice tune into things without it. 50 pounds makes a difference, or about a half-turn of that turnbuckle, and it is hard to find at times without it.

Again, of course making sure that the mast is in the boat straight up and down, tighten up the upper shrouds. Make them snug. As you tighten up the rest you'll find that these will loosen a bit as the whole boat compresses—you'll begin to see the issue. Then, it is best in my mind to go to the forward lowers and do the same. Then do the after lowers, though these are usually not as tight as the forward lowers. I usually tune to put a little pre-bend in the mast, perhaps an inch and a half of deflection at the top on a 30 foot stick. The purpose of this is purely to flatten the main a bit, as a lot of them are cut too full or perhaps are a bit blown out.

Now you grind the forestry and the backstay down in conjunction. The forestay is going to be the tightest wire in the boat, perhaps a 15 percent load. If it is soft, your pointing will suffer. I like to set the main at this point for fiddling with these wires will change my mast bend a bit, and I like to tune some good shape into the main by working the mast bend a bit. You'll find a bit of mast bend makes quite a bit of difference in where the draft in your main will sit, so if you've been having weather helm problems here is a good place to tune some of it out. The backstay usually ends up with a load about the same as the shrouds or even a bit less. If you've got a tunable backstay, this is easy.

After you've done all this, start at the top again. You'll usually find that things are no longer even, but it won't take much to make them so. Sight up the mast track, you should be able to shoot a BB straight up it—it needs to be utterly straight. If you've got real trouble, it's likely because the hull is floppy—we've talked about that—so you might consider doing some glass work to stiffen up the hull in the area of the chain plates. You may as well expect any production boat to be a bit floppy and to need some strengthening to really sail well.

Lastly, you go sailing and check things out from on tack to the next. It's normal for the lee shrouds to go a bit slack but they shouldn't go sloppy—if so, you'd better snug things up perhaps a turn all around. If nothing helps, you've got deck compression trouble or the like so you'd better look for it.

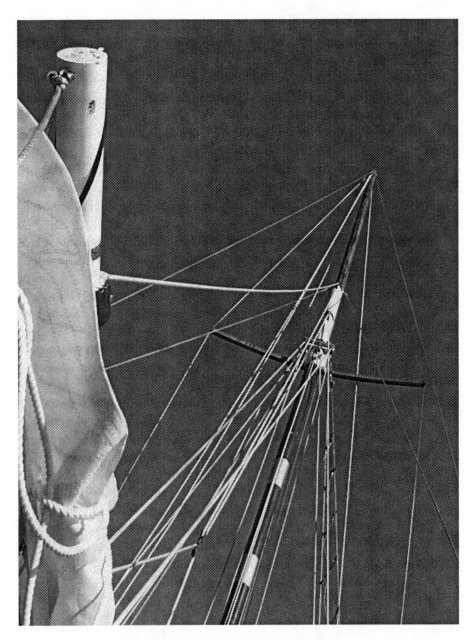

Figure 22: MACHA's topsail cutter rig.

13

TRICKS OF THE TRADE

There are an unlimited number of little bits and tricks that this lifestyle demands, and it becomes a daunting proposition to attempt to organize them into any sort of coherent manner. This chapter is an attempt to collect a number of these and supply them in a useful manner. Besides, for this to be a good book on sailing, it needs to be comfortable aboard a boat. A good book on sailing should contain some weighty discussions, but it should also contains some quick morsels—so that on those late nights, after a long hard passage, as the port wine is working into a sailor's blood in some stormy anchorage, the sailor has a thing or two to idylly peruse as he watches for the signs of a dragging anchor....

Anchoring

Heavy anchors always set easier than light ones.

The presence of kelp indicates a good deal of rock and a good deal of current.

Do not ignore the time honored practice of tying to kelp if there is no other option. It is remarkably secure.

Learn a good anchor flake that will allow you to get a rope rode over the side quickly without fouling.

Having the anchor rode marked off in Roman numerals stitched in dark twine makes anchoring much easier. Mark in fathoms from the head of the chain shot. Chain rodes can be shot with bright colored spray paint.

Look for signs of the security of the anchorage—remember that a sandy beach almost always indicates wave action—that driftwood driven high indicates where the waves (and your boat would) go.

If one doesn't secure one's halyards too well, they act as a wind alarm...

If anticipating a blow, put a reef in the main before the blow. Keep all sails bent on and at the ready. One may be forced to leave for the safety of the boat.

Don't trust your depth finder for the final reading of the depth of the bottom in an anchorage. Use a lead line. The depth finder may be reading the top of a deep kelp bed...one needs to know this.

When forced to leave a tight anchorage, with a small boat, realize that the act of hauling in the anchor rode can give one a powerful head start and steerage if done with a good bit of beef. It is nice practice to haul smartly, break the anchor free and be underway at speed all in moments...

Often, if one is alone and faced with an anchor that is tough to break loose, the boat will sail it out. This is done by tacking into the rode, back and forth, to weather of course, and on each tack gaining a little more cable. This action of working back and forth will usually break the anchor out with ease. Some boats will do this more or less by themselves, if the main is sheeted nearly amidships and the helm left free, or even lashed amidships, one can sit on the foredeck and haul the rode easy as it comes—holding it on the deck cleat when it wants to pay out again. As it snubs up, the boat will be put about. One can almost steer in this manner. Again, some boats do this nicely and some don't, but it is certainly worth a try. This technique is especially valuable if one must haul anchor against a stiff headwind.

In a large boat like MACHA a different technique is called for, as well as a great deal more caution. The power of the main is such that at some point the anchor will be jerked out and the boat will go galloping off more or less in the direction that the boat is pointed. Hopefully this will be the right direction but if it's not, you'll have a disaster. We had one such early in our sailing and we escaped with the skin of our teeth. We broke loose on the wrong tack and galloped towards a beach in a tight cove—immediately tried to reset the anchor but this was done poorly as well and it fouled with a mass of kelp. As we blew towards the beach dragging the mess, I was able to get a kedge set which held us just off the rocks—we fought for some time to kedge ourselves clear with multiple sets. A bitch, for sure, but I learned a lot and lived to fight another day.

First lesson. Keep the boat on the proper tack. This for us means setting a headsail aback much the time—this alone works in light conditions. In heavier air, we sail back and forth with a deep reefed main—to keep the power down. Sail up on the wrong tack, tack the boat, and haul chain like hell. If you don't get the hook clear, you'll tack back, and do it again. It is a matter of careful timing. If you're getting to short cable (less than a 2 to 1) and you're going hit the rode hard on the wrong tack, you'll be forced to veer chain as she comes through irons to avoid breaking the hook out. At some point, you'll find yourself on a close reach, on the right tack, coming up fast on the anchor. Haul chain like hell as it comes. When it quits, hold. With a jerk the hook will come clear and you haul like hell again, leaving the anchorage behind.

Lesson two. Take nothing for granted. The skipper, regardless of the trust he has in the crew, must keep account of the chain that has come aboard. Crew are seldom conscious enough in their moment of hauling to keep this figured out. If you come up hard on the wrong tack and the anchor hand has been having a mental vacation—you'll be plain screwed. On MACHA, I know one turn of the crank of the windlass hauls one foot of chain. I can both hear this and see the whirl of a tailbone as this occurs. So I keep count myself, and this has made all the difference. I swear, it's only one time in 4 the crew has an accurate count.

When the anchor breaks loose, give it a good jerk to be free of the bottom, but it is best to immediately head for the helm leaving the anchor trailing under the boat. Sail on it a bit for deeper water and to be well clear of other boats before finally hauling it aboard and stowing it. You'll find you've likely washed all the mud off of it by this point too.

In an anchorage that you expect might be foul, the use of a tripping line is a good idea and can really save the day. Beware, however, where you use it. If the anchorage is a busy one, and you put a float on the trip line, some bonehead in a powerboat is going to pull it, thinking it is either a mooring or a crab pot. Don't laugh—I'm not joking. Keep an eye on it.

Kedges should be large anchors on short chain on rope rode. They're far too heavy to haul otherwise. We on MACHA have 3 bow rollers. One for the bower on chain in the middle, and one on each forward quarter for rope.

If you carry a regular inflatable, they're nice for hauling anchors out as the plywood transom works well for supporting the anchor, and the aft leading pontoons made to carry the weight of the outboard keeps the boat well balanced.

Figure 23: My favorite job.

Do your kedging or set your extra anchor before it starts to blow. Don't expect to effectively haul a rode to weather in a skiff in much more than 15 knots of wind. By the time its blowing, your only recourse will be to fall back on existing rode to set the secondary. You might not have room.

The further out you anchor, the easier it is to leave, the fewer bugs get aboard, the quieter it is, the sooner the wind fills in, and the less likely that anyone will drag down on you. Unfortunately, you also are more likely to get bashed and rolled by powerboat wakes.

Beware of this trap: At the head of many bays is a stream, river, or small lagoon. It might look innocent enough, but these can be notorious boat eaters. If you find yourself anchored near the head of the bay, near the entrance to one of these, and you find your self needing to leave with an onshore breeze and a rising tide, there is likely to be quite a set into this mouth, over shoals, and in the worst cases, through breakers. BEWARE! As well, debris from the outgoing current is often all over the bottom in this vicinity and makes fouling an anchor likely. Keep well clear!

If you anchor for any period of time with irregular currents, you're very likely to foul the anchor. Set a stern hook or haul the bower every few days to make sure things are OK.

Cooking

Make sure one always has a meal on board that can be prepared in a hurry.

Make sure one's cooking arrangement is secure and functional in a seaway.

It is awfully hard to beat an oven full of baked potatoes as underway food in tough conditions.

Make sure you are prepared for a cooking fire.

Unless a stove is universally gimbaled, you're going to have a very hard time cooking in a sea-way. Some sort of single burner device for heating soups and the like is very useful—I'd really call it a necessity. While we use kerosene for fuel throughout the boat due to its low cost and easy portability, consider a single burner propane stove for this purpose. The cans are expensive, and don't last long, but the fuel itself doesn't need priming and this is a big plus when it's really rocking.

Burning a small cup of fresh coffee grounds on the stove for a while is a good technique for deodorizing a boat of funky boat smells.

Crew

"No crew at all" is better than "bad crew."

Beware of crew sporting deck shoes and sail gloves…

If you ignore that last bit of advice and end up with one of these "heavy swells" aboard—make him (or her) the navigator. That will make them pleased as punch—until you hand them a hand-bearing compass and ask for a running fix and speed of advance. Make sure you're sailing to weather when you do this. Make sure you tack a couple of times while they're working on it. If you can find really rough water, that's better yet.

There are people—sometimes partners and sometimes friends—who just are too lazy or insolent by nature to learn to become good sailors. Do yourself and them a favor—send them packing. Unless you want to be in a situation where you nearly always single-hand and are forced to double-check everything that they might want to do when it's convenient for them, and then eat the contention that this belittlement inherently contains—you've got to demand a certain level of attention be paid to the "ways of the ship." If you don't heed my advice here, you're doomed. They'll get hurt, or hurt someone else, or screw up the boat—and you'll end up holding the bag. Actually, you're probably screwed either way as you'll either be condemned as a hard-case or as irresponsible once the event occurs and hell comes to pay.

It is unlikely that any crew member will know the boat as well as you. Make sure that the crew is trained as much as possible. Insist on certain ways to secure lines, etc., as these things matter on a boat that sails. Insist on the proper names for items and parts of the boat as well. Don't be dogmatic about—give a realistic how and why for every request. If a crew member is casual about these things or uninterested, take note. It is a good idea to find other crew.

A good skipper has trained his crew so well that he need give no commands…he certainly never need scream at the crew. A screaming skipper is a shithead, straight up, no exceptions. It doesn't matter what situation is, it is a simple mark of panic brought on by incompetence.

People on the foredeck are generally slow to learn that if they yell while facing forward they can't be heard by those in the cockpit.

Know the difference between crew and *passengers*…

Figure 24: Perry Fizzano, a fine sailor, a good friend, and the best crew one could want, keeps a tight ship, as we relentlessly overhaul the competition. A little more throat halyard, please!

Drag

A three bladed propeller may contribute thirty percent to the total drag of a boat.

Don't believe the data about folding feathering propellers—their drag figures are misleading at best. Folding propellers often don't fold at low speeds, exactly when you need them to fold the most. Gear driven feathering propellers are better, but still assume a flow stream parallel to the keel to have minimum drag. Which, of course, you don't have, as the flow stream comes off the keel at an angle (which is how it gets it's lift, right?) Hence, they often drag through the water at 5-10 degrees of incidence and feathering gets you not nearly as much as you'd think. The tank data neglects to notice this, somehow…

On MACHA, towing the skiff costs us almost two knots.

A 3 foot shaft, ½ inch in diameter, and not faired creates as much drag as the entire hull of a thirty foot boat.

Keep the bottom clean, it's a safety issue!

Line handling

Make sure one knows what a *fair lead* is on a line and why it is important. Foul leads indeed jam cleats, and this is a serious safety issue.

If anchor rodes have eyes spliced into each end—with good solid thimbles—it makes the job of bending them together with ultimate security as easy as a galvanized shackle.

Always mouse a shackle! Zip-ties are fast and dummies can use them.

For quick and simple exits from a dock or a mooring single-handed—consider the use of a toggle. A toggle is a wooden fid, perhaps a foot long, tapered, with a light line attacked to one end. If a mooring line with a generous loop in the end is taken to the ring on a mooring—the loop can be passed through the ring, and the bight from the standing part of the line passed through the end of the loop. If the toggle is inserted in this loop in the bight, and tension applied to the line, the bight will draw up, pinning both legs of the loop against the toggle—and will hold securely. If the line to the toggle is given a jerk, all will spill and the line will release. Of course this can be easily done from the cockpit of the boat and is a nice way to maintain control while shorthanded. Of course, always again watch for the fair lead…

Consider a toggle with a line lead to the cockpit for dropping the anchor if you're shorthanded. It might make things on some boats much more simple.

The key to coiling line is in the lay. Modern three strand line is coiled in a clockwise fashion, with a slight twist imparted in each turn to keep each turn of the coil laying fair. Braid line has no lay and has a tendency to generate twists if coiled—so it is often coiled with reversing turns—much more of a hassle. Fortunately, on modern boats, we seldom see long lines anymore so this is less of an issue than it once was in the days of tall ships with huge multi-sheave blocks. Perhaps the only place where coiling a line remains critical is in the use of a heaving line—which every sailboat should have and at the ready. A heaving line is best thrown with half a coil in each hand—and it is imperative that both coils be *flawless*…

Quarter inch three strand spun Dacron makes a nice heaving line. Choosing a reasonable weight that is comfortable for the monkey's fist in the end, one should be able to throw a heaving line at least a hundred feet.

Navigation

Learn to judge distance by eye. This can be done by learning one's personal eye resolution. For example, one may be able to see, buildings at several miles, but make out individual windows at one mile, and further benchmark details at less than that. This is a very useful skill if deliberately developed. It is often very difficult to judge distance across water, and all tools one can learn are of good use.

As well, different colors of light generally have different ranges in different conditions—with experience this can be used to judge distance too.

Don't ignore one's sense of smell. Often reefs, especially, can be smelled a good distance to looward.

When taking bearings, of course it is wise to choose objects that have as many degrees difference as possible—for example, three bearings 120 degrees apart would be ideal. Practically speaking, however, this is seldom the case, but in consideration one must choose as close to the ideal as possible to diminish the envelope of error.

Pay good attention to reciprocal tacks, and be honest about what one is making good to weather on each. Hopefully it will be 90 degrees or better, but don't expect a lot better, especially if a sea is running. Looking at reciprocal compass headings is no good for this, obviously, at it doesn't give one's course over ground, just the direction the boat's bow is pointing, and a boat can look like it points high and is quite weatherly but actually is making a good deal of leeway.

When you get involved in celestial navigation—be careful how you learn it. A great deal of the celestial navigation books available are written with a strong naval tradition behind them, and some of the techniques taught are not so applicable for the small boat. First and foremost the large tables, HO 229 and 249, often used—are touted for their convenience, ignoring the fact that they are huge books and take up a great deal of space, as well as being expensive. It should be well noted that the only reason one might want to use HO 229 on a small boat is because one is very sloppy with one's math, as there are several fewer entries. Otherwise, the short tables are very nearly as accurate, and practically certainly so—though again, they require a few more table entries. Yet I feel the advantage of having a short table perhaps 60 pages in length is a major advantage, and I would heartily recommend it. I agree with others that HO 208 is one of the best to be found.

Remember that a celestial line of position can be combined with any other type of navigational data—say a sighted magnetic bearing, to provide a fix—but remember to account for declination.

Sail handling

On many boats of about 30 feet in length, rather than sheeting a mainsail in and across in execution of a gibe, it is easier to grab one fall in the middle of the mainsheet and pull it like a bow—this accomplishes the same thing but leaves lines coiled and the end on the cleat. It is often faster as well. I can get away with this stunt often even on MACHA.

When furling the main, using the mainsheet to secure it does double duty. If one daisy-chains around the sail—this technique called "Swedish furling"—the main and the main sheet are secure but ready for use in a snap.

The "racers" technique of flaking a sail on the boom is reasonable for harbors—but a sailor needs a sea furl that is secure and will not hold water. The best way to do this is to grab the leech of the main at perhaps the first reef point, and pulling away from the boom. This forms a pocket which is in essence all the cloth of the first reef. The rest of the sail is tucked into this pocket, and the whole works neatly rolled up on top of the boom and secured.

Never stand on a sail.

Never pull a sail down by its leech.

Never let a sail flog any longer than necessary.

Try to never fold a sail the same way twice. Modern cloth is vulnerable to creasing and fatigue.

I personally believe that tell-tales on sails are a bad idea. I don't like wind direction indicators either. The reason for this is simple—they are unnecessary, one can learn to trim sails effectively without them and should. Besides this, the presence of tell-tales often encourage the bad habit of staring at them, when a sailor, especially a single-handing one, has better things to be looking for. A boat can be sailed effectively entirely by feel—and this should be learned. Lastly, the reality is that if one becomes dependent on tell-tales and the like to steer a good course, what does one do when sailing at night? One needs to be able to anticipate an accidental gibe by feel, once again, or night sailing may be unnecessarily dangerous.

At times it becomes useful to be able to make a quick headsail change. Foil headstays and the like are indeed quick, but of in my opinion a bit fragile for a cruising boat. Twin headstays, as one used to see on older boats, seem to me to be heavy and clumsy. Actually, with good practiced hands, a relatively quick headsail change can be made in the following manner with little gear.

The trick is to have the second headsail bent on as much as possible before the first is lowered, and thus be without a headsail for as short a time as one can. Obviously this concern is more important when sizing up a sail than sizing down—as if one is overcanvased dropping a jib altogether is of little concern. What one does is to release perhaps the lowest piston hank on the working jib, and to hank the sail to be hoisted onto the forestay in this space. Then the halyard is lowered and shifted to the new sail, the hanks on the dowsed sail are removed quickly, and the new headsail is hoisted. It is useful as well to have a pair of shackles at the tack for this maneuver. A headsail can change can probably be made in a third of the time it would take otherwise in this manner.

A shackle on the clew of a jib sheet is fast and convenient but a good way to loose teeth…it is best for each jib to have its own set of sheets and for them to be spliced on. Splices are far less likely to hang on the shrouds than anything else to use to attach to the clew.

Self-Defense

This can be a sticky issue. We've had some problems in the past with bad folks and I'm sure you will to from time to time. I don't think it matters much whether one is on land or sea, in one's home country or abroad—there is a segment of every population that is trouble and you'll occasionally meet it.

I'm not real impressed with the response many people have towards being robbed. Many people will glibly say that their strategy is to give the robber whatever he wants to avoid being harmed. First, I've got to say, people have got a lot of confidence in Mister Robber's ethics. There's a lot of people who may take what they want and then shoot you—more of those all the time. Second of all, you've got to think a bit about what you're doing—subsidizing the robber population and teaching them that cruisers are easy targets. Hell, just bully one a bit and they'll throw their wallet at you. *Thanks a lot for that.* I just might be the next guy in that harbor.

Lastly, somebody might be wanting to take from you something you're not willing to give. Think on that. Or, they might just be on the prowl with the intent to hurt people. There are people like that too. What then? Well, you'd better be prepared. And preparation here is going to take some commitment.

The obvious answer is firearms—but law around the world is increasingly uptight about honest people in possession of guns—a good reason to be suspect of the law. You've got to be very careful. Going to prison over a weapons charge could be as bad or worse than being shot dead during a robbery. Guns as well have a certain danger to their use. I think their danger is hyped a lot—uh, guns are designed to be dangerous?—but learn to use what you've got if you go that way. Still, most anywhere you want a firearm it's likely to be illegal. Still, there's a lot of stuff most boaters carry that are pretty damn fine weapons and are totally legal. Machete? How about a fire axe?

Actually, I think the biggest problem that a Seasteader faces is simply a product of living on the fringes of society. There's a lot of kooks that hang around docks, boats, and yards. You'll meet them. Watch like a hawk. Some of these sorts just want a victim to freak out on. Don't be that person. Keep your distance from those who've got the funny twitch. Especially problematic in the United States are the growing ranks of methamphetamine users. These folks are bad, bad, news. Their brains are cottage cheese, and they are unpredictable as hell. I'm no Nancy Reagan, but watch out for these folks. Dealing with a raging meth-head is going to be a Dawn of the Dead kind of experience…Don't expect much help from law enforcement—the cops are perfectly aware of the wharf-rat kooks. They probably think *you're* a fringy kook too, and figure that if only one of you two kooks are left standing that's all the better for those who actually pay property tax.

REFUSE TO BE A VICTIM! This is a good motto to live by regardless of what you do, but, seriously, consider for a moment: Does a victim somehow share in the ethical ownership of a crime? What if there was a world where *everyone* fought oppression.?

Don't look like a victim. Look like *trouble*. Keep yourself fit. I'd really, really, really recommend a year or two of martial arts training. It will do wonders for your fitness, your balance, your flexibility, and your confidence. Take it seriously, and learn a style that teaches the real deal. Some don't. Find a school that emphasizes live sparring and be serious about it. I'd recommend Jiu-Jitsu in one or another of its permutations. Don't freak out—you'll probably have a good time. Just be sure that you learn skills that actually work—beware of schools that teach "self-defense" techniques that don't demand much of you, but promise the world in results. These won't work. Remember, you've to physically tangle at least as much as the kook in the boatyard who's going to jump you. Hey, if you take your training half as hard as you take your sailing—you'll be a match for most anyone.

A hint: if in your self-defense class they start teaching you groin kicks, quit. That's baloney: a groin kick won't stop anybody, and any fool can defend against it.

Tactical Sailing

Always plan for a destination *and* plan for an alternative if things don't work out.

When faced with entering a new harbor for the first time, try to time one's passage so that one can do so under oars in a near calm. If this means one must anchor outside the breakwater for a couple of hours—so be it. This is seamanship.

In sailing tidal races, unless the wind is strong and constant—try to sail them to weather, at the slack, with the current filling in behind. This way as the current fills in, apparent wind increases and one maintains good control. Otherwise, one risks becoming becalmed and loosing steerage as the current and wind move in the same direction. This effect is more pronounced than one might think.

Again, favor the starboard tack unless there is a good reason not to. That reason might be sea-state, as typically one tack will be more contrary to the waves than another.

Remember than any place you can touch bottom is an anchorage in a flat calm.

Any place you can anchor to avoid loosing way is reasonable too.

A twenty knot blow in January with driving rain may carry nearly twice the *force* of a twenty knot blow in July. The force of the wind is dependant on speed, but of course also greatly dependant on density of the fluid medium—thus temperature, humidity, and carried precipitation.

Speaking of force—as sailors are more concerned with force than with velocity—the traditional Beaufort Wind scale still does make far more sense than describing wind speed in knots. Note that each force is described by a range of velocity that manifests a given effect—this effect is the expression of force. Thus, I believe it good habit to use the Beaufort scale although many find it a bit archaic and pretentious—the fact is, for the uses of a sailor, it remains the most *accurate*.

When crossing a strait, or a set of traffic lanes, do so more or less perpendicularly to avoid spending any more time in the hazardous middle than necessary.

Tide

It has been suggested that one can determine the likely duration of slack water by taking the maximum anticipated velocity of the tide in knots, and by dividing this number into sixty, a result is derived in minutes that corresponds to the duration of the slack. That is to say, for example, a 6 knot current gives a 10 minute slack.

I would suggest that any time you've got in excess of a 4 knot current—you're not going to have a slack water at all.

The maximum speed of a current is not necessarily dependent on its position within a tide cycle, which is to say that the current cycles may be asymmetrical. Full flood or ebb is not necessarily at mid-tide.

Strong winds can accelerate or stop tidal flow. For example, a strong onshore wind may delay the onset of an ebb—the resultant ebb being significantly stronger than normal.

The change in tide often can induce a change in weather.

Current is usually least near shore, with the exceptions of spits and points which accelerate current.

It is really difficult to get bashed into the rocks by currents, in spite of how it looks. Water flows around objects, not through them, and you'll drift around objects, not into them, unless you give some effort to do so.

Underway

A ship is only as safe as it is ship-shape. Keep all lines coiled and ready to run.

Remember that unless it is specifically ballast, all weight on a boat slows it down. Weight high and in the ends is the worst.

Weight on board makes a boat gives a boat more *initial stability* but less *ultimate stability*. Which is to say that weight makes a boat more resistance to heel but more likely to capsize.

People say that loading a boat helps it pound through waves and makes it faster. This has been proven again and again not to be true. While it is true that heavier boat does slow less while encountering each wave, it also accelerates less each time it gets through it. No, loading a boat only makes it *slower* unless it significantly increases its power to carry sail.

Always know both the tide and weather forecast for every sail. Always have the proper chart at the ready.

Oil lamps make excellent interior running lamps at night, as they draw no electrical power and effect one's night vision minimally if kept low.

Anything that can come adrift certainly will. Practice good stowage.

Make sure the bilge is kept clean. A dirty bilge can sink a boat.

All through-hulls should have read damage control plugs lashed to them and at the ready. In the case of a flooding, one only has moments to get it under control. Once the cabin sole is awash, most survivors report that they could no longer determine the source of the flooding…

Keep a large, handheld spot-light on the boat and ready. It will draw far more attention than running lights will.

If underway at night, and one finds oneself in a situation where one must wait for conditions to change to make a harbor entry, etc., because of bad visibility—a good place to sail to kill the hours is in the immediate proximity of a large navigational buoy. Certainly, sailing around and around a buoy for hours is tedious, for certain, but it is a very safe place to be and eliminates a good deal of worries. One knows that all large ship traffic will be watching for the buoy, and while they might not notice you they will notice *it*, and will avoid the general area. Likewise, being a hundred yards from a navigational buoy makes one's personal navigational problems relatively simple...

Always have a couple dozen gaskets at the ready for use in securing sails and anything else that might want to come adrift. Pieces of ¾ inch nylon webbing are convenient. One should always have at least one of these in a pocket, especially when heading for the foredeck.

14

SEA STORIES

The following are a few selected accounts of some memorable voyages in sail-boats—selected because they convey the atmosphere and attitude of the sorts of situations sailors encounter—perhaps one will hear an encouraging call in these accounts...

Figure 25: RENEGADE moving out.

A quick trip on RENEGADE.

So at 1 in the morning I hear a knock at my hatch. Since bad folk rarely knock the shotgun stays where it sleeps and I get up and peek out the hatch. Well, hell! A sailor buddy of mine back in town after being off in the Sea of Cortez for the last eight months. Coffee's on: lots of sea stories follow—some of which were even likely true. We decide to go sailing, visit another friend in a port about 100 miles to the south in Port Townsend—I haven't got any work lined up next week so we'll leave on the ebb first thing in the morning. The barometer is high; it has been blowing northwesterlies for the last three days—there are rumors of a depression working up the coast. Sounds like a great sail. Four or five days, reach down and reach back.

We leave in the morning. It is absolutely flat calm so we row out of the harbor. We are not far out when a light southerly comes up. Not a real great sign—with a high barometer a southerly in our area can only mean local effect stuff—but it is on the nose and with the 180 genoa set we're actually making good time on the flat water. We decide to hug the gradient of a large mud bay on our way in case the wind totally dies—when can just drop the hook right there. Everything is an anchorage in a flat calm.

The wind dies. It is just a tad before noon, and the current is still taking us in the direction we want to go, so we simply break out lunch and the stereo and drift along. After about eight cans of beer the expected northerly starts to fill in and we take off. After about an hour we've got a decision to make—tide is starting to change. We look at the charts and it's not going to be a big run-off. We can either take a longer route and face less current or a shorter route with more—at any rate we want to be in harbor in Anacortes an hour before sunset because the wind nearly always dies. We opt for the short route and pile on the sail; we are determined to make time while the wind holds. It turns out to be a good choice; the wind holds nicely and we bomb into the harbor several hours sooner than we thought.

We leave next morning on the ebb again. We've got a good northerly as soon as we're underway. Tack through a narrow channel with wildly variable winds and out into the Straits of Juan de Fuca. Wind starts to fall light about noon again, and our speed is greatly reduced. We desperately want to make Admiralty Inlet before the late ebb—it is going to be a big one and there is no way we'll hold against it in this air. We claw our way along making as much way as possible, even rowing a bit from time to time, and we make the Inlet just as the tide turns. We've got about five knots of air, we've got a dead down wind approach, and the current is dead in our face and building. Looks pretty bad.

Desperate strategies evolve. We'll see how far we can get and if we start to loose way we'll turn around and hang for the night in a small mud bay about six miles off. It will be a long night, but that's playing sailor. We notice that there is a bit of a lift off the south point—it's pretty shallow over there but deep enough, especially at our rate of speed. We sneak over there and actually discover bit of a back eddy—we're actually now making 2 knots over ground! Will it hold? Don't know—it's pretty small, and we can see the ebb really starting to pick up only a hundred yards to the north. We scope it out with the glasses. Well, it sure looks like it holds around the point—there is a lane of glassy water all the way around the corner. We don't think it's flat (windwise) there because we would anticipate the wind to actually pick up a bit due to the topography. We guess the glassy flatness can only be due to the water moving in the same direction as the wind—hot dog! We're going for it. Yes, the water does get a bit thin but we've careful, and we sneak around Point Wilson at sunset and into harbor at Port Townsend with the feeling we cheated things a bit. A useful note is entered into the log.

We fiddle around in town for a day. The front from the south has deepened a bit and is expected in the morning. Small craft advisory southerlies posted. We're going to make great time heading back north.

We leave in the morning on the ebb again. Very little wind, actually, but the barometer has fallen—though not as much as I would have expected. We whip out through the Inlet on a heavy ebb into a sloppy low swell running in from the Pacific. Breakers out over there; I believe we'll avoid that. Yup, it's blowing out there somewhere. A couple of hours later we've still got very little wind, and we've only made but a couple of miles to the north due to the lumpy sea state. Barometer is falling. I don't like it a bit.

Neither did NOAA. They've got a gale warning posted now for 40-knot westerlies.

Aw, Damn! Sounds like we get to play sailor after all. We make a quick strategy pow-wow. Our first priority it to be out of the Straits before 40 knots shows up. Pretty hefty tides all day today and with the typical 2 knot currents it's going to be LUMPY. We harden up sails and blast off in a northwesterly direction: it isn't where we want to go but there are a couple of good bays up there that we can hide in if it comes to it. Now that we're on the wind we're making good time. If the wind comes up we want all of the extra distance to weather we can get in case we have to fall of and run under my spitfire jib—even in that case we ought to be able to find a place to hide.

Wind builds. We are driving the boat. We are making excellent time. Can you say performance? Can you say performance? Wind is clocking from Southwest to West as we head on north. Actually, that's becoming close to ideal. We are really hauling ass now, running in the high sevens in a four-foot slop. I don't like it and I've got the boom preventer really tacked down, but this is one of those times when driving a boat hard is prudent seamanship.

We blast in around the corner, into the lee of the islands. The wind builds; the slop moderates. We're now heading north on the full flood. GPS is reading and holding 9 knots over ground. The main gets a reef and now the helm balance is reasonable. We blast into Anacortes, it's about 3 in the afternoon. It's blowing a very irregular 25 and all over big powerboats are running for shelter. There is no way I'm going to sail into the harbor right now. We think for a moment, gybe, and point the bow north for Bellingham with Van Halen thumping the speakers.

It is a sloppy ride through the islands. We get to see everything from a flat calm to thirty knots in gusts and we have a regular sail change drill. We get into Bellingham before dark and it is still blowing pretty solid in Bellingham Bay. I'm not too keen about running into the boat harbor with the lump that is running across the entrance, and I'm going to have a hell of a time keeping the speed off once inside. We sail up, check it out, don't like it, and stand off. I drop the headsail. We noodle around off the waterfront waiting in hopes of the wind to die at dark—else we'll have to find a spot to hide for the night. I make supper—the wind moderates a bit—though not as much as I'd like and we come jamming on into the marina under bare poles. I back water hard with the sweeps and crab my way down the pier to my slip. Pause for a moment, and we're home. Gosh, that was easier than I thought it would be.

Put stuff away. Have a beer. Have another. That's sailing.

Down the coast in PHOCA:

In May 2000, having owned and sailed the 28-foot Atkin designed ketch, Phoca, for five years, I decided to remove the diesel engine. We planned to sail north into British Columbia, then head down the west coast to Baja and the Gulf of California. I suppose I had entertained the notion of removing the engine for quite some time, feeling that it would give greater storage of water, tools, and food, increase her speed and beauty as a sail craft, and test my sailing and seamanship skills in the "sink-or-swim" way. Some people had dark predictions about our upcoming trip, but there were a few encouraging adventurers whose voices rose above the backdrop of naysayers. These people had stories I wanted to listen to, and their knowledge through experience I integrated into my own. My sailing partner and girlfriend Djuna and I have come to feel that that the fun-less moments (which can last from minutes to days) of engineless sailing are balanced by the more fun ones (which can last from minutes to days).

After a 14-day nonstop passage from Neah Bay, Washington to Newport Beach, California, and followed by two months of living in the heart of materialistic and sta-tus-seeking Southern California, Djuna and I were ready to make southerly tracks. Thankfully, things had worked out well for us; we had found work, kept our meager stash of money intact, made some minor improvements to our little floating world, and had met some great people. The hurricane season was ending and Djuna had hinted that she might lose it mentally if we did not leave soon.

We had decided that our first landfall in Mexico should be Isla Guadalupe. This island lies about 180 miles offshore Northern Baja, and is roughly 375 miles, as the crow flies, from Newport Beach. I had dreamt of seeing this island for myself ever since I had read Lin and Larry Pardey's stories of adventures in Saraphin, and there was definite appeal in sailing to a small, offshore, volcanic island where elephant seal breeding colonies exist—as well as the Great White sharks that prey on them. We knew that the "anchorages" on the island were sketchy at best and that if the weather was iffy, we might not even stop, opting to sail on towards Isla Cedros

It was 1200 or so, November 18ᵗʰ, and our friends had said they were coming to say goodbye before noon. We had spent the previous evening preparing for sea and cramming tools, sails, and lots of water in various containers into what had once been the engine compartment. We did a good job of it too, for we had learned our lesson about "loose items" after being becalmed on our previous passage…Unfortunately, our friends were nowhere in sight and I was antsy to get out of the harbor and across 12 miles of one of the busiest shipping lanes on the West Coast before the wind died in the evening. We bade them a mental farewell and pivoted the boat 180 degrees with lines to mooring buoys. Once pointed downwind, we raised some sail and let go. A little improvised slaloming and we were in the clear and headed for the harbor entrance two miles away.

Once clear of the breakwater and we steered west-southwest, beginning to feel the Northwest swell and wind. We were scooting along, on a beam reach under full sail, with our self-steering gear working well. The coast was clear (so to speak) for ships, so I went below to do some last-minute stowing and grab a snack and a couple of bottles of water to ensure that we would drink enough over the next day. Both of us were too excited to sleep, but I went below anyway to try to rest before nightfall, leaving Djuna to be captain. By nightfall we were 8 miles off the southeast end of Catalina Island and experiencing very little wind. I was starting to feel seasick—no surprise since I suf-fer from that curse—but knew from past experience that no matter how horrible I felt, so far I'd been able to do anything which needed doing, as had Djuna.

The night was calm, but after a little while I could hear approaching wind from the land. Sure enough, about 20 minutes later a light wind was blowing from the

Northeast and we were moving though the water once again. I silently gave thanks to the Wind God for sparing us the discomfort of wallowing in the swells and for giving us our mobility. I had just settled into a cozy area of the cockpit when I was startled by something out of the corner of my eye. My pulse slowed when I recognized the strange orange shape of the moon rising from behind the mountains of the coast which was to be our last glimpse of land for the next three days.

Day 2 dawned high overcast with a light northwest wind. Too light for our liking, in fact. That day passed by, us repeatedly raising and lowering the drifter in exchange for the light-wind jib—sometimes taking down all sail to save our ears and sails from the slating in the much larger swell. Preparing myself a lunch of tuna, salad dressing, and instant mashed potatoes (I highly recommend these) I wished the wind would increase. Djuna and I traded watches in what felt like a natural rhythm of 4-6 hours and about 3 hours at night. This schedule seemed to afford us enough sleep, but with so many sail changes we were up a time or two on our off-watch. However, that night I had my first restful sleep while Djuna kept and eye on things out in the cockpit, listening to tunes on the Walkman that were written in a world much different from what was now ours.

Day 3 was celebrated by the return of my appetite, and the absence of nausea. We paid our dues and from now on our lives at sea would be much more comfortable. The sky was still a high gray overcast, with a building northwest swell, we were sailing under light-air jib, whisker-poled out to one side and drifter sheeted to the end of the main boom on the other side, our preferred downwind combination for light air. I checked the barometer regularly, wanting wind yet sighing with relief at the needle's reluctance to move. At one point in the afternoon I happened to glance aloft and notice (to my dismay) that the leech of the drifter had flopped over on a roll and had hooked itself into the bronze clip which serves as the upper end of the jib downhaul. As the boat rolled the other way, the drifter inflated and ripped along the leech. I could see what looked like two feet of tear so it must not have been hooked for long, but I wanted to save the sail from as much damage as we could. Djuna was down below sleeping and I realized that to solve the problem, we needed to drop both sails simultaneously, or more ripping would occur. I yelled for Djuna to "come up ASAP! Skip the foulies, Skip the harness! Just get up here! The longer you wait the more it will rip!" She woke up about half way though my ranting, unsure of who I was yelling at. Once she came up we got the drifter down with a little more damage, and Djuna volunteered to renew about 3 feet of the leech. She was now standing on sea legs. Without the drifter up, our progress was halved at least, and I will stress to any prospective engineless sailor my opinions on the importance of large area, light-wind sails...

The rest of the day passed uneventfully. We hadn't even seen a distant ship, let alone any marine life since our first night, so were feeling a bit lonely, and the monotone of the gray of the sky had an ominous feel to me. "Oh well," I thought, "If anything's going to happen, it's going happen." That evening we were about sixty miles north of Punta Del Norte, the north end of the island, and after an uneventful night with the same light air exercises, Day 4 found us about 25 miles off. We knew that soon we should be able to see the island; it rises out of the water to a height of 4000 feet in about half a mile of horizontal distance. We kept moving forward, and we kept not seeing it. Finally, and about 10:00 we spotted a dark shape up in the clouds, and realized that this was Isla Guadalupe. Within minutes, the island shed its clouds and it appeared in its entirety, looking larger than we had anticipated.

Our first island landfall had me feeling awed yet wary. The island resembled a huge dragon rising out of the ocean; with a volcanic spine of a central ridge, slopes cut with more weathering-resistant dikes and sills, and seemed to communicate a message to keep away. The stationary ventricular cloud which clung to the main ridge was visible as this strange conveyor—clouds appearing on the leading edge of the lens, blowing across the ridge, then disappearing at a precise line in the sky. The sound of the huge surf four miles away definitely added to the vibe.

A distinct edge of the cloud-cover which had been our company for the last three days was visible further to the west, moving south, and soon it was hot and sunny, and the wind completely gone. We broke out the 11 foot sweeps we call our "two-stroke" or "sympathy sticks" depending on the situation, and began rowing the last two miles towards our anchorage. We traded off for the next hour, and were closing in when fishermen in pangs started coming in to their little camp which we were hoping to anchor near. One of them, noticing our less common method of travel, came alongside to ask if everything was ok. We conversed in English and Spanish (their English was better than my Spanish) and they introduced themselves. They seemed exited about having visitors and asked if we were hungry. We were, so they grabbed three lobster from their coolers and gave them to us. They asked for nothing in return but we had some beer and soda—none of it cold, of course, but they were as pleased as us with tepid soda, so we chatted while sipping our drinks. They warned us not to swim or dive because of the sharks, invited us to come fishing with them the next day, to come ashore and shoot a goat with a shotgun they would be glad to loan us, and many other things. They made us feel quite welcome but we declined, wanting to rest and clean up, thinking we could talk in the morning.

Having eaten a large meal, Djuna and I finally relaxed into the awesomeness of the scene surrounding us. It felt like we were looking straight up to the top of the ridge 4000 feet above, and the ever-present ventricular cloud we were now viewing from behind and below—though it continued to disappear at a distinct line far above our heads. I was very psyched, energized, and glad we had decided to come see this place. Soon it was dark, so we broke out the soap and bucket, got clean, then made up the 2-person berth. Snuggled into our warm little be I cultivated the dream of a leisurely wake-up after a full night of worry-free sleep. I lay awake listening to the diversity of sounds bellowed and belched with abandon from one of the many seals ashore, underlain by the sound (transmitted though the hull) of gravel and cobbles being swept up and down the beach slope by the refracted swells. That sound was a bit unnerving…

At 0227 (exactly!) we were both awakened by the sound of chain on the bottom and the whistle hum of wind blasting over us. We had read and heard about the williwaws that which the area hosted form time to time, so we knew what we could be in for. We quickly dressed (with reluctance) and readied PHOCA for sail, then went back below for sleep (if possible) fully clothed until first light.

Three and a half hours later, we were ready to go. The gusts were about thirty knots, some maybe higher, and we didn't like the way that sometimes they would blow about 45 to 90 degrees off the shore, and at other times it was more like 20 degrees to parallel. We wanted to get the anchor off the bottom while falling off, headed away from shore. I believe we did, and I remember the feeling of relief tinged with wistfulness that grew as we fell off, never having touched the island.

It was a beautiful day, the sea was alive, and if this wind held, we could make Isla San Benito, 150 miles distant, by the next morning…

Matt Nelson

Getting one's sealegs:

I got into sailing just a couple of years ago. Why, I'm not sure, but it seemed like the thing to do. None-the-less, I bought my first boat—had a friend tear the engine out of it—and I was ready to learn what to do.

No, I didn't know a thing about sailing when I bought the boat, and I didn't know how to sail when I had the engine tore out. The only other boat I had ever been on, however, was owned by a friend of mine, it had no engine and we went places in it just fine. I sure liked the idea of a sailboat without an engine. I liked having lots of room for stowing things. I liked how the engineless boat was so much faster than most all the other boats we'd see. I also really wanted to learn how to sail, and while I didn't know, I could certainly tell that nobody else did either. It was a circus every marina we got into. My buddy knew how to sail, that was clear, and I understood that came from not so much being more talented but rather really having done it.

So, yeah, I had the engine tore out. I bought some oars. I've never even been on a boat with an engine in it.

I took my first cruise in Yggdrassil, my Albin Vega, last summer. I hadn't ever been out of the local bay before, and I needed to learn some things. I had my sailing buddy along for crew so I wasn't too worried, but it was good to use my boat and see what it was capable of. I had learned a lot so far, sailing in the bay and in and out of the harbor, but there are decisions and issues one faces only by making long trips. This would be the first long trip.

We left Bellingham early in the morning, rowing out of the harbor in the morning calm. It was supposed to blow pretty well that day and we wanted to make a good deal of time north, but it was also supposed to blow hard enough that we could have gotten stuck in the marina so we left. Once we got outside, though, there was a little wind and we took off at a couple of knots. We had Hale's Passage to deal with about 7 miles to the south, and we needed to hit that on the flood tide. It looked like we'd be a little late and more into the flood than we'd like, as we were hoping to ride it north, but one doesn't always get to choose what the weather is.

A couple of hours later we were still only making a couple of knots, the wind hadn't filled in. My buddy didn't like it, we could make it through Hale's but we'd end up in the straits on the north end and in the shipping lanes. We didn't want to drift around there. There was a small bay at the south end of the passage that we thought we'd anchor in if the wind didn't fill in. The wind didn't fill in. We sailed into the bay and anchored close to the entrance to make it easy to leave once we finally got breeze.

No wind all day. We sat in the sunshine, listened to the stereo, and enjoyed the solitude.

Until about six o'clock, that is. All of a sudden the bay started filling up with other boats. They anchored everywhere. As the bay got more and more crowded, people anchored on shorter and shorter scope to be "considerate" of each other. Some fat guy came out and played the bagpipes. It was weird.

My buddy didn't like it. The weather, that is—he didn't like the bagpipes either. We'd been watching the barometer and it was still falling but no wind. We figured it was going to show up at some point or another and that when it did, it would show up quick. We hoped it would be next morning.

Just in case we put a reef in the main, got everything stowed, and had everything ready to make sail at a moment's notice.

Good thing too, the wind came up at midnight with a howl. Halyards were slapping, motors were running instantly—you could see people running around in waving flashlights and hoping they weren't dragging. Boats were starting to swing around and bump into each other. It was time for us to jimmy out of there.

We did. We set the main, hauled the hook like hell—five shorts on the horn and a wave at the spotlights across the exit (there was a reef out there we wanted to avoid) and we were gone in a heartbeat. When we got outside the entrance of the bay the wind was really rocking, probably 30 knots, and we decided we'd sail on under the reefed main alone to keep the speed down a bit. Visibility was good and we stormed north in the dark trailing huge plumes of phosphoresce behind us.

A few hours later we were miles away, having sailing into a nice anchorage at dawn, the sails stowed, we had a real breakfast, and spent the day fiddling around and catching up on sleep.

The next morning we were hoping to head north to Vancouver. There was supposed to be some wind but not a lot. We had traffic lanes to thing about and pretty big tides. We weren't really sure we wanted to go but finally got antsy and left. Once we got away from the island and into the flood stream the wind all but died. We were able to make way but only a knot or two under the huge abomination spinnaker. The weather was warm and nice and it wasn't too bad. We got across the traffic lanes as quickly as possible and sailed in the shallow water of the Fraisier River delta with the idea that if the wind died we'd just anchor right there amidst the crab pots. We had done that before. Not a protected anchorage, obviously, but if the wind came up you left.

The wind died. We anchored. A light wind came up in the early morning but only enough to stir cat's paws and we didn't get too excited about leaving until we were ready.

The cat's paws held and we set the big spinnaker again and went north once more. It was hot and sunny and comfortable early—we took turns at the helm and just glided along. The wind more or less held all day, not much happened except we saw a big cruising powerboat run up on a beach in English Bay, which was fun. We got to the entrance to False Creek in the late afternoon and took the spinnaker down, and the wind started to fill in from the north.

This was a little bit of a problem as False Creek is one of the few places you aren't supposed to sail. It's narrow, it's got crazy boat traffic, it's got a Coast Guard station right there watching everything but the "no wake" rule. We'd rowed in and out of there before but it was too windy for that. So, we took the sails down and "motored" in under bare polls and the incoming tide. Wasn't a problem, we had to drudge a bit with the anchor to get from one anchorage to the next, but we snuck in, dropped a hook, took a stern tie, and thought we'd enjoy the Vancouver night life a bit.

It blew while we were in Vancouver. We didn't care at all.

After a couple of days we felt it was time to leave and head for home. We rowed out of False Creek in the early morning hours on the ebb tide. The people zipping by in the rowing shells stared.

Very little wind all day, but we kept making time somehow. A lot of wallowing around in the straits in a sloppy swell. We kept sailing south all night as the wind was supposed to fill in again. It kept acting like it would and then almost dying. I sailed in the dark for hours and watched the big ships go by.

My buddy took the early watch and the wind came up just before dawn. I awoke to the sounds of water rushing by and a glorious reach. My buddy was tired and said he'd try to sleep, but the wind kept building and soon we were tearing south in rolling four footers and only hitting the high spots. He tried to sleep for a couple of hours and finally gave up. The seastate got pretty rough as the flood tide caught full strength, but the little Vega was fast and didn't care at all. We made great time back to the island where we had spent the night a couple of days before, but as we got within a half mile of the entrance the wind suddenly backed and almost died. We scrambled to change to the big headsail—a pretty strong tide runs across the entrance and we didn't want to get swept by. A few touchy moments and some worry, but we threaded past the reefs and got inside the bay, found a little harbor breeze again and within the hour were tied up and making supper. We were glad for that and were pretty tired.

The next morning we awoke to sun and a 15 knot southeasterly. We set sail and were home in a just couple of hours. It was the weekend and we passed a number of other cruising boats—although just a couple of them were under sail. As I packed the sails away back in the slip I was glad for the choice I made to go without an engine. Having an engine would have made our voyage easy and uneventful. We didn't, so it made it interesting and challenging. I was a bit saddened to see so few people realize that...

Tom Weber

15

FINANCES, GETTING STARTED, AND THE FIRST BOAT

So now it is time for a serious conversation about economics. How much is this project going to cost? This is one area where many "cruising" books are sorely lacking—the primary reason being that most cruising books are written by people who do not have the finances of the Sea-Stead worked out. Thus the writing of the book, with an attempt to pay for the current habit. I hope one can take it on faith that I am not in this position, although a royalty check or two would be nice, the limited return is unlikely to make much difference in my position at this point. Hopefully, though I can offer some insight on how to get into the same position. This issue is very important, and perhaps the main reason people fail at the project of Sea-Steading.

I can say with confidence that simply equipped, rugged ocean cruising sailboat of proper design can be purchased second-hand about a dollar a pound. It will require some major refitting, likely, and to acquire the necessary tools and gear will cost a minimum of another dollar a pound. These are round figures, of course, but very reasonable estimates coming from my own experience and the experience of those I know who have followed much the same minimalist path I suggest as necessary for the Sea-Stead. If these figures seem low, there is one major reason:

I advocate sailing cruisers. Sailing a boat without the aid of an engine is far, far, far cheaper.

Let's be clear. People think sailboats are powered by wind. This is not true. They are powered by **money**. It is simply a fact that person A with income X leaves *sooner* and goes *further* in a <u>less</u> expensive boat than in a <u>more</u> expensive one. Don't listen to the advice of the XXXXXXXXXXXX crowd. Do you have income X minus 1 and want to leave now? Our way may be your only way. Time to face facts and buckle down.

Now for the numbers. Pay attention. Much of this no one addresses fairly.

You need to know that it is pretty reasonable to expect that the cost and maintenance of a marine diesel engine is going to run fully half of the maintenance cost of the entire boat. This doesn't seem like a really big deal if the boat sits at the dock all the time—like most do—and rots into the water. You'll hear people boasting about how little the motor costs them and how little fuel they use. Bullshit. This is a boat that sits at the dock. But we're not talking about sitting at the dock. We're talking about a boat that goes places and is used hard. I think you'll blow the rig, engine, and sails out of a boat every 5 years if you're cruising hard. You'll need to replace all of them to maintain safety. Now, I build my own sails and I can get by relatively cheap on that, and the rig isn't bad, but the engine is a *tough* one. I can rebuild engines, sure—but fixing a marine diesel engine is ridiculously expensive—parts are terrible, and you'll have complicated yard time. If you can't fix stuff yourself in a big way—repowering is going to cost you multiples of thousands of dollars. To put a new diesel engine in my old 28 foot boat it would cost me upward of 6000 bucks. I can pretty well cruise for a year on that much money…As well, most honest cruisers report that when the boat is reliant indeed on the diesel engine, they run it a *minimum* of two hours a day, underway or at anchor, to keep systems charged. Considering passage-making as well, four hours a day is not an unreasonable figure. The fuel dock a quarter of a mile from where I sit here in Canada working on this manuscript has diesel at 3 dollars a gallon. We are then talking about a likely minimum of 6 dollars a day in fuel costs—which, in reality, will be a quarter to a half of an average cruisers budget, *excluding* maintenance! If you add in yearly maintenance, you'd be hard pressed to get by on less than 500 dollars a year, or generously, a dollar a day, so now we're up to 7 dollars a day. The sails and rig will cost you 500 a year, much of which is a deferred cost, on a thirty foot boat. That's another dollar, say two, a day. Now we're up to nine dollars a day, or in round numbers 300 dollars a month *known* costs before you even start to eat, and nothing else just craps out.

Suppose then, you tear the engine out. Now a whole new set of issues present themselves. By removing the engine—you have removed the heart of the modern cruising boat. Without the aid of the engine—most modern "necessities" that boats carry simply won't work for you. There is no way you can possibly generate the power needed for water makers, nor radar, nor SSB, nor refrigeration, nor even some depth finders, nor even perhaps a diesel stove a lot of the time. Not having all this crap saves you a phenomenal amount of money as well, in fact, not having an engine simply prohibits the use of a lot of this gear. You'll be forced to learn the skills to do without. I do see boats decked up like space probes with panels and generators and stuff—I get asked about the viability of that sort of thing—I've come to respond with this: "unnecessary windage." You don't need that junk—there are all sorts of alternatives—and we'll show you how to run a boat with NO electrical power if you'd like. You only need a hull that doesn't leak, and a rig that sails. Starting there, add reasonable technology for a reasonable amount of comfort…but I'm getting ahead of myself…

Now pay big attention to the next point.

The next big point is this: a "cruising" sailboat *must* carry a certain amount of gear on board. It must carry a certain amount of fuel, even for cooking, water, sails, repair supplies and tools, a tender, clothing, extra line, ground tackle, etc,. A Sea-Stead, as it is a full time home, even more so. On a small boat, this can take up an impractical amount of room—and you understand why you see the kind of boats that look like the "Grapes of Wrath" gone to sea. Now certainly—the amount of gear one needs is often overstated—and a good amount of skill can reduce this amount to a large degree, *but somewhere there is a bottom line of what one can carry and still be properly equipped.* This argument persuades a lot of people to buy bigger boats than they can afford—a catastrophe! You can't catch up. A bigger boat needs more and larger and heavier gear!

Take a look at what happens when you remove an engine, however. You gain a HUGE amount of stowage. On my RENEGADE, the engine compartment took up about 60 cubic feet of stowage space. The engine, tank, hoses, and all other assorted gear ran into nearly a thousand pounds. That's enough size and weight for carrying all the gear I would need for a serious ocean passage. MACHA, obviously a much larger boat, the abandoned hull I purchased, had an engine installation in when I bought her. The installation was a 10 HP SABB. The installation effectively filled the *after 12 feet of the hull,* or at least made it unusable. In this case we are talking of perhaps 160 cubic feet of hull volume! One gains a cargo hold—located in the ideal place—and of an ideal size and shape in many cases. In other words, an engineless 28 foot boat might have the carrying capacity of a 32 foot boat with an engine in…this makes smaller boats FAR more functional than they would be otherwise. MACHA carries a full ton of cargo—gear and trade goods—and the effect on sailing performance is all but unnoticeable.

Figure 26: Large waterproof hatch that is the access to our cargo hold.

PERFORMANCE: You cannot believe what taking an inboard engine out of a sailboat does for its performance. The change is jaw-dropping. Pulling an inboard motor is the simplest, cheapest, and most certain way of gaining a knot under sail. I'll run quickly through a few numbers to show as to why, which demystifies (and validates) things a bit—but it is *such* a big deal that I don't see why more people don't talk about it.

On my RENEGADE:

Removing the engine raised the boat 1.5 inches on her marks. That's almost 6 square feet of wetted surface area. It lowered the center of gravity about 2 inches, because of the huge impact on overall displacement, vastly improving its stability. Removing the prop and strut most likely removed 70% of the hull's drag—hard to believe this; but the data shows that a round strut, three feet long and an inch in diameter generates as much drag as the ENTIRE HULL OF A THIRTY FOOT BOAT! What did it mean in performance? 1.5 knots on every point of sail and 5-8 degrees of pointing. I think that's pretty reasonable to expect and every boat that I've torn the engine out of has gotten close to that in gains. What it really means as well is that a boat without an engine hardly ever needs one...I put over 15,000 sailing miles on that little boat, in inland waters, I got everywhere I wanted to go, in and out of anyplace I wanted to go. I didn't ask for a damn tow once, thank you! Andrew, the new owner, is hot on my heels to do the same.

On MACHA the change in performance was not so profound but certainly noticeable. More noticeable than an increase in speed was a significant increase in the ease of handling, and much more confidence in stays than before the rudder aperture was filled. Hence a boat that one can sail in tight quarters with confidence and before, this was not the case. Again, a boat without a motor that doesn't ever need one.

So what I see is this. A 28 foot sailboat has as much stowage as a 32 foot motor sailor, it goes as fast as a 32 foot motor sailor dragging a screw—it is much less work to sail—you're far more likely to have anchorage or moorage available when you get to port—moorage is just that much cheaper all the time...

Again, a quality, outfitted, engineless 28 foot boat can be put together for less than 20 thousand dollars including all the gear for extended ocean passages. A quality, outfitted 32 foot boat with a good engine installed would be tough to have for less than 80 thousand dollars. Sounds to me like if you pull the engine you get the circumnavigation for free...or maybe a couple of them! What I'm getting at is this—all in all, I see one saving perhaps *three quarters* of the cost of purchase and of cruising by going engineless once everything is considered. Take note! MACHA, with this simple gaff rig and no systems aboard that I didn't have on RENEGADE—a sixteen ton cutter again—cost us perhaps 30,000 dollars to build and equip. THIS IS A NEW BOAT! I think most people would agree that this is a hell of a lot of boat for the money.

So now, I've got to counter the objections. I hear this all the time—that having an engine is a safety issue, not an economic or aesthetic issue. I usually hear it with a bit of a snort. I reply: Safety against what? Seriously, against what? Against anything that skill should not have been the first safety aid? With the skill to avoid the problem, what need is there for the engine? I will admit that the engine is a powerful aid to incompetence—but as such in my eyes perpetuates incompetence—and so is a safety issue in itself. When one realizes that the presence of the engine carries inherent hazards with it—increased risk of fire, asphyxiation, injury by mechanical parts, through-hull failure, or even the cases I've read about where the prop strut came undone and the whirling propeller chopped holes in the bottom of the boat—when one realizes that the presence of the engine

GREATLY impairs a boats sailing ability and its ability to claw off a lee shore in a gale—it is pretty tough to look at the engine as helping with safety much at all.

The engine "issue" is purely one of convenience and comfort. It takes a lot, if not most all of the work out of sailing. It does allow one to be in the harbor on schedule, for cocktails, when one could not have entered without under some conditions. But we've already talked about this, some people don't get into sailing for convenience. If convenience is such a big deal to you—why take up sailing? What on earth is supposed to be convenient about sailing? It's a lot more convenient to stay home.

Figure 27: Sometimes it's pretty nice.

Anyway, what this means for many people is that many of you could sell your car, and with that money, have the means to see the world, or at least have a very solid start of the Sea-Stead project. Once the boat is purchased, and you have moved aboard, now comes the time of learning to sail and learning the boat, and outfitting the vessel so that it works flawlessly. This will take some thought and time. I would expect that the novice realistically has three years to learn these basic skills. I have certainly seen certain individuals make much more effective progress than this, but these were people who brought many skills with them to the environment. This may not be you. Skill acquisition is *critical* to this environment—this is another area where many people fail. They keep a vacation mentality. Sure, you're going to have some free time to fiddle around and have cocktails—but just as importantly, you'll have time to learn new skills and move forward in improving the viability of your Seastead.

Do you have the skills for this environment? If not, *now is the time to start acquiring them.* Any frontier lifestyle requires a great deal of skills—one must become an expert in everything. There are two reasons for this. First, the vessel itself will require maintenance and this burden will fall upon you. For example, you will not likely be able to afford to purchase sails; one can save two thirds the cost of sails by building them by oneself. As of 2005, most cruising material suggests that 1000 dollars a month is perhaps the basic low end of the cost of cruising for a couple. I would suggest that in a modern boat with modern systems, the real cost of cruising plus maintenance may be at least 1500 dollars a month or more. This is a lot of money to earn on a fixed income, as well is it a hell of a lot of money to save by casual employment. Again, by going simple, and by going without the engine—and having the skills to get along comfortably without it, which you can indeed do—this cost can *easily* be cut in half. I have cruised comfortably on four hundred dollars a month in the United States and Canada and did not feel burdened by this. I know others who live more primitively and get by on less, but as some point living really cheap seems to me to be more work, not less, than the occasional job. The key is to success is determining what level of expenditure you can indefinitely maintain with your current earning potential and to stay within it. What is lethal to the cruising lifestyle is spending too much, either on the initial boat, maintenance, or goodies underway—so that one must return to the work-a-day world on a regular basis. It is often so expensive to return to the higher earning "professional position" that it takes a disproportional amount of time away from sea to earn the necessary cash. As long as one can make ends meet with funds earned from casual labor and a bit of trade—one can fly under radar very cost effectively. *It costs a great deal to return to port—to come home and get a job!* The slip rental, now the car, now the professional clothing—it can cost a thousand dollars to earn 1100. Pay careful attention to this trap!

Make sure, then when in calculating earning potential not to sweeten the numbers. Earning potential *must* be calculated from portable or casual employment. This will always pay less than time-card punching long term employment. There are, however, jobs, especially in the trades, where the turnover rate is so high that a reasonably good wage can be earned on short term notice. I, for example, work in construction primarily when I feel the need to—as it is often on a per job basis and requires little background resume other than a tool belt. Still, as another rule of thumb, I would expect that it is unreasonable to expect to earn more than twice a US minimum wage in the states and less overseas in the tourist trade. This may be enough, however, if one is very careful.

Figure 28: Boat building under a CDX lean-to in the middle of winter.

Don't be so gung-ho or hung-up on the idea of sailing off to the ends of the world that you lose sight of the project as a whole. A successful Sea-Steading lifestyle can be had many places—one can live this frontier lifestyle in the heart of a major city and sometimes there is good reason to do just that. There are times to sail away and there are times to not—one must follow not only the weather but economies and politics as well. As an example, we in August of 2005 were set to sail for Mexico. I'd been cruising the Pacific Northwest for about a decade and while it's a good spot for a Sea-Stead, I was feeling that I'd seen it, and that it was really time to go. We were *one week* away from heading south, we were provisioned and ready to go, and suddenly the opportunities for income popped up. Everybody has got to save some cash at one time or another—some times are good for this and some times are not. So, we jumped at the chance and delayed the plan to sail—certainly one can get by on very little but it is *much more fun to get by on more.*

Diatribe:

Blue water sailing! Blah Blah Blah Blah BLAH BLAH! Everybody is so fired up about blue water sailing! Well, so am I, to a certain degree, but let's put it all in perspective.

Every sailor has the dream of sailing off to some distant and exotic place. Sure, sounds great! But there is a problem with this dream. You've got to sail at sea. Sailing at sea, to my mind, isn't any sort of great adventure—it is purely long duration uncomfortable drudgery. Some people do like it, a lot of people claim to like it—I'll be an honest one and say I don't like it at all. This isn't to say that you should be discouraged in your dream if you'd like to sail off across the oceans. This isn't to say that all of us shouldn't be prepared to do so if the need or opportunity arises. Still, realize, that the vast majority of sailing is done within the sight of land—and most all effective Sea-Steading is certainly coastal in nature. There's not a lot in the deep ocean that would entice me to stay any longer than I needed to in order to get somewhere else.

If you haven't done any blue water sailing, don't let blue water sailors wipe snot on you by talking about how many miles they've got under their belt. The majority of blue water sailing is done completely automatically, with very little time involved in the handling of the vessel. The fact that one sleeps mostly on an ocean passage is fortunate, because if one could not it would be even more boring than it already is—the problem is that blue water sailors make the claim that "miles" somehow equal "experience" and they'll use that to belittle coastal folks, especially those just getting started.

This is a crock of crap, and you should be aware of what you need to know. First of all, let's assume that a 100 miles of tactical inland sailing (sailing, right?) at an average of 3 knots of advance will take 33 hrs of helmsmanship and pilotage without relief to complete. A hundred and twenty miles underway at sea might take an average of 4 hours of chart work and maybe a sail change as well—while the rest of the time requires only minimal attention. If my assumptions aren't far off—we've got to say that inland sailing requires ten times the effort than ocean sailing. I'd say it certainly feels that way. We might fairly say then that 10,000 miles of inland sailing would teach much more about sailing than 100,000 sea-miles. I certainly think this seems to be the case, as I don't infrequently meet ocean sailors who couldn't make a 20 mile passage under sail if their life depended on it. To be completely fair, each activity does teach somewhat different things, but don't think for a moment that ocean sailing is a "superior" activity, whatever that means. Bar Pilots are worth more money than Ocean Master tickets, right? While crossing oceans can be intimidating, it also takes a lot of balls as well to *sail* where it counts and the water gets thin and the edges crunchy. Most sailors die on beaches, no?

So why all the hype? Well, ocean sailing is a dream, and a big expensive dream, and it sells a hell of a lot of gear to those who dream that dream. It is quite the industry in itself, so the drum really gets beaten. So, in conclusion, don't get all freaked out about sailing off to Tonga. It will cost you a lot to do so, and you might be surprised at the number of people who are sailing around the world to get to the "paradise" where you already live…

This being said, don't let finances trap you. It is very easy for one to get trapped by the notion that one is always ten thousand dollars away from what one really needs. You *can* sail away on damn near nothing, and people do—but as I say, it's simply much more fun with more cash in your pocket. This hazard cuts both ways, for certain. One can get bogged down in the money earning mode—which provides for very little quality of life on the boat—and get jaded about the whole project and quit. As well, one can sail away in fine minimalist fashion, but one can get tired of a rice and rice diet, of always being anchored out on the boat, of always scrimping—and get jaded about the whole project and quit. The key is to be happy, right? Whatever that takes then! Baby steps; guard your enthusiasm. Still, *always* keep the boat in the trim and condition that it could leave at a moments notice. Keep yourself and your attitude in a place where you could and would be willing to, at any given moment, untie the mooring lines and sail away. I see people intent on sailing away so often suddenly showing up with dogs, kids, debt, career options, responsibilities, etc., etc., and suddenly the boat is up for sale. Don't think for a moment that this cannot happen to you. *Always* keep a plan, a goal, a destination and move towards it. Have a time, date, and financial threshold of security that you work towards. Be serious about it; write it on paper and staple it to a bulkhead. If things come up, or opportunities arise; well, sure! We're nomads, for sure, but being nomadic is nothing if not being opportunistic. Still, move forward with more purpose than just getting by year to year. Have a passage making mentality—don't just be adrift. *I'd say that if you are so currently attached that you couldn't up and leave with 12 hours notice you run a grave risk of never leaving at all.*

I have been successful enough in this game that in the last 10 years to actually have saved some money, which brings me to the next topic: investing. Savings, especially those earning a return, even a small one, are a *huge* boon to the Sea-Stead. By the time one has saved a year's worth of living expenses the pressure comes off immensely. No longer is one forced to find employment by necessity—one finds employment by opportunity. This alone makes a huge difference in one's hourly rate. Every ten thousand dollars saved and safely invested earning perhaps five percent earns almost a month's worth of cruising—at least in the manner I suggest—one month that is paid for *forever.* Five percent is a modest rate of return indeed and often one can do better than that. It is useful than, to think of the existence of some magic robot within the Sea-Stead that works and provides one all the supplies one needs for a month of living—this robot costs about ten thousand dollars per unit. Why spend more money than needed on the boat? The 2500 dollar paint job earns no income, nor does the flashy inflatable, or the fancy yachty foulies. Remember that every dollar spent not only costs, *but costs lost income as well.* This income can become very important. At some point, at some day, and a day perhaps not so distant with a serious application of effort—complete financial self-sufficiency can well be had.

Listen to me. You will *never* cruise successfully unless you develop some smart business sense and the ability to make and save money. The experience of sailing will surprise you—everybody expects the "engineless" sailing experience to be a sort of "zen" laid back drift-about: hardly, you'll sail harder and more aggressive than ever before. Just as this is the case—even if you live in the most non-material way you'll have to learn to be shrewder than the most material cooperate executive. You've got to count your beans, even if it's just a few. This doesn't mean you've got to make a lot or save a lot, but you've got to know how to live within your means. Fortunately, the boat life is one place where the level of overhead can be very low.

Important!

You've got to always think ahead, in sailing, in boat handling, and in life. Remember, people go to the frontier to get ahead in life, *not* as a vacation. That was the case with me, and still is. Think! The sailboat is your frontier home, your bread and butter, and your save all fall back plan. That is all fine! But it's also your jailor to some degree, like any business venture might be, and there's going to come time where you'd like to get away. Mark my words: you're going to want to get off the boat after a while. You're going to want to take a vacation away from the sea. This is all good, so make sure you save your beans so that you can afford to do so. *You may even, at some point, decide you'd like a "vacation home" ashore*—some place to take a break from the rigors of the boat life and maybe even take a bath. Go for it! This isn't selling out on the boat life, this is *success in it!* You've achieved the dream—you've just done it backwards of what most people try to do. You can feel justifiably smug for pulling this little stunt off.

But even before you achieve this point, any income at all that is guaranteed and coming on a perpetual monthly basis is very, very valuable. It will come when one is working and when one is not, a precious little salt mill just grinding away. One can get by on *so* little money in many places, if one needs to, that very small amounts of cash can provide surprising amounts of security. It is indeed, a balance between earnings and spending. This is a unique environment where one has much control of both variables. Use this to your advantage! There are times when earning is good and spending is not, and times when spending goes a long way and earning is hard to come by. Take advantage of this! Have as much cash in your pocket as you can reasonably come up with, and don't spend a bit of it. This is the key to a life of freedom that will last you through the years.

Two Year Program for Escape!

Assumptions:	This plan assumes you're single, you're employed, earning a wage of between twice and three times minimum wage, that you live in a marine environment where the opportunities exist—that you don't live some place so expensive that you're broke all the time—that you've saved at least $5000 dollars with which you can make a move and you're ready to go.
	If you've got tons of debt you've dug yourself a big hole and you'll need to fill it somehow before you start on the Sea-Stead.
	If you've got no savings at all you should ask yourself as to why. Do you have the discipline for this style of life?
	Perhaps you've got none of this, and you're screwed, and you're desperate. Well, you can still make this all work but I probably can't legally advise you as to how. Necessity is the mother of invention, no? It's your life we're talking about…
	If nothing else, start saving some cash so you've got an option or two!
Month 1: Try to make this early in the year! Boats are cheapest in the winter.	Find a slip in a local marina that will be open for you. Find a boat for sale that can be had for less than a dollar a pound. It should be rough, but something you can sail if you need to. Purchase it and move aboard. Now you will have much more income at your disposal as you're not paying rent any more.
Month 2:	Start acquiring critical systems and supplies. Start with anchors, if and when you need to move or if you lose your slip. These will be expensive. Start research on learning basic repair skills, such as fiberglass work. If you can find yourself a sewing machine, get it, and practice.

Two Year Program for Escape! (Continued)

Month 3:	Begin basic repairs as you can afford materials and the weather permits. If the weather doesn't permit, keep with research and start really learning frugal living to keep your costs down. Rice!
Month 4:	If you're making progress, now is the time to consider whether or not you can be rid of your car. If you've gotten far enough that you can, do so, and use the equity to invest in the boat. You're going to need sails so start shopping. Headsails can be found second hand but you'll need to build a main yourself. Do this out of a kit the first time around.
Month 5:	Learn some sailing! Make a trip or two. Learn! At this point the weather is going to get worse soon so you'll be learning a thing or two. Insulate as things dry out or get wet—install the heat if you can. Continue with repairs and learn tactical sailing as you can. If you've applied yourself, you should be getting to the point that you can sail in and out of your slip pretty easily by now.
Month 6:	More of same! Enjoy the weather while it lasts. Save some money, right?
Month 7:	Try to have your sail suit built or acquired and ready to go. Take a longer cruise of a week or two if you can. Learn those anchoring skills, and start paying a lot of attention to weather. Do you have a shore boat solution worked out?
Month 8:	Get ready for colder temperatures or life will be hell. Finish any last repairs and pay a lot of attention to deck leaks or leaks around port holes. Start thinking about where you'd like to make your way in the world, and hook up with other sailors to find the good spots. By now you should have an idea of what you want.
Month 9:	If the boat needs a rig, you can do some of this while the weather is a little rough. At the very least replace the headstay. Go over the whole works and look for trouble. Budget for what you need. Make improvement in the leads of lines and cleats so the boat sails slicker.

Two Year Program for Escape! (Continued)

Month 10:	Save some money and start learning skills that will serve you in the Sea-Stead. You've already learned a good deal about boat repair and probably can handle canvas work. What else can you do to earn money underway? What else can you do to spend less?
Month 11:	The same. Take some classes if you need to. You've probably spent most everything you've made this year on the boat but make yourself a list of what you still need to break clear from the dock and be effective wholly underway. The level of complexity you have will depend on your budget. If you can't swing complicated, start right now on the very basic no motor, no electricity Sea-Stead. Make this workable and learn the skills. You'll be fine. You can always add these things later as you go along.
Month 12:	You've almost made the hump. You're dealing with bad weather perhaps, and it's best to just hunker down and learn to do everything better every day. Again, and again, save as much cash as you can. If you've got health benefits, use the hell out of them. Find a Doctor that will get you a ship's medicine chest!
Month 13:	The anniversary is past! If you're still hip on the whole lifestyle now is time to think about cutting loose from the dock. Is the boat capable? It isn't trick, for sure, but is it capable? If not, consider what needs to be done to do so and get on it.
Month 14:	As the weather is still poor figure out where you'd like to go as for the next step. Plan on going somewhere, even if it isn't far, just so you don't get stuck in a rut. It happens to a lot of people. Consider when you can quit your job! Oh yeah!
Month 15:	Continue with the plan. Try to time your departure so that you get a couple of months of good cruising in while the weather is nice, whenever that may happen to be for your area. Start acquiring charts, which can be more expensive than you think. How good is your weather reading by now? Study!

Two Year Program for Escape! (Continued)

Month 16:	Haul, paint, and pull the motor. Revel in the new found stowage you have, and be utterly amazed at how well the boat sails now that she isn't handicapped. Watch out for Captain Piddlemarks!.
Month 17:	Save that cash and be ready to bolt...
Month 18:	Bolt! Get some cruising in and find yourself a new home. Where? That's up to you.
Month 20:	You should really know your boat by now, and have some sailing ability. Can you handle coastal sailing? If so, you're in really good shape. If there are problems with the boat, get them fixed so that you can. Meet some new folks when you find that new home, and make a good effort to get hooked up.
Month 21:	If you haven't headed south, you're going to be facing another winter, so plan for it. Hunker down, put in a mooring or find a temporary slip, get some work ashore, and save cash for another season. Else wise, cruise in the tropics and live on mangoes!
Month 22:	Wonder why the hell you didn't head south?
Month 23:	Mangoes or work, it's up to you. Anyhow, be planning the next step...Be always afraid of being stuck in that rut. Always have a plan, a goal, and a destination. You must keep that dream alive. Be sure you connect with those that are engaged in the same dream. You'll find them, if you look. They're as hard up as you. Don't forget the Oar Club Website, right? We're eager to know what's going on.
Month 24:	You're a Sea-Steader, aren't you?

16

GETTING BY ON NEXT TO NOTHING

Frugality and practical ingenuity are the heart and soul of any successful frontier lifestyle. There are certain basic human needs that need to be met in any home to keep one's self sane, and a boat is no exception. In fact, boats offer unique problems, in some ways, to land based homes. First is simply the amount of useable space, second is the reality that there is an upper limit to the weight of stores, food, and fuel that one can carry. Third is that the sailboat must still sail, and any modification that is made to the boat must not effect sailing performance in any way. There are all sorts of widgets and devices available for many jobs—many of them require a lot of electrical power, which, on an non-auxiliary Sea-Stead you're not going to have. All of these "solutions" are a compromise in many ways, none are ideal, and all of them might call for other solutions in different circumstances. So than, rather than advise, I'll try to make you aware of the problems and let you know what we've done to solve them. At this point, we're pretty happy with the results. There's no system on MACHA that I didn't have on RENEGADE, so I've lived with all of these things for about ten years now, and I think they're pretty sensible.

Heat:

If you live outside the paradise of the warmer climates, which most of you will at least at some time, you're going to want some heat on your boat. A cold boat is misery indeed, and the long months of damp, wet, moldy misery will drive you to despair. Most "liveaboards" have very poor advice on how to keep boats warm, as they often live chained to docks and all one needs is a big power cord to fix this problem. Many cruisers only cruise when the weather is warm, so they have little advice to offer either. Most of the successful cabin heaters are forced air types that use waste engine heat—you may well not have this option either. Realize, however, that most of the really good, undeveloped, remaining Sea-Steading environments that still exist are chilly to cold places. You'll need heat. What then to do?

There are three lines of defense against cold: Heat generation, heat retention, and moisture elimination. If any of these lines are missing, you're going to suffer. Let's talk about heat retention first.

You're going to need to insulate the boat. If you for some reason have purchased a wooden boat, I have nothing to tell you. I don't know a good way to insulate a wooden boat, as anything I can think of is likely to be a rot trap and I wouldn't suggest it. True, wood itself is an insulator to some degree, but it is a poor insulator compared to foam types of insulation, and I think you're just going to be a bit colder, hence, skip ahead to discussion about big stoves, which, of course, will dry out a part of the boat if you're not careful, and make it prone to leakage.

Fiberglass hulls don't have this rot problem, or leak problem, of course, but they do sweat well. What does one do? Well, the best option I know for insulating a hull is to use a closed cell flexible foam such as Insulite and to contact cement this to the hull everyplace one sensibly can. The problem with Insulite, and it is the only problem, is that it is quite expensive. Still, in living spaces and on small boats where one is in contact with the hull surfaces, I think it is a good option. Go with at least a ½ inch all around, and potentially double that in the fore-peak if you sleep there. Do the overhead in the fore-peak if you can possibly do so.

On MACHA we used Insulite in exposed areas, but the rest of the hull living spaces are faced in 1.5 inch regular construction grade Styrofoam insulation—the kind with a plastic skin face. It is reasonably flexible and will stick with Liquid Nails or the like to the hull—we covered this with strip planked hull ceiling. In the fore-peak we did the overhead as well—and faced it all with aromatic cedar as well. Very nice, tight and dry. There are many ways to solve this insulation problem, but there are pit-falls. Make sure, especially, that whatever you use fits tight against the hull or you'll get condensation behind the insulation and grow mold in there like nothing else. I haven't, but one might consider an application of some mold killing paint in a few areas as well. Don't apply insulation over wood, as the same concern applies, you're likely to start rot there. If you have to, like in the case of plywood decks, be sure to seal the hell out of the wood with epoxy to make sure it doesn't matter. Be vigilant, and then you'll probably be ok.

Now for the heat itself. On RENEGADE I spent my first winter with one of those piddly little propane burning piece of crap heaters, you know the type. I routinely woke to a soaked, and sometimes frozen sleeping bag, and just about went nuts. Save yourself the trouble—install the biggest damn stove you can fit into the boat, and one with a real chimney flue. Don't worry about being too hot, you can always open a hatch.

There are really only two sensible systems that I can see for heating a boat. One is solid fuel—wood, coal, etc. The other is oil. I've lived with both, and both have advantages and disadvantages. Ideally, I could see a stove that might burn both, but haven't had the opportunity to build one yet.

On RENEGADE I had a small woodstove. It was a cast iron, two burner affair about the size of a mailbox with a 4 inch flue. It certainly dried the boat out and made as much heat as one could want. It was a bit filthy, with the ash, but if one was careful it worked fine. A couple of years into using it I became very clever and installed a couple of propane burners into it, so it could match light and burn solid fuel. This was very slick, as I could run on either propane or wood, and wet wood at that, for I'd use the propane to light it all. This was also very nice for getting rid of trash, food scraps, bacon grease or what have you—more useful than you now know. Lastly, I could use it as my chemical defense system—because as you all know it is written somewhere in the Bayliner manual that upon entering a completely open anchorage with one sailboat in it, that one must, repeat must, anchor within 30 feet of said sailboat and play country music for hours. Chemical defense system? I found that 120 weight crankcase oil burned really nice in that stove too, and made such an unholy smoke that no one could stand to be within a quarter mile. Especially on a cold, rainy, windless night that smoke really hung around—thick, greasy, stringy smoke—down below it was warm, bright, and cheery. Ah, I miss those days! I'd sit and drink my tea and make mental bets about how long they could take it.

Wood, by itself, however, is often too hot and then not so hot, and it takes a lot of skill to keep things going nicely. It can be done, however, and it works. Driftwood is not the best source of firewood, for certain, but it is free and not a bad option if one has time and not cash. Woodstoves for small boats can be hard to find now, but one shouldn't be afraid of welding one up custom to fit the place one might have. Remember, the wood stove is going to get good and hot at times—you'll want to keep any structure at least 6 inches away from any surface including the stack, and more is better. Mount it as low in the boat as possible to keep the heat down and the stack long..

Figure 30: MACHA's hearth.

Now we've got a diesel burning stove. This is very handy indeed, as it's nice to be able to light the stove, set a thermostat, and not worry about it. It draws some electricity to power a blower fan, but the fan uses such little current that I'd not worry about it, even on solar like ourselves, even in the winter. They say you can run these without the fan, but I'm not a believer. On very cold still nights the smoke can condense and soot up the stack, which, at two in the morning, will plug the stack and flood the cabin, with potentially lethal results. In any case, have a smoke alarm on board!

Now in the picture above you'll see a few things. First of all, the two stainless steel tanks above the stove, which are re-cycled fire extinguishers, are part of the system. One is the gravity feed fuel tank for the stove, and the other is a hot water tank. The stove itself has hot water coils inside of it and will make more hot water than you need—you can boil a 4 gallon tank in about an hour. This was a problem, so I installed a hydronic heating system to cycle the heat around the boat. The hot water leaves the stove coil, and rises in the copper pipe, continuing upwards into the forepeak to a set of coils well forward, forming a simple radiator above our bunk. From this point, the water is starting to cool a bit, and falls back into the tank, out through another pipe and to a radiator just above the cabin sole. Thus the water thermally cycles without any need for power.

This system works very nicely and distributes the heat well around the boat. As well, all coils are soldered with potable water grade solder and brazing compounds, so the whole provides hot tap water as well, which is a god-send in the cold winter months. A slick system, and one ought to give some thought to something similar.

The problem with oil—diesel, kerosene, or what have you, is that it is expensive. You can burn two gallons a day in this stove, to keep the boat barefoot comfortable, if it's really cold—say 10 to 15 degrees F. At this point, you might not care, but the budget will be strained. Of course, you might ask why one would be out sailing in these conditions, and true enough, that is a good question. But, if one is in the northern latitudes, the winters are like this. You've got to be prepared. Smarter, likely, is to take that money and sail south! Spend it on liquor rather than heat!

Note both stoves move a lot of air through a large flue. This is critical to keeping the boat dry. Both do so nicely, don't consider anything that does not. Remember, if you're at the dock, and you're going to go with electric heat for that first winter, that electric heat will not dry anything out at all. Seriously, do yourself a favor and spend whatever it takes to get the boat nice and warm. You'll end up crazy, single, or both, if you don't.

Forage Foods:

One thing that we get asked a lot is whether or not one can "live off the sea." I answer, of course, yes! The large question is whether one would want to. It is easy, in many areas, to make forage foods a large portion of one's diet, and that this can certainly supplement one's diet in a large and cost effective way. I enjoy fishing, especially, and it seems pretty simple to catch as much, or more, than one would want to eat.

So then, yes, for certain, with a big sack of rice and a few fishhooks one can get along a very long time for very little money, or none at all. Even if one can't catch fish, most people can handle catching clams, limpets, mussels and other things that don't run—you won't be starved for protein. There are, however, practical problems. First is the law, which might prohibit where and how you catch your meals. Licenses can be really expensive, and for certain cruises not cost effective. How much you care about the law is up to you, of course, and I wouldn't accuse anyone of a moral lapse for sneaking a clam or two, but if you get busted it can be a very big deal. Fortunately, where there is lots of law there are often very few fish, and the reverse is true as well, so one can get by with a little common sense.

The second problem is pollution. Clams, especially, which could and should be a large portion of a forage diet, especially susceptible. Again, the rule applies: lots of law, pollution, and crappy clamming are to be found in the same areas. Yes, again, forage foods can be a big part of one's diet, but to use them requires that one must be pretty far a field—more so than is easy to come by anymore.

The future is looking a little brighter, however, on this front, at least for the Sea-Steader. The reason for this is the price of oil, which, as I write, broke $60 a barrel for the first time yesterday. The price of fuel is making commercial fishing much more difficult, as it is hugely fuel intensive, and this coupled with declining stocks is going to put an end to the commercial viability of a lot of harvests—permanently. Fish-farming, for whatever you think about that, is the way of the future, for good or ill, and is *vastly* more cost effective. Shrimp fishing, especially, is a good example—as pond raised shrimp are cheap, a reasonably good product, and don't involve dragging nets on the bottom of the ocean killing everything with wild abandon. Hence, commercial shrimp fishing is really on its last legs. Salmon is not far behind. For the Sea-Steader this is only a positive development, as we don't need a ton of fish, we just need one or two, and it's nice not to have to compete with the 80 foot steel war-wagon from Sitka. Or the recreational fisherman, for that matter, who doesn't want to blow 100 bucks in gasoline to catch a crummy little rockfish. Hell, I've got all day, it doesn't cost me a dime, and that rockfish can taste pretty nice after a week or two of lentils and rice!

A skiff is just about a necessity for good fishing, as the sailboat is just too big and fast moving for good effect. As well, much of the good fishing is right in and among the rocks, a place where keels don't really belong. One person rowing and one person jigging is a time-honored and proven means for dinner for both! Watch out for the spiny sorts of fishes around inflatables. They can deflate you in no time!

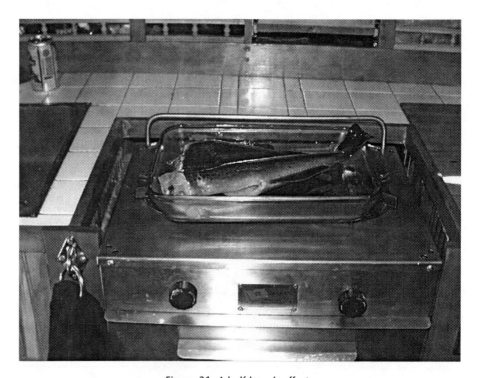

Figure 31: A half-hour's effort.

Fishing, forage, and subsistence gear:

Clams and Shellfish	A simple small rake is a very effective tool, as well as a regular clam shovel for the larger varieties such as horse clams. Many types can be gathered by had and varieties abound. Be ware of Paralytic Poisoning as well as pollution.
	Clams: Nice with pasta or simply steamed
	Horse Clams: The necks make exquisite sushi.
	Mussels: Served as clams
	Limpets: Easy to catch, even for stupid people. The small ones are the best as the large ones can get tough.
Crabs and Lobsters	Traps and snares work well. Can also be caught by clever folks while diving.
Fish	I don't believe you need much in terms of gear for most fishing. I swear you can catch everything with a heavy pole and either a black or white jig worm. In some areas the problem isn't so much catching fish as it is catching reasonable sized fish—what do you do with a forty pounder? Reef fish tend to be smaller a lot of the time than ocean or bottom fish.
	In coastal sailing it is often worth while to trail squid jigs for mackerel or tuna types.
	Scuba is very effective, with a Hawaiian sling, if you need to score fish for a crowd. You'll always nail the biggest thing down there.
	A skiff is just about a necessity for good jigging.

Fishing, forage, and subsistence gear: (Continued)

Kelps and Seaweeds	A little bit of this in meals eliminates just about any need for dietary supplements. Most all sea-weeds are edible, with very very few exceptions. The rule as I know it is this: Don't eat any grasslike or stringy seaweeds, and don't eat any that taste acidic or like bitter lemons. Otherwise, they're all fine to eat. If you're vegetarian, sea-weeds can eliminate the need for expensive manufactured protein.
Hydroponics and Seed Sprouting	Many types of *dwarf* plants can be grown aboard a boat to supply fresh foods while away from stores. The seeds required take up next to no space at all, and only minimum space and soil is needed for the plant types. Most dwarf hybrids have very short growth times and can be harvested in weeks, not months. The following work well and are available from specialty seed suppliers:
Continued...	Beets Radishes Tomatoes Eggplants Herbs of all types: especially basil, oregano, parsley and cilantro. Strawberries.

Fishing, forage, and subsistence gear: (Continued)

Seed Sprouting	Sprouting seeds in jars or trays can greatly diminish cooking time and need for fuel, as well as supplying fresh foods when none are to be had. I've had very good luck with the following. All will take a few days so think ahead. If you're just sprouting to cook, two days will suffice, or until you see the seed break. Get 4 or 5 jars and keep them cycling so you've always got something fresh. Build a rack for them if you need the space with clear circulation of air.
	Beans of all types, especially pinto and black beans. Chick peas Lentils
	Wheat: excellent meat substitute, even for me, and inexpensive. Wheat last a very long time in stowage and sprouts readily. Three day sprouts are good for salads and added into breads. I think you could live on this one
	Alfalfa, of course. Fenugreek
	Rinse carefully and beware of mold!
Water underway	We've not had any problem with water, as we either catch it or find it ashore. We treat all water as it joins tanks, needed or not. Rain catch systems do work if you take the time to be smart about it. We've got a through hull in the bottom of the cockpit that allows us to use it as a cistern, and we shed everything off the mainsail into it. If you think ahead, you can get a great deal of water this way. Filter it if you need to, it is way easier to filter fresh water than salt…Again, set the system up and test it. The improvational systems are less than effective.
	I've built solar stills, and they do work, but I've found them inconvenient and prone to failure as the acrylic faces are very hard to keep sealed. The stills get hot, and the plastic expands hard. Be careful of any design that doesn't take this issue seriously.

Fishing, forage, and subsistence gear: (Continued)

Dehydrating Food	I've done a great deal of this and it is a nice way of preserving those windfalls that you can't keep otherwise. Dehydrated food lasts well if properly prepared. In northern climates you'll need to build a dryer with a heat source in it or things will mold, but if the ambient weather is warm and dry trays will work, but still heat is useful. A solar hanging tray system with a black cotton cover works quite well and keeps the bugs and birds away. Make it large enough to process a useful amount of food, perhaps 10 pounds raw. This will require at least 20 square feet of screen space.
	Store dehydrated food in plastic bags. If you put little bits of dry ice in the bags as you close them, you'll drive all the air out and food will last a very long time indeed. Another solution, which we use, is to use the air out of a scuba tank, as it's had the moisture removed to keep the interior of the tank from rusting.
	We dry fruits, vegetables, mushrooms, and some meats. Even fish can be dried nicely if the weather permits, but it must be warm and dry indeed. The thinner you slice things the faster they both dry and reconstitute, so good clean preparation is important to good results.
Solar Ovens	The use of a solar oven is not to be underestimated, as there are times where cooked foods are to be desired, perhaps even baked goods, and to do so below in the interior of the boat would be uncomfortable for certain. Designs abound, so find one that fits the stowage area and capacities that you expect you will need.

Fishing, forage, and subsistence gear: (Continued)

Pressure Cooker	The pressure cooker is indeed a god-send to the sailor, and well worth learning to use. If you're a meat eater, like us, and poor, you'll find the first use you appreciate is the ability to transform tough cuts into very nice tender meals. This alone is worth a lot. Use of the pressure cooker for other things, as soups that might have extended cooking times, is also valuable. We use ours perhaps not daily but close. If you can, get one large enough that you are able to can with, so the day you nail that huge fish you've got something you can do with it.
	If your boat is too small for an oven, the pressure cooker can fill that need too. If you get one, get a good one, and the biggest one you can fit on your stove. You'll be glad you did.

Provisioning without refrigeration:

Let's talk about provisioning for a voyage. I have never seen a good book on provisioning—I think it is a lost art. Everybody seems to assume that you've got refrigeration, something that is completely unsustainable on a Sea-Stead. I've had none for 10 years now, so think I've got a knack or two for going without it which I'm going to share with you—but as it is with so many things, again one must understand what one is doing before one understands how to do it.

I learned to provision as a backpacker. This activity teaches one frugality like nothing else; as I've said before, if the load is on your ass you generally pay more attention to it. Let's take some of those lessons and apply them to sailing.

One really doesn't learn much about backpacking unless one has a transit in excess of 150 miles or so in one shot in tough country. Less than that, one doesn't need to provision: one's probably got enough fat in one's butt to stumble through the backcountry for that long and suffer no ill effects—even if one didn't eat a thing. That would be pretty unpleasant, however, so don't think I'm suggesting it. At 150 miles, two weeks or so, things change. One gets off borrowed time. Actually, there are not many places in the world anymore where a guy can walk for two weeks in one direction and not hit a place where he can resupply unless he's trying to make things difficult. I know of only two in the United States. The issue really doesn't come up much, but we'll talk about it anyway. It will teach us something about sailing.

Say we have a transit in high alpine country that will take 14 days to cross. Say a lot of it is trail-less and tough, so one needs real boots and can't get away by going really light and just running; that risks injury anyway. It can snow too, so one needs real clothes and gear. It is easy to carry too much and/or too little, either is a serious mistake. Carry too little and one is forced to move unpleasantly and irresponsibly fast. Carry too much and one won't cover enough distance before one runs out of supplies. Either mistake risks injury and is a good way of ruining knees.

So setting aside gear weight, let's concern ourselves with food. First, one cannot provision properly unless on knows how much one eats, and how much one will eat in a given environment. People are really sloppy about this; I suppose this is because the presence of the refrigerator provides for a convenient place to let food rot, but there really is no reason why, with a little practice, one cannot cook a meal that provides as much as one wants but no more, and there is no waste. I never have food waste, ever. It can be done. So if one is interested in provisioning; practice—it really doesn't take practice so much as just paying attention—until one can predict ones appetite within a tablespoon. It's surpassingly easy. As a rule of thumb, which works even for people I don't know most of the time; people in an active environment eat the equivalent of ½ pound dried food per meal as a base; that is 1/2lb past, rice, flour, lentils, beans, whatever. These are big portions, for big guys. Size down if you need too, but to call it a ½ pound or a pound and a half per day per person is a decent guess.

Also, be sure you take a look at what it takes to cook a meal in totality. This means food, fuel, and water—all of which are necessary to figure when provisioning. A good example of this, if ignored, could lead to trouble. Soybeans, which I hate and never eat anyway, are generally touted as a excellent nutritional source. Lots of protein, lots of calories. Here's the problem: they have to be cooked so long in order to be digestible that one uses a tremendous quantity of fuel. Oh boy—don't ever try to eat them undercooked—remember Challenger? You'll feel like that or worse.

Anyhow, soybeans need to have the hell cooked out of them or to be sprouted or otherwise processed in some pain in the ass way. This makes them pretty unpractical for a boat. By the way, an interesting lesson in this and a great thing to taunt your vegan friends with (not really, no one ever really has a vegan *friend*) is the details on the huge amount of carbon intensive fuels that need to be burned to make tofu...

Seriously, fuel for cooking is a reasonable concern, unless one makes the mistake of transforming ones boat into a tanker of sorts. Makes beans look bad for extended voyages and things like lentils look better ever if they're more calorie poor. If you sprout them you greatly decrease their cooking time but it takes a bit to get used to the flavor. At any rate don't starve yourself either: we're going frugal, not acetic. Cook what you like but be aware of the costs and the limitations it may impose upon you. Fish a bit and catch some extras.

One must compare food value in not only weight per calorie, but quality per calorie, and cost per calorie. This is really tricky but if you're interested in it makes for an interesting study. A case example, once again, from backpacking. No one believes me on this, so check it out for yourself to see—this makes an good point. Hikers and even the military now (which should know better) have been sold on the freeze-dried food stuff that is really expensive. Everyone thinks freeze dried food is the best, because it is so light. So barring the absolutely fraudulent stuff, like freeze dried pasta—uh, I thought that was dry to begin with—it is indeed light in weight, especially the meats, largely because the fats have been removed in the processing. This, of course, turns this stuff into food lint and is practically worthless. If for, example, one compares the best freeze dried meats around with a can of "Spam," there are quite a few more calories in a can of Spam, more well balanced calories for someone out in the wet and cold, even including the weight of the can! Sure, not gourmet far, but neither is. The difference is this, however, eat a can of Spam and you'll stay warm longer than if you eat a block of meat lint. This may matter to you in the middle of some night on a tough beat rounding Pt Conception. Or above the snowline, where I first learned about it.

Another example: peanut butter. The calories per weight are great, and so is the price. But in reality, peanut butter isn't very digestible to a lot of people, so you may only get half the calories out of it. That makes it not looks so good. My system, however, burns it like rocket fuel so I usually carry a lot of it.

My baseline? These figures are generous and work like clockwork for my crew and I.

1 gallon of water a day
2 pounds of food and goodies per day
5 oz of fuel, per day.

Now most backpackers will look at these figures and thing this is really reasonable, "living it up" even, but a typical yachtsman will think it impossible. It sounds that way: 3000 miles in 30 days-needing 30 gallons of water and 60 pounds of food, and a gallon of propane, for a total weight of 300 pounds or so; in round figures 10 pounds a day per person. Obviously the big figure is water and if one can cut that back by cooking in salt water, etc.—one can go a really long way in a really small boat. Face it, a 30-day passage is a long one, and few people ever do that. Provisioning just doesn't need to be a problem. On MACHA we've got tanks for 150 gallons of water—which in essence means a long time without support at all.

So what do we eat? Well, we have a rice, beans, lentils kind of diet—all of which store very well on a boat, are good for you and are as cheap as dirt. Actually cheaper, if you're talking potting soil. We do carry canned foods but mostly canned meats, and a few treats, but whatever it is it must justify its own weight. I can't imagine stuff like canned soup: can one really justify carrying cans of salt water on a boat?

Again, we have no refrigeration and need none. If I carried fresh milk—which I don't—I suppose I'd need one but I've been without refrigeration for years and I can't imagine needing it. Most wholesome food is quite resistant to spoilage—even fresh meat will last for days if cool. I've never has eggs go bad, never treated short of rubbing a little petroleum jelly on them and kept them for months, but if it were really hot I'd use them up. I've seen far too many vegetables ruined by refrigeration, or worse, iceboxes. Keep them cool and dry, the dry part being tough to do in an icebox, and the best will last six months, like the onions I've got hanging out right now; not because they're rotten, but they want to turn into plants now, so they need to get fried.

Cheese lasts a very long time. I love it and carry a lot, mostly hard white varieties of low grade bought in bulk: these being dry and mild lend themselves to keeping and eating. There's a dozen different ways of keeping mould off of cheese. I can't recommend any because I've never needed to use any other than the occasional careful trimming. Once again, my weather is cooler than yours might be and if I lived in the Tropic of Rot I'd likely have to be a bit more careful.

One last trick I find super useful—salt junk. Yes indeed, keeping meat packed in salt like sailors of long ago. This works exceedingly well. Yes, I too have heard the horror stories of salt junk, but seeing no alternatives to going without such useful foods such as bacon and other cured meats, I thought I'd give it a tentative try. What I did is create my own little salt barrel out of a five gallon plastic bucket and packed about 15 pounds of bacon in it buried in salt. How long does it last? I have no idea; nothing has spoiled inside of a year—I've always ate it before that but that's usually when I'm about four months into the game. I'm not sure bacon or meats stored like that in a quality fashion will ever truly spoil—but they might get a bit like boot leather finally and become increasingly unpalatable. I'm sure if things ever got wet they'd rot quick. After not too long this gets too salty to eat for breakfast straight up, though absolutely excellent for soups and stews. Soaking meats in water a bit pulls most of the salt out. On my next experiment I may pack it in a salt/sugar mix and this may help the versatility. TRY IT.

Figure 32: Produce drawer. Notice coarse screen drawer bottom to allow good circulation of air.

◆   ◆   ◆

And back by infamously popular demand, here's that recipe for one hell of a fine sailor's meal. This makes a highly indulgent and filling meal for 1 big guy.

1 can Jack Mackerel

2 Tablespoon minced garlic
4 tablespoons olive oil
One bottle tawny port wine

Half handful of dried vegetables, any, what ever—but I hate peas.
Just enough tomato paste to taste, this works out to be about ½ of those little cans.
Bread, crackers, or sea biscuits
Some Hungarian paprika.

Open the bottle and start sucking on it. A glass? You must be joking…

Sauté the fish, oil and garlic together. If you bought really cheap fish like I usually do there'll be a bunch of pressure-cooked bones in there which bothers some people, so, if you're one of those, mash them all up as you stir.

Once this is pretty well cooked up, add some water to it to make about the volume you want to eat, and then once this boils, pitch in the handful of veggies. You could use fresh too, doesn't matter. In about 15 minutes this will be pretty well cooked up—add some bits of bread or crackers to thicken it up. If some dock bum smells it at this point and invites himself over, you can add a bit for him too. If it's too thick, add some water. It isn't critical.

Add tomato paste and paprika. Salt and Pepper to taste.

Boy-oh-boy! This is a manly meal—best on a particularly grim night. If you get it right you'll enter a transcendent state-you sing odes to sack-you will find wisdom and peace. Your breath, however, with be a zone effect contraceptive so plan accordingly.

Note: Most women hate this recipe and think it tastes like puke.

The Reflux Still:

Now I'm going to really do it. If you don't think I'm nuts already, you're about to. One of the biggest obstacles to success in the Sea-Steading venture is the cost of alcohol. If you don't drink—good for you. Things will be easier. But if you're like most sailors who think that alcohol is the lubricant that greases the gears of life—the costs at times will be staggering. Rightly so, too, I think the taxes on booze and cigarettes are half of what they ought to be, and doughnuts, soda pop, and other shit like that should be taxed as well. Still, on our last trip to Canada, a bottle of Budweiser was almost six bucks at a pub, and a price like this will give even a thirsty drunk pause.

So, the solution? Really embrace the frontier image and build a still. No kidding, I shit you not. A small reflux still can turn cheap fruit into high grade vodka with ease, and gin with a bit of know how. Most anywhere bad fruit can be had for free, sugar is cheap—use a wine yeast and you're good to go. You don't care a bit what's in the mash, as long as it's obviously not toxic, as you're just making pure, super clean booze which you're then going to cut with distilled water. It's all good in fruit juice, later, and will allow you to indulge your habit without breaking the bank. As well, you'll be amazed at the friends you'll make, as the gift of a bottle of booze is something that anyone in the world (that you'd want to be friends with) will appreciate, especially somewhere where it is expensive.

A ten gallon pot still full of sludge should make about 10 percent alcohol crud, which will distil to about a gallon of 180 proof vodka, once it's been run through a few times and been made good and clean. A gallon of 180 proof booze is *plenty* for some time, with some left over to give away.

Plans for these things abound on the web, and there are people who are greater experts than I. Find a design that fits on your stove top. The distilling process is stinky, but not too bad, so don't panic about that. You could always do the job on the beach if you needed too, which is an occasion for a grand party.

Legality varies. Owning the still won't bring you grief, only using it. Pay attention and be discrete. Most places allow you to distill for fuel purposes. If that's the case, do it, use it your lamps and stove, and just be really sure no one drinks any of it, right?

Figure 33: Sparrow makin' bacon. Note the sprouted beans on the counter.

Basic produce staples to have on board and how to stow them:

Apples	-I don't eat a lot of fruit but some people do. Apples go a long time. Green and firm apples last the longest and we both prefer them.
Asparagus	-We get it in season or pick it where we find it. It doesn't last well at all. We both think it's pretty rotten canned.
Avocados	-We'd eat these until we popped. Very important to keep from bruising. They don't keep too well unless really green. The fact is we eat them faster than they spoil anyhow.
Bananas	-They keep well. If in growing area be sure they're not full of the worst sort of nasty bugs.
Black Beans	-Cheap and our favorite. They cook fast from dry and are not bad canned either. All beans can be sprouted to reduce cooking time.
Garbanzo Beans	-Or chick peas, we use them mashed in hummus and in salads. They are very fine sprouted and raw for salads.
Navy Beans	-The backbone of bean soup with a bit of salt junk for flavor.
Fava Beans	-Raw and dipped in olive oil
Kidney Beans	-In cans for chile. I don't like them much.
Refried Beans	-We use refried beans in two forms, from cans or dehydrated. Both have advantages. If from cans the flavor is more traditional. The dehydrated ones are good and nice to through in as a quick thickener for soups.
Beets	-When we get them. Love them pickled.
Broccoli	-I've never had any luck storing it for more than a few days. It's expensive anyhow. Once a plant gets up to a certain cost we'd rather eat an animal.
Carrots	-I hate them, basically, but they keep and I'll eat them grudgingly.
Cabbage	-We both love cabbage. It keeps well until cut so buy small tight heads. If you peel leaves rather than cut for usages it helps as well. It can be buggy in places. Cabbage rots fast if at all dank. Try slabs of it fried in oil with soy sauce!

Basic produce staples to have on board and how to stow them: (Continued)

Cauliflower	-Again, much expense like an animal.
Celery	-I hate celery and it rots, all to the better. Celery seed, however, is indispensable around here for flavoring soups.
Corn	-I like corn canned or prepared. Corn on the cob isn't so good as it's buggy and takes up a lot of room.
Cucumbers	-They keep well if cool and clean.
Eggplants	-Don't expect them to last very long. Types vary as well, small ones go longer. Bruising rots quickly
Garlic	-Ah, the stinking rose! We use a lot of it and it stores well if kept dry.
Grapes	-if you find them. Eat them quick. Seem to draw a lot of flies that end up on everything else.
Grapefruits	-Buy dense firm ones. They last pretty well like all citrus fruit.
Lemons	-Often very cheap. I love them and the good ones I eat like oranges. People wrap them in foil, but I never have so I can't comment on that.
Limes	-Ditto. Often use lime juice as potent antibiotic.
Mangoes	-Can't keep them because I'll eat them until I blow mango out my ass.
Melons	-If they're available. We've little experience with them.
Mushrooms	-Dirt fruit! We love mushrooms and I've spent a good deal of time picking them in the Pacific Northwest. It is well to learn to do so if you're in the area. Chanterelles and Boletus are safe places to start. Know what you're doing as there are deadly ones too. Eat them fresh or immediately dry. Dried mushrooms are often better. Can be very cheap at Chinese markets. We keep some on board as well but are frightened at times when dealing with customs, as they do look suspicious. Be careful with that and stick to the more common varieties when crossing borders.

Basic produce staples to have on board and how to stow them: (Continued)

Onions	-buy firm onions and peel. They go well but don't put them near apples. Who knows why they don't get along. Dried onions are fine.
Oranges	-as all citrus.
Peas-black eyed	-These make a fine soup much like navy bean.
Peppers	-Know your types or get your head blow off. They last a good while if un-bruised and dry.
Potatoes	-We eat a lot of potatoes. Potato soup with salt junk bacon is a staple, and fried for breakfast with the same as well. We find that smaller, tighter, denser potatoes last longer than big baking types. Keep in a dark and cool place and watch for sprouts. I hate sweet potatoes and forever will, but you'll see a lot of them around the world.
Squashes of variety	-They keep for ever, it seems like. I don't use them much but like them tossed in curry dishes and the like.
Tomatoes	-Canned tomatoes are good, dried tomatoes are good, green tomatoes can be easily pickled in a hot brine and are very useful that way. They last longer than you will expect. Protect them by wrapping them in newspaper.
Tomatillos	-Much the same treatment, great in salsa and cheap.

Water and Keeping Clean:

A Sea-Stead must have adequate tankage to support its crew on the passage that it is designed to make. We've already suggested a gallon of water per person a day—one can do with less but it becomes tight. Obviously one can do dishes in salt water, and clothing as well, but the salt keeps clothes dank and not comfortable—it takes so much fresh water to wash the salt out that it doesn't seem very practical. One must be careful of salty clothing for long period as sores are reality and salty clothes don't help. The key is to have big tanks and to water up as often as possible, especially where it's free for the taking. In the winters of the northern latitudes a bit of creativity with a rain catch system will provide more water than you can use—some people are afraid of caught water as being dirty but not to worry. Run the rainwater through a filter if you need to and chlorinate with a 5%

bleach solution, at a rate of ½ teaspoon for 5 gallons. Perhaps double this if it must sit in tanks for a while as the chlorine leaves the water at a rapid rate. We treat all water, regardless of the source, before it enters our tanks, as they are large enough that water stays in them for quite a period of time and we've had it go slightly green on us.

A mild bleach solution bath for fresh produce goes a long way to reducing mold growth. We use this on all firm skinned produce.

Showers are a hassle and it's nice to get them ashore when you can. If you can't, a pressurized weed sprayer is a very nice alternative to an installed unit, and if you've waterproofed your head with a drain to the bilge, a very practical and low cost solution. If you can, and the weather is moderate, it's far nicer to clean off in the cockpit, but in the interest of not being raunchy you should have a down below solution.

Hauling water in jugs isn't the most fun in the whole world. Plan ahead, and do it when it is convenient. If you're hardcore and get to row on every trip you'll like it less. This is where the Phase Three Sea-Stead or group effort can really be worth a lot, as a big communal skiff would be very valuable. As well, it seems to me that most of the time water makers for small boats are unsustainably expensive and impractical, but one that could service a fleet of boats makes a great deal more sense. But, as of yet, we'll leave that for the future.

Electrical Power:

Our power demands are very modest, and we use two 50 watt semi-flexible panels to provide all of our power. I've always kept the policy of making sure that my boat was capable of functioning in complete absence of electrical power, hence the solar panels, batteries, and convenient electronics are only just that—conveniences. They are truly helpful, however, and I'd hate to be without, but if the system were to fail, we'd have backup for everything.

I think this is a good policy. I advise a good quantity of quality oil lamps on board, of a rugged enough type that they could be used for running lights if you needed to. Interior electric lights are nice, for sure, as to live under an oil-only mood all the time can get a bit moody indeed. Navigation electronics use so little power that it would be hard to get a deep cycle battery so dead that it wouldn't run them—but make sure you can do without. Get that sextant and know what you're doing!

Figure 34: Our pair of 50 watt Solara panels. These are semi-flexible types with a non-skid face. They provide all of our power. Yes, you can walk on them but we make an effort not to as it can't really do them any favors.

I think you'll find running lights to be your biggest current draw. When I built MACHA I installed fancy LED lights all around. They were expensive, and didn't last six months before they fell apart. So, we've got the regular bulbs now, which use too much power, but I'm going to wait a bit to try the LED thing again.

We use an oil lamp for a anchor light, and it is really the best option, besides looking classy. We hang it under the boom. I think this is better too, because I've always found masthead lights hard to see as they blend in with the stars. I've got a friend that uses a Tiki torch for a anchor light, which has got an image to it for certain, but makes some good sense in an area where bugs abound and you burn the anti-bug oils.

My navigation lamp for underway at night is oil as well. Most crew find it much easier to sleep around oil lamps than electric anyhow.

The Head:

Marine heads are truly obnoxious devices. They stink, the complicated structure doesn't lend itself to cleanliness, and they're prone to leakage, plugging, and failure. I hate them, but we've got one of the big bronze Skipper heads on MACHA, and I must say, it is the best and most rugged of any that I've used. Still, it is a hassle, and there is no getting around it.

Holding tanks are trouble too, as you're required to have them but no one is required to have pump-out stations that work or are reasonably accessible. For a sailboat, the hassle of the pump-out is very large and you'll get very tired of the issue. To get a slip, however, in most marinas will require an approved head with a holding tank and locked valves preventing accidental discharge. Some will allow porta-potty arraignments and I've found these workable, but not all marinas approve. Hauling the container down the dock is much easier to deal with than moving the whole boat, and you'll find you'll fill it slowly if you're wise and if you do your personal purging elsewhere you'll need to purge the boat less.

One will quickly discover that for all things considered, while cruising, not many solutions to this problem beat the traditional cedar bucket. I'm going to go that route as soon as I get a regular partner talked into it, which hasn't happened yet, but is getting closer for sure. They're much cleaner, they don't plug (unless you're *really* a champion) and they don't involve through-hulls. The sole problem that I see with them is that a trip and fall in the companion way on the way out for the flush could really be trouble—but I suppose this reality would be present enough on each usage to cause a bit of prudent caution.

The "bucket and chuck it" method is uncouth for marinas, however, and probably not a good option there, unless you really hate your neighbor. I have a friend, however, who will remain nameless, that installed a little seat in his head that a standard five gallon paint bucket would just slide beneath. He found a place in town that had these for sale, and for less money, he felt, than the treatment "blue de-stench" stuff would cost him for a porta-potty. So, he'd buy a new bucket, once a week or so, and he'd crap her full. Once it was full, or when he just couldn't stand its persistent presence anymore, he'd put the lid on it and cart it up the dock—pitching it in the dumpster—much to the outrage and dismay of the marina dumpster divers. Hey, whatever works, I guess. Anyhow, you'll need some solution and it pays to be creative, as there really isn't any good one.

Whatever you do, unless you want to be single forever, try to install in the boat some closet or such for the bucket business or the head proper as crapping in company strains the relationship and just putting a bag over one's head for privacy isn't too effective in fooling anyone, as everybody knows as to what you're up to.

The law is heavy and the penalty for being busted for overboard discharge is extreme: be careful and take this seriously. Really, if it's a big deal, just go shit on the beach, because if you were to do so in your boat and pump it overboard, you're potentially facing thousands, maybe tens of thousands, of dollars of fines. Shit on the beach, in the marina parking lot; hell, on the hood of the harbormaster's car for that matter, and you'll only get a ticket for some silly thing. In reality, however, I find it ridiculous in the extreme for people to worry about my pissing in the ocean. Every study ever conducted about the impact of boater waste has found that except for the most bizarrely crowded harbors—where you wouldn't go anyway—boater waste is difficult to detect let alone count as a problem, and the vast vast majority of pollution comes from septic systems ashore, agricultural run-off and development. Seals, dogs, seagulls, geese, and the rest create just as much shit or more as people, and it's nearly impossible to separate the impact of this from the impact of the boater. Still, you're a target, as you're the easy "solution" for law enforcement, so beware. It would really be a shame to lose your home and your livelihood over a turd

Tools:

It is very important to remember the motif of the homestead and the frontier again: what sort of tools would one bring to the frontier with them? Assuming repairs might be six months away or financially unaffordable, would one incorporate a tool into the homestead lifestyle that would cause failure if lost, stolen, or broken? Not to say that one should not take advantage of such tools; be an enormous convenience—but rather to never, ever *rely* on such tools. One must face such issues with serious integrity.

The auxiliary motor is one such tool. Even if one disagrees with me and chooses to keep an inboard engine, one *must not* be come dependent on it. In order to *demonstrate* that one is not reliant on this convenience, <u>one *must* sail wholly without the use of it for some period of time, and completely develop the skills to do without</u>. If this is not done, the auxiliary motor remains a necessity, not a convenience, and so is a dangerous liability. It is a doubly dangerous liability to deny the existence of this liability. If you're going to have a motor, have a back-up if the motor fails. This back-up *isn't* the sailing rig, as the sailing performance is probably too hampered to be helpful in that pinch, and you've not earned the skills. *You'll need an extra motor, and one big enough to be useful.* Can you afford that? We have discussed this at length.

Electronic navigational items are another potential issue. Certainly less invasive and expensive than motors, at least in this day and age—they too can easily become necessities, and not conveniences. Can you pilot successfully and confidently without the GPS and the depth finder? If not, the failure of either is dangerous. Build a lead line, learn basic triangulation—and when one can perform these skills easily and confidently, and only then, can one accurately judge the value of these items.

In all cases we should ask ourselves:

Is the tool needed at all?

Can an increase skill level eliminate the need for the tool?

If the tool is incorporated, will the use of it diminish currently possessed skills due to lack of use?

Is the loss of the tool capable of putting an end to the Sea-Stead?

Can one justify the cost and the resultant loss of income?

Tools I think you would be really happy to have aboard:

Brace and Bits	A good brace and a set of standard auger bits are very useful when away from shore power. They'll drill fiberglass actually quite well.
Chisels	A good solid firmer and a couple of others. Good ones are expensive and almost impossible to find. Look second hand.
Drill	12 volt cordless drills can run off your batteries direct without an inverter, with a little creativity. Drilling stainless steel will be hard without one.
Drill bits	Probably better go cobalt all the way around. Expensive. A luxury item worth considering is a drill bit sharpener. If you've got much work to do you'll pay for it quickly.
Epoxy and fillers	Necessary. Carry some underwater type epoxy such as Z-Spar Splash Zone for emergencies. I like System Three for regular work. Silica is a good all around filler, but wood flour looks nicer. Micro balloons are only for fairing work. I only carry the fast hardeners as it seems, I never work on boats except when it's cold. Maybe I'll change my ways.
Grinder	Necessary for fiberglass work
Hack-saw	Got to have this. Since it's going to be used mostly for stainless, carry fine tooth blades. If you need to cut wire, you'll find you can easily if you wrap first in masking tape and saw through the tape.
Japanese Back-saws	These are precise saws for woodworking. They are very sharp and fast cutting, even in hard woods and plastic. Available at most tool suppliers now. Carry a couple of types, but I use fine tooth saws the most.
Lanolin or Bag-Balm	For lubrication and anti-seize, as well as leather dressing
Mapp gas torch	For soldering, brazing, and burning ends on line, even if they're wet.
Needles and Palm	You've got to have this, at least, for sail repair and whippings on lines.
Porter Cable Quick-Sand	The nicest sander I know of. You'll use it.

Tools I think you would be really happy to have aboard: (Continued)

Screwdrivers	Very hard to get nice ones, so carry a few of the types with re-placable tips. Carry a lot of tips.
Seizing wire	For shackles and repairs. Monel is nice.
Sewing Machine	Very useful and a source of income if you can carry it aboard. They do not draw much power and can be used on small inverters. The hand crank ones work well too. Go with a heavy one, not a dress-makers machine!
Scuba gear	This is expensive, alright, and bulky. It needs to be maintained, which is expensive too. Invaluable in certain circumstances, however and can be a source of income
Wrenches	In all the sizes you need, and of a couple of types. If you've got no engine, now is the time to start gloating. These kits are cheap in the US and make nice gifts when cruising, as every guy in the whole world can use a new set of wrenches. A big quality pipe wrench is good too.
Vise-grips	Do the impossible. I could not live without. Have a number of sizes, especially the big jawed pipe size.

Oddball Really Useful Stuff:

Flashlight	A really big spotlight for getting the attention of other boats, because running lights don't work. They make rechargeable cordless ones that are handy. Very useful for odd jobs and roaming through dark lockers also.
Hand planes and draw knives	If you need them, they're invaluable…
Hand swagers	For pressing Nicopress in small gauges of wire, up to ¼ inch. Very useful for all sorts of stuff and can be profitable too.
Wire cutters	For rigging work. The big ones with 3 foot handles. They won't cut chain.

Figure 29: Dive gear is a good example of expensive but potentially very useful gear aboard a Sea-Stead.

17

REVISITING THE RIDDLE

Now that you've stuck with me for this far you must have more than a little interest in the Sea-Steader's lifestyle. Good! It is indeed a wonderful, rewarding life, and even in the worst moments I ask myself what else I would do if I didn't live the way I do. Still, there are those worst moments, and I want to caution you. You'll be surprised, I think, of what our troubles have been.

It hasn't been bad weather or storms that have threatened to put me out of commission. Nor has it been finances. Reefs, rocks, and whirlpools neither. I've gotten tired of the cold and the rain, which is why we want to leave for warmer climates, but the weather in itself wouldn't put me ashore either. Actually, there is a single greatest problem, and one that is seldom spoken of. We've talked about it already, but we're now to put this difficulty in practical context. This problem isn't a new one, and has been the wolf at the door of frontiersmen since the beginning.

The problem, of course, is alienation and loneliness.

You will need to realize that the choice to Sea-Stead is a very encompassing project. Again, hardly a vacation: it's going to end up more or less being your *career*. You'll be busy. At first, when you get started, no one will believe you're serious. After a while, people will, partners will too, and will begin to grow uneasy. The life of a Sea-Steader is a *very* counter-culture lifestyle. It is so counter culture that it is nearly what might be terms "extra-cultural"—it is a choice very much against what most everyone else chooses. It is a choice to bet, in fact, on the failure of the conventional lifestyle. You're betting that within the average every-day work-a-day life happiness and fulfillment *can't be had*. You're expecting no improvement in this state of affairs. You probably don't see much of a future. You may well, rightly, expect turmoil and economic collapse. You may well expect violence and upheaval. You are, again, *betting* that these developments will occur—and you're checking out in search of a better life. Everyone at some level understands this, and, at some level, most people perceive your choice against *their* choice to carry a certain level of insult in it. They may well agree with you, inwardly, but simply be too cowardly to attempt what you attempt. They will resent you for your strength. Again, this is bound to cause you a certain amount of alienation.

Sea-Steaders are rare. Most people that cruise do so for weekends and holidays, and their life is still within the culture at large. A large portion those who cruise extended periods of time are wealthy retirees, obviously people again who have a good deal of investment within the values of the culture at large. Much of the world hates the American Yachtsman, and, I've got to admit, so do I. There is an awful lot of affluent, ignorant, materialistic, self-entitled arrogance in this crowd. The people tend to be "important" sorts in their shore life and tend to feel that they're "important" sorts everywhere they go. We had a distasteful encounter with a boatful of these last summer. Two couples on a new 50 foot plastic fantastic sailboat. They motor into the harbor, and proceed to anchor square in the middle of the local ferry lanes, less than 500 feet from the ferry dock itself. The ferry boat comes in, all 300 feet worth, and wiggles itself around them and into the dock. The ferry captain, on the loud hailer no less, tells them (and the whole island) that "they've chosen a very bad spot for their anchorage and it would be nice if they moved.) But, hell, they're in the middle of cocktails and nothing doing. The ferry leaves again, they decide dinner in town would be nice and leave the boat un-attended in the same spot. Mind you, this isn't a crowded anchorage, there are only two boats at anchor, they and us—we're about ¾ of a mile a way. We run into them at the pub as they sip their beverages and whatever—unfortunately they recognize us and feel like they'd like to talk to the "cute couple on the nice little gaff cutter"—no joke, their words! We talk a bit—I'm not too supportive of the conversation but no matter. They're Real Estate developers, one couple in Sun Valley, Idaho and the other couple in the Virgin Islands—two places where, of course, we desperately need even more development. Sparrow, my partner at the time, finally, exercising all of her natural Kodiak Island tact, tells them that the ferry is likely to run their mother fucking boat over and that the captain wants it moved. The response? "Oh well, they got around us once and I'm sure they can again" and "we can take care of that after dinner." And so they do. Two more ferries come They motor across the bay and anchor, of course, right up against us.

You'd better be in the mind to not let this sort of encounter get to you, because it can be a pretty common experience and you'll be pissed off daily. These people set the stage for you and give you your reputation. This is rough, and you've got to go some distance to make sure people can see you're not this kind of ass. What is still rougher yet to stomach, I believe, is this: Sometimes sailing is hard. Sometimes you've got to really work to get places. This is to be expected. But what was hard for me to stomach from the start, and is still hard to stomach, is to have a hard day of sailing and to get to an anchorage, only to find it *packed full* of these sorts of folks. This is disheartening, and will impact your experience if you let it. It is no different than for a mountain climber to struggle up a peak, risking life and limb, and upon making the summit, not finding the reward of vista and solitude for your discomfort but rather a Wal-Mart parking lot. You'll have to swallow hard to like it. I don't think you'll ever learn to do so.

With the "sailing" crowd, as well, if you follow my good advice and go with at straight sailing vessel, you'll be surprised to find that people are going to give you a good bit of heat for this as well. It will shock you at first, and then you'll learn to do as we do—keep the fact under raps. People do not understand what you are doing. Ninety percent of "sailors" are just cross-dressing power boaters. They'll accuse you of being a starry eyed novice and not knowing what you're doing, or an expert who's simply out to rub other peoples faces in their skill. They'll accuse you of not being able to afford an engine, or accuse you of being so rich that you can afford to take all the time you need to get anywhere you want to in your "engineless" style. You just can't win, I'm telling you, so keep the secret in the gang that understands. Still, it won't help the alienation factor. It will be hard to do, as you learn, because you'll learn so much that you'll want to share it with everyone who, obviously, doesn't have a clue. Forget it, take it easy! If you need to chat some folks up, do it on our webpage...

As you get started in this game, you're not going to have the ability to get very far a field, and you'll likely be earning a wage at least part of the time. This means you're going to have to sail in areas that are accessible to the average person, which simply means overdeveloped, crowded, and gutted of any sort of spirit. You'll just have to live with this, but the reality is that in this day and age you're going to spend a lot of times anchored in places that feel like someone's back yard. As some point these anchorage will be developed with private docks and moorings, and you'll not be able to anchor there even if you needed to, so you'll need to anchor further out and be punished by the roll of the powerboat wakes left by boats on the way to the marina in the inner harbor. Some places, where rich really have sway, they'll just prohibit you from anchoring legally. Other places they'll hire thugs to smash your gear up or cut your boat loose while you're away. Don't be shocked, *this happens*, it has happened to me, and if it happens to you you'll begin to find warning tales of pirates in the South China Sea to be a lot less intimidating. So be very careful where you hang, and who's house you anchor in front of, no matter whether you're legally entitled to or not. This will make your first years hard, and this problem is only going to get worse with development, so the longer you wait, the more of this you'll need to stomach. Keep a low profile!

If you're under the age of 50, you're not going to meet very many people cruising of your age. If you're under 40, there will be even fewer. If you're female, you'll meet few women sailors. You'll meet a few "drag-aboards" but that's about it. If you're male and single, and live on a boat, you're likely to remain that way for some time—as this lifestyle can be a pretty hard sell for a lot of women. Not to say that any of this is impossible, or that these observations are absolutes. You are going to meet some very, very wonderful people as well. But, as is the case in life anywhere—the assholes you'll meet greatly outnumber them. Be prepared for this, as there will be difficulty enough in just learning the ropes of your new life and developing the skills to live in your new environment with ease and comfort—which you will, if you stick it out—without having to have a steady diet of interpersonal difficulty as well. The interpersonal stuff has been hard for us, and we want to warn you.

Should any of this prevent you from pursuing this dream? NO! Unless you completely sell out and become ordinary, *you'll have the same problem ashore.* Not at all to scare you off, but forewarned is indeed forearmed and I want you to know the dark side of what you're getting yourself into. As well, I want you to take seriously the need to create good relationships that will stick with you as you move through this transformation. You're going to find them hard to come by. Of course, and again, this need is a large part of the reason for this book—it is an attempt to build these bridges and create that network of like minded individuals. Again, unless you really want to go play "old man and the sea" by yourself, which some do, get started and get yourself hooked up with others. Our website is a great place to start.

If you find yourself in dire straits and don't know where to turn, and you find yourself thinking about giving up on the whole project at some point—take the traditional remedy. Try a life ashore for a while. Don't get rid of the boat, or do anything stupid that sews up all your options, but give the life ashore a try. Many find that an extended vacation away from the sea can really give new steam and focus. Don't view this as a failure; view it as an adaptation to the necessity of this rapidly changing world. To be a Sea-Steader is more of a frame of mind than anything…

Last summer I went through a set of circumstances that might illustrate this point. As we were planning to leave for Mexico in the summer of 2005 I began to develop some pretty dehabilitating arthritis problems which made boat life pretty uncomfortable. It became aware to me that certain changes and remedies were going to need to be made or my sailing days were numbered. This, of course, was a bummer—but bummers happen, you know. I've found that if I'm very, very fit and conscious about my diet I can keep the symptoms under control, but we've not the skills right now to maintain this level of fitness on the boat. We're working this one out right now and attempting to find a solution. For us, it looks like it's all coming together nicely but again sometimes you're going to get complications. Sometimes sailing is waiting in port while a storm blows out. Expect this sort of thing—don't let it cripple you.

In some ways the future looks pretty dim for mankind, but in many aspects better for the Sea-Steader. Demographics and aging populations are going to keep the anchorages likely more clear than they have been before. Rising oil prices will make access to remote places much more expensive for everyone. The two of these phenomenon together—which are certainties—will also have a negative impact on the economy of the world at large, and I believe that there's likely to be fewer cruisers in the future, not more, and this will be good for you if you can hang on in the mean time. As financial security in a land based lifestyle becomes more and more difficult to be had, the lifestyle you hold will look more and more appealing—hence the alienation may start to fade and many more people may desire to join our ranks. Hard to say, but I think these developments are pretty likely. Still, it looks to me that for the average individual there's likely no better time to start than today, as wages aren't so terrible, and material costs aren't so high. If you wait, you may not be able to pull things off.

We escaped by the skin of our teeth. Only a year after launching, the yard we built in no longer allows the activity (nor does any in the area.) There is no safe place to anchor within 25 miles of Bellingham that isn't restricted or claimed privately. I know of no place in the Puget Sound where one could effectively live an anchor-out lifestyle anymore. Today, we couldn't get a slip in Bellingham either. We couldn't do today what we did then. Don't let the grass grow under your feet...

Lastly: Partners-

Many people have a hard time finding people to take up the Sea-Stead lifestyle with them. This can be difficult, as it can be a drag to be chronically single, especially, I think for women. Men can get a long pretty well with the "Siete Mares" lifestyle, and maybe that's best for us after all, but a lot of us are romantics, and enjoy a steady partner in life, and someone close to share these amazing experiences with.

Most women, however, have had bad experiences with boating through other guys and the like—they generally don't like the less than ultra comfortable environment that a boat may have, and they often like to have a lot of stuff. Not all, but many. Men as well can fall victim to this. It is important, however, that if one is looking for a partner that one doesn't waste time looking among normal people. You've got to find the niches of folks that want something else other than a McLife, and find them you will *if* you look.

If you've got a partner, be very very clear about what it is that you want to do, where you want to go, and how long you want to be gone. We're talking about Sea-Steading here, a lifestyle, not a vacation. Many people secretly think of cruising as a vacation. Be sure, as I've seen many couples get involved in a big project together, and incur a lot of cost—he thinks he's sailing away, she thinks they'll be gone a year or two and then come back and raise a family. You can tell the cruise is over when the family just happens to show up one day, unexpectedly. Again—be very clear of what your expectations are. Whatever you do, play fair and honest. This project will be a lot of work, and it's really a shame if someone throws it in and someone else ends up holding the bag.

18

SO, BUILD A BOAT OR BUY?

So, should you build a sailboat or buy one when getting started on the Sea-Stead project?

This is a pretty tough question. First off, I'd really recommend that if this boat is one's very first boat, it would really be a mistake to try to build. Building a boat is a much bigger project than it appears from the start, and will always cost more than one thinks—unless, of course, one is really aware of the costs of materials and has a good idea of quantities. Which, obviously, at this point in the project, one isn't and does not. Besides, it is very hard for a new sailor to have a very good idea of the needs and ways of a ship, and one is likely to waste a good deal of time, effort, and money installing parts and hardware in unworkable ways. Any reasonable production boat has these issues more or less under control. They may not really be set up to sail without motor assist—they may likely be clumsily rigged and under canvassed—but nothing will be terribly wrong. One would be better, I think, to make a really good attempt at finding an older quality production boat and refinishing it. You'll get a lot of hardware in the deal that would cost an awful lot to buy by itself.

So what should a used boat cost? I've used this benchmark for years and it has worked nicely. You shouldn't pay any more than a dollar a pound for a used boat, unless it is very well outfitted and ready. Even so, I don't think an outfitted boat is worth more than two dollars a pound, as it very unlikely will be outfitted in the way you'd like. Many people bolt all sorts of expensive nonsense to their boats and consider them upgrades—you'll likely disagree. Ideally, what you want is an older boat with good fiberglass and a minimum of nonsense, and hopefully with a blown or almost blown motor. These boats exist, and you'll find them if you look. I'd not get a boat any smaller than 27 feet overall, and I'd not get a boat any larger than 32 feet overall for that first boat. If the sails are shot, and the rig is dated, and the motor is blown—you'll not have much to argue about in the price. Many times these boats can be had for *less* than a dollar a pound. Don't worry much about the fiberglass, if it looks good, it's likely fine. Avoid boats with blisters, of course, but few old boats have any. As well, be cautious of boats with a lot of jel coat crazing. People say its all in the jel coat, but I'm here to tell you it's often not. Some times the crazing will go clear through the laminate. What this is caused by is an overly resin rich and sloppy lay-up. The resin shrinks over time and hence the cracks. It might be thick, but it's still relatively weak. You'll find boats that don't have this problem, so I'd just keep looking unless it's really a deal.

So in many ways, you'll be rebuilding, not building, but you'll have the benefit of now having a place to camp (which is hard to do in a partially completed hull, but I've seen it done) which will save you money, and the boat will likely be functional enough to get you out and around the bay, although you'd likely not want to take it to Fiji. That's OK, you'll have time. But get started, get rolling, and don't look back. The initial enthusiasm you have for the project will carry you a long way, but it needs to get you through that first winter and the early hassles that come from boat life. Don't, at this point, try to live on the hook. Get a slip if at all possible. You'll have enough trouble without trying to drag power tools and materials out in the skiff to work amidst the incessant roll of powerboat wakes. Even being in a yard that will allow you to live and work at the same time is better. These, however, can be hard to find, and for probably good reasons.

But, if you really want to build a boat there's nothing I'm going to tell you that makes any difference—and actually, for a second boat, I'm not sure it's such a bad idea. Just know it's likely not going to save you a lot of money, especially when you factor in your time. While I suggest that these projects are for those of moderate means—to build a boat you're going to have to do better than moderate. People of moderate means no longer commonly own property, especially own property large enough to contain a boat project. If you need to rent a place to build, it will cost a lot, and you'll be liable to the whim of the owner who might just get sick of your project and tell you to leave. All of this will cost more than buying a boat, and you'll still need a place to live while you're at it. So again, if you're convinced you can build a boat quickly and for much less money than a purchase, well then, go for it. A lot more people start building boats than finish them. But you've been forewarned!

You will, however, if you do a good job, gain the invaluable reward of knowledge and confidence in that knowledge. This is worth a lot and perhaps a reason in itself. There are real traps, though. It can take a lot of time to get the project done, especially if one is really a fiddly sort with tools. You need to set yourself a strict time schedule and stick to it. Keep the boat a simple as possible, don't get hung up on a lot of finish details—you must get this thing working and in the water as fast as possible or your likelihood of joining the ranks of those who have *almost* completed a boat are very high. These projects abound, and can often be had for a song. Perhaps this is a good place to look.

I think there is another grave error that a lot of people make. There are a number of boat designers out there who make their trade by peddling designs for the "home builder." Invariably, these are chine hull, plywood sorts of boats. While there is nothing wrong with this style of construction, there is a very often understated problem with these designs. Without apologies, these tend almost without exception to be very poor sailing boats. Sure, they're inexpensive, I guess, and rugged—but there will come a day where you'll feel handicapped by the boat design—you can only shrug off 4 knots to weather for so long as everyone else flies by. It's really a shame, because while these hulls are indeed easy to build and a place to start, as you'll go along you'll develop the skills to do a nicer shape and you'll at some point really wish you had. Listen to me, *this is really good advice.* It's sad to see the really nicely finished piece of shit designs sailing along poorly with their mostly proud owners grinning as best they can. Just go ahead and get a good book on cold molded construction and read it cover to cover. Steal a classic wooden boat design out of some other book, you'll find a table of offsets and that all you need to get started. Don't consider any design that doesn't have an easily achieved hull speed of *at least* six knots. You'll need a staple gun and a table-saw and a place to build. You'll be fine. Build it out of clear fir, upside down, and glass the hell out of it with epoxy and several layers of light cloth. Bring up the weight in the ballast keel about 15 percent to make up for the lighter hull. It will be a very nice hull and will last longer than you.

I bought MACHA in December of 2003 as a partially completed hull project. The hull itself had been owned by a friend of mine since 1977, and he had made a nice start on it. But, life happened, and happened again, and he had a heart attack. At that point it was clear that the boat was not going to be finished by him, and it was going to be hard to sell. He had been trying to sell the boat for four years with only very little interest generated. I was looking for a larger boat at the time, although not this large, but I had the cash, and the deal was done. At the time, I knew of at least two other boats of the same type in the area that I could have had for the same sort of money, in about the same state of completion. Basically, in all cases, these boats had decks more or less built, although slightly deteriorated. Some had tanks, some had gear, mine had an engine—although nicely installed and new was much too little power by modern standards. None had masts, rigs, or sails. Any of these boats could have been had for under five thousand dollars, and people would have been very glad to have them hauled out of their yards.

Figure 35: Taking a pause in a late night. It's 20 degrees, no heat in the boat, and it's tough to get the glue to set.

Figure 36: A couple of weeks later…sailmaking while the glue dries.

Figure 36: Building the rudder out of scraps and Dad stuffing foam.

Figure 37: The moment of reckoning!

Figure 38: Does she float?

Figure 39: We step the mast…

So I took possession of the hull, chased the bat colony out, and set to work in the snow of January. It sucked, and it was cold. I was working driving fork lift at the time making just under fifteen dollars an hour—I'd get off work and raise hell in the dark, in the snow, building boat. Did I mention that this really sucked? Definitely not a Center for Wooden Boats sort of experience...I remember one dark frozen windy night where I was trying to get a couple of sheets of plywood up on deck—I couldn't climb the ladder because the wind would blow me off—I was throwing sheets of ¾ inch plywood up on the deck trying to get them to stick as they slid and blew off the ice covered deck to the ground on the other side...Well I persevered, and quit the forklift driving job as the weather got better, and then really put in some days. We built the sails, finished the interior in clear fir—all salvage lumber. And when I mean salvage, I mean salvage—our cabin sole is built out of rip sawn pallets. We did all of our own upholstery work with nice help from Mom and Dad. We launched MACHA in early July of 2004, I finished the rig in the slip, and we went sailing for the first time on July 22. And sailed she did. We still had the 8 hp Sabb diesel installed in the boat, for I wasn't sure that I really was going to like the boat and I wasn't going to pull the motor until we gave it a test, but MACHA absolutely exceeded every expectation. Once we had the topmast on, she leaped to life and we knew that we'd keep her, and the motor was history. I designed a new mast for her, as the original was a simple deck stepped pole and I wanted a keel stepped rig—out of steel, and had this welded up at IOTA metal works in Bellingham who did a very nice job indeed for a very fair price. We in February, contracted for week of yard time in a shed, and raised hell once again. I sawsalled the cockpit out, pulled the motor, and glassed the cockpit back in. We filled the rudder aperture, and installed the new mast, and 6 days later we sculled her back into her slip. Putting the rig back together took a week—I had a few days of dragging lead and concrete down the dock in carts to finish the final ballasting (1500 pounds worth, Damn!) and we were good to go.

By the way, I sold the engine for as much as I had paid for the hull. All in all, the project, ready to go to anywhere cost us about thirty thousand dollars.

Figure 40: She's a pretty girl, isn't she? This is July of 2005, as we cruise British Columbia.

Now, I list this not to boast but to inspire. If one has the will and the means, one can get a hell of a lot of boat done right quick of one really puts some ass into it. Sparrow was working at a marine supplier at the time (which gave us a discount on materials, a big help) and she early in the project would come home quite disillusioned at times, as many folks soon knew we were building a boat and had a lot of advice for her. Especially, when people heard our time frame they'd simply snort. I said all along I'd have the boat in the water by July, as we simply *had* to. *We needed a place to live, and the time frame was non-negotiable.* Still, some or the other old Captain Piddlemarks had a lot to say about that. Simply couldn't be done. It will take four years, at least. Well, when the boat went in the water in July, old Captain Piddlemarks wasn't much to be seen. He snuck back a while later, with advice about the sailing performance of gaff rigs, but then, out in the bay, he learned a lesson or two about that. He had some advice later about sailing in and out of the slip, and how that just couldn't be done—but he had piddle-marks aplenty the first time he saw us scull out of the harbor in the calm of the morning, and sail back into the slip under a triced main in the afternoon. Old

Captain Piddlemarks and his crew had advice on everything, even the steel mast as too heavy, etc., etc., etc. This got really old, I'll tell you. I expect, now that we've left, he's looking for someone else to offer his seasoned advice. Don't listen to old Captain Piddlemarks when he comes to comment on your project. Keep your nose to the grindstone and just go for it.

So that's about it for this book. If I've got a final message, it is this. Know the dream, believe in the dream, and be relentless in your pursuit of it. If you're careful, you will succeed where many do not. Don't take the task lightly, but don't be afraid either. Don't let anyone, including me, tell you what you can or cannot do. You will succeed if you mean to. I hope to inspire you to believe that you will succeed.

Mean to succeed. The world is changing fast. The Sea-Stead is one of, if not *the* last option available for a life of peace and freedom, but even this option may not last. You may well lose your chance if you dally. Start today!

Hey, we hope to see you out there! We monitor Channel 72!

Figure 41: Still pursuing the dream...

Afterword

If you really like this sort of thing, and are intrigued by the whole sailing motif, I'd encourage you to check out The Oar Club on the world wide web. The Oar Club is a sailing club dedicated to people who sail real sailboats—at the time of this publication we were about 500 members worldwide and growing. No, you don't have to buy into my flaky philosophy—but you must have a passion for sail, and know what sailing is. You'll not find a more skilled, experienced, and pleasant group of sailors anywhere else. We can be found at www.oarclub.org. We offer classes, training, crew positions—we build sails and fix boats—help with pretty much anything that is involved with running a sailboat can be found there. So far, and hopefully forever we've also found the means to keep money and funding out of it and offer all this for FREE to any good person that comes our way. If you're not a sailor, but you'd like to be, this is the way to get a hold of us...our entire purpose in this project is to create a community, so please partici-pate!

Lastly, if you've got any questions about the material in this very incomplete book, don't hesitate to contact us either! It's the point of the whole gig, after all!

In Memory of
Peter Kittel
An inspiration to us all

Under the wide and Starry sky;
Dig my grave and let me lie;
Glad I did live and gladly die;
And I laid me down with a will.

This be the last verse you grave for me;
Here he lies where he longed to be;
Home is the Sailor, home from the Sea;
And the Hunter home from the hill.

978-0-595-38758-8
0-595-38758-6